STRANGE
YELLOWSTONE

STRANGE
YELLOWSTONE

Weird True Facts about America's Premier Park

SCOTT HERRING

RIVERBEND
PUBLISHING
ESSEX, CONNECTICUT

RIVERBEND
PUBLISHING
An imprint of Globe Pequot, the trade division of
The Rowman & Littlefield Publishing Group, Inc.
4501 Forbes Blvd., Ste. 200
Lanham, MD 20706
www.rowman.com

Distributed by NATIONAL BOOK NETWORK

British Library Cataloguing in Publication Information available

Library of Congress Cataloging-in-Publication Data

Names: Herring, Scott, 1963- author.
Title: Strange Yellowstone : weird, true stories about America's premier
  park / Scott Herring.
Other titles: Weird, true stories about America's premier park
Description: Lanham, MD : Riverbend, [2024] |
Identifiers: LCCN 2023059396 (print) | LCCN 2023059397 (ebook) |
  ISBN 9781606391419 (paper ; alk. paper) | ISBN 9781493085774
  (electronic)
Subjects: LCSH: Yellowstone National Park—History—Anecdotes. |
  Yellowstone National Park—Description and travel—Anecdotes.
Classification: LCC F722 .H48 2024 (print) | LCC F722 (ebook) | DDC
  917.8752—dc23/eng/20240108
LC record available at https://lccn.loc.gov/2023059396
LC ebook record available at https://lccn.loc.gov/2023059397

♾️™ The paper used in this publication meets the minimum requirements
of American National Standard for Information Sciences—Permanence of
Paper for Printed Library Materials, ANSI/NISO Z39.48-1992.

Contents

Introduction   1

Chapter One: Unsolved Mysteries   9

Chapter Two: Bats for the Bellhops and Other
            Structural Surprises   45

Chapter Three: Weird and Wonderful Wolves   75

Chapter Four: Northern Nuttiness   111

Chapter Five: Geysers Are Stranger Than You Think   147

Chapter Six: Landscape Bizarre   185

Chapter Seven: The Departed   223

Conclusion: Our Strange Future   269

About the Author   281

INTRODUCTION

A traffic jam on Yellowstone's Grand Loop Road—perfectly bizarre anywhere else, perfectly normal here. The whole place is like this: a constant surprise. SCOTT HERRING

INTRODUCTION

If you give it a little attention, you will be struck by how very, very strange Yellowstone is.

Where else can you find a spot called "Fishing Bridge" where no one fishes, where it is actually illegal to fish, and the main pastime, in fact, is fish *watching*?

Where else can you find a lake that is over seventy-seven hundred feet above the sea and is crowded by seabirds?

Where else can you find a volcano so big that, for much of your visit, you are driving around *inside* it? And you do not even *notice*?

Where else can you stand in a dense, old-growth Douglas-fir forest, then walk a hundred feet out of the shade and into a treeless desert where one of the main plants is a kind of cactus?

Where else can you find a threatened species of fish, nearly extinct in the park, that lived a hundred years undiscovered in a creek that went right under the main highway?

Where else can you find a few nondescript hot pools with goofy names like Mushroom Spring—from which came discoveries that helped kick off the revolution in the science of genetics?

You get the idea. Everything about Yellowstone is a surprise. It routinely leaves you shaking your head in wonderment at how strange it is.

It was strangeness that led to the creation of what we now know as Yellowstone National Park—and it was the world's first national park, another unique feature of the place. During its prehistory, the land that became Yellowstone exploded with surreal violence over and over. It explodes on a cycle of roughly six hundred thousand years, and the last really big blast was six hundred thousand years ago, so we may be due. What is driving the violence is what geologists call a hot spot, a plume of magma that wells out of the hellish depths of the earth. It stays in one place, and the surface of the United States—the North American plate, they call it—rides over the top. If you

approach Yellowstone from the southwest, through Idaho, you
will see the lava it ejected when that part of the plate was over
the hot spot. Yellowstone is many things. Among others, it is
one of the biggest volcanoes in the world, and it is still plenty
active. That magma plume is what heats the water in the hot
springs and drives the geysers, of which Old Faithful is only the
most famous.

When the nation of the United States was young, mountain
men penetrated what is now the park. They were mainly
searching for beaver pelts, but what they found up here was
quite a distraction. They wandered through the great high
plateau and saw the geyser fields with their myriad surprises.
They saw the canyons of the Yellowstone, the largest a bright
white and yellow and red void in places two miles wide and over
a thousand feet deep, with a pair of waterfalls at its start that
rivaled anything on the continent—and that was just one of the
canyons of the Yellowstone. They looked out across what we
call Yellowstone Lake. We now know it to be the largest high-
elevation lake in North America, an impossibly big, impossibly
blue bowl surrounded by peaks that never entirely lose their
snow.

Those are only the most dramatic secrets the future park
revealed to them. They got a thousand other surprises. When
the mountain men returned to civilization and told the stories
of what they had seen, they were not always believed. Indeed,
the record suggests they were regularly mocked. Still, the stories
accumulated until, after the Civil War, the more isolated corners
of the West began to give up their secrets. Beginning in 1869,
a series of more-or-less organized expeditions penetrated the
area. Detailed accounts began to appear in the news media,
but the printed word could only convey so much. In 1871, an
expedition led by the geologist Ferdinand Hayden included
two happy additions: photographer William Henry Jackson
and painter Thomas Moran. They captured the beauty of the

place . . . but also, of course, its strangeness: the water jetting two hundred feet high, entire valleys obscured by steam, the travertine at Mammoth covering the hillsides like the icing on a wedding cake hundreds of feet high, the waterfall—Tower Fall—with a boulder like a bird's egg in a nest sitting balanced on its verge, where it would hang for another century and more.

Faced with this—and much more—evidence of its uniqueness, Congress passed a bill that Ulysses S. Grant signed in 1872. It made Yellowstone into a national park, the world's first—another mark of its uniqueness.

And it only got stranger when, over the course of the coming decades, people began to visit from the rest of the country and the rest of the world (the park's original inhabitants, tribes like the Shoshone, Crow, and Bannock, were at first still around; they just tended not to hang out with the tourists). A road network gradually took shape, and at the most popular stopping places, villages sprung up. The park was—and it really remains— far from the centers of civilization, so every year an ad hoc army of temporary employees assembled to run the businesses that catered to park visitors. Then as now, it is difficult to the point of impossibility to get fine, upstanding, boring citizens to do temporary work away up in the mountains for the summer, so from the start, the employees have been odd. Their eccentricity is usually charming and only sometimes criminal.

The villages and roads were eccentric in their own way. The road builders were forced by the absurdities of the landscape into improvisations not to be found in the outside world, like one of the only corkscrew bridges in the world. It is gone now, but it was what it sounds like, a road that crossed a bridge, then turned in a circle and crossed under. Elsewhere, the road passes through Mae West Curve, named by park employees for the curves on the actress Mae West (the rough equivalent, named by employees in the 1970s, is a pair of mounds near Midway Geyser Basin called Dolly Parton Peaks, which I shall leave to your imagination). In places elsewhere, the asphalt looks funny, because a new thermal feature is coming up underneath. The villages grew in no planned manner, and you never know what you might find there, from the world's largest log structure (the Old Faithful Inn) to a roadside eatery that looks like a UFO (the old Canyon Lodge). Among the employees who work in these places, a culture grew over the decades that reflected the peculiar nature of the work, and of the life: sometimes dull, often grueling, but also emotionally intense to the point of being regularly joyous.

I lived that life myself and know it well in all its weirdness. Long ago, I worked for the little company that ran the service stations and wreckers. It was fun, but it was strange, too. Many of you have heard—we will look into the matter later in this book—about the ghost in the Old Faithful Inn. When I first arrived, I was surprised to learn that the bunkhouse where I lived housed a ghost, too. It was supposed to be the spirit of a woman. She had died when the structure—a ramshackle, barn-like thing built in perhaps 1920—was being moved by road to a new location in the late 1950s. She came around a corner too quickly and was decapitated when she slammed into the corner room of the structure. The mechanics I worked with claimed to know she was driving a 1956 Austin-Healey 100 convertible. "And because it was a low-slung convertible," one of them told me, "she went under the building, and her head come clean off." Her spirit now inhabited that corner room and specialized in turning on lights and radios and the like when no one was around.

I shook that off and got on with the summer. I discovered that the whole operation was a maze of eccentricities. We did business the same way we had in the 1950s: all full service, a half dozen of us charging a single car all at once, filling the tank and cleaning the windshield and checking the oil and even airing the tires. Confronted by this assault, the tourists did not know what to do or think. It was the 1990s, but we even used equipment from the 1950s—it had never worn out, so we kept right on using that tire machine from the Eisenhower era. The really strange part was that no one could explain why. We did it because we had done it always. Our social lives were just as rooted in tradition. We had a whole series of parties that took place every year and had since at least the 1970s: the tip fund party, the steak fry party, the Pink Passion Punch Party, the Handlebar Mustache Party. We had a toga party every June with the odd regulation that all the Texans in the group had to attend in a toga with cowboy boots and a ten- or twenty-gallon hat.

I loved it and stayed for years. At the end of that first summer, though, I found myself in the bunkhouse in the early morning hours. I was the last resident; we were getting ready to shut down for the season. The weather was turning toward winter, and as happened during those final weeks, a frosty wind blew hard out of the north. The building was all wood, and the wood had come apart in places. We repaired the cracks with duct tape, but now the tape fell off and the wind whistled through the building. The windows all had old-fashioned shutters, and one had worked halfway loose. As the wind gusted, it swung to and fro, banging rhythmically, and loudly.

In the lobby, a light switch had broken, although the lights worked well, too well, in other places. I sat in the darkened lobby for a long while before I could work up the courage to walk down the hall and turn off the heater and lights, in the haunted room.

The whole park is like that. Everywhere you look, you find nature behaving in the most extravagant ways, and as often as not, its weird moods are tied up with the human society that has grown up here, itself full of plenty of weirdness. Those two features of the park—strangeness both human and natural—are the subject of this book.

INTRODUCTION

There is method to the madness on these pages. Each chapter has a major focus, as you can see from the table of contents, but within each chapter, there are subdivisions that are more specific. You will regularly see there some guidance that will allow you to find your way around the park and its surroundings, and that will lead you to some of the stranger sights in this very strange place. Some can be seen from a car. Others are fairly easy to scare up during a walk around the famous locations in the park.

This book is not after sensationalism, although some of its elements are sensational. The stories are carefully researched and factual to the greatest possible degree. In the process of writing the book, I also spoke to park insiders who know the place as well as anyone alive, and who have been persuaded to spill a few of its secrets.

If you are reading this book while on your way to Yellowstone National Park, congratulations. It is a wonderful place to go—indeed, a hundred years ago, people routinely called it Wonderland. It is big and truly beautiful, one of the genuinely gorgeous places in North America. It is also surprising, outlandish, and sometimes eerie.

In a word, it is strange. It is stranger than you can imagine . . . but if you are on your way there, you will not have to merely imagine for much longer. Yellowstone will soon be there right in front of you, demanding all your attention. There also will be all its weirdness, demanding an explanation.

Having read up on it, you will at least have a clue. But understand this: some things about Yellowstone are so weird that a clue may be all you end up with.

UNSOLVED MYSTERIES

Abyss Pool, at the West Thumb Geyser Basin, where the shoe turned up—with the foot in it. SCOTT HERRING

Yellowstone is a big place. In fact, it is a good deal bigger than you probably realize. When we talk about "Yellowstone," we usually mean Yellowstone National Park, the 2.2-million-acre block of the Northern Rockies that is administered by the National Park Service. Scientists, however, talk about the Greater Yellowstone Ecosystem (GYE), a stretch of terrain extending far up into Montana and, in the other direction, halfway to Salt Lake City. The GYE covers more than ten times as much land as the national park. To keep things under control here, we will focus only on the park itself and the terrain just outside.

Which is big enough. Furthermore, except for the road areas and the villages (like Old Faithful and Canyon), the park is composed of the most rugged, raw wilderness. It swallows things, and it does not spit them out. In fact, over time, it swallows them more deeply.

An example, a big one: during the Second World War, on the night of May 23, 1943, a B-17 bomber was flying from California to Lewiston, Montana, when the wings iced, and the plane went down. The bombardier, a lieutenant named William McDonald, was the only one who managed to bail out. The plane slammed into the earth four miles south of the town of West Yellowstone, Montana. A ranger found McDonald three days later. The bodies of the other victims were recovered, and at least a few old rangers remembered the crash, but the forest absorbed the wreck so completely that it disappeared, unexploded ammunition and all.

This was a B-17F, the kind of heavy, four-engine bomber that was known as a Flying Fortress for the mass of defensive machine guns it carried. It was the same type of aircraft that did most of the work pulverizing Hitler's Germany. It weighed perhaps 34,000 pounds empty, and this one weighed a good deal more because it was still carrying much of its fuel and all but one of its people when it hit the ground. Still, the few rangers who knew where it had landed all retired and went away, and the wreck was entirely forgotten. Yellowstone had swallowed it whole. The wreck was not rediscovered until 1988.

If the park can absorb an aircraft like that, you can guess what it can do to people. They disappear so completely that they leave nearly no trace. Consider the case of LeRoy R. Piper.

In his classic *Death in Yellowstone*, Lee Whittlesey, the park's official historian for years (he is retired now), tells the story: "On July 30, 1900, Piper, 36, of Saint Mary's, Ohio, was staying at Yellowstone's Fountain Hotel at Lower Geyser Basin. He purchased a cigar from the cigar stand, stepped out onto the porch of the hotel, and was never seen again. Piper, a bank cashier, had been en route to San Francisco to settle his deceased uncle's estate. . . . He was carrying a considerable sum of money with him as well as valuable jewelry. Friends feared that 'his mind became unbalanced,' detachments of cavalry searched for a month for him, his brother-in-law came to the park to conduct a personal search, and a one-thousand-dollar reward was posted for his return, but it was all to no avail."

Whittlesey has a theory about Piper's fate that, for the strange environment of Yellowstone, makes perfect sense: "I believe he walked out into the night and inadvertently stumbled into one of the many hot springs that were and are located nearby. Persons who fall into hot springs disintegrate, and there is often no recovery of them. Two hot springs there, Gentian Pool and Deep Blue Geyser, are very large and very deep, and I believe that a search of them or other springs there, could it be done, would yield Piper's silicified bones, perhaps covered over by years of hot-spring deposits."

Such a search is nearly impossible, so Piper remains in the same category as Amelia Earhart and Jimmy Hoffa. The same can be said of many other park visitors who walked away and simply disappeared. Whittlesey devotes a whole chapter to them.

So the park is full of mysteries, and not just from disappearances. It is full of things that are hard to explain. Among them is a riddle arising from one of the great environmental crimes of the twentieth century . . . although were the criminal ever caught, the charge would never equal the harm done.

Who Killed the Lake?

Or tried to, at least.

Yellowstone Lake is one of the gems of the park. As noted, it is the largest high-altitude lake in the country, and it has an advantage that other lakes—Tahoe comes to mind—do not enjoy: it was set aside before the surrounding land could be developed. It lies now in nearly pristine condition—with a big exception.

The main fish in the lake has always been the Yellowstone cutthroat trout. It was, in fact, the main fish in the park when the park was first established. It is a handsome fish, of a color that it hard to describe—green from above, brown on the sides, and regularly golden overall. The name comes from the characteristic red/orange slash under its jaw, and so a cutthroat is easy to identify. Holding one in your hands, you have the strong sense that you hold a little bit of America before Columbus. If you fish, however, do not expect lunkers in Yellowstone. An adult cutthroat can be anywhere from six to twenty inches, but in most places, a large cutthroat could be a foot long. The Yellowstone winters are too long and severe for them to get much larger. Still, quite a few creatures depend on them as an important item in their diet, including creatures that even casual visitors have a shot at seeing, like otters, osprey, and even bears.

In a number of places in the park, cutthroats are doing well. In others, they are victimized by the fish-stocking that happened in the park's early decades. Many of the fish an angler will encounter in the park do not in fact belong here; they were hauled in from elsewhere in an effort to improve fishing that we might have done without. Brown trout came from Scotland and Germany, brook trout from the eastern United States, and rainbow trout from the far West. The latter have been a problem for the cutthroat. In places like Slough Creek in the northern part of the park, the rainbow trout interbreed with the cutthroat and produce a fish called a cutbow, a kind of jackalope of a fish that is neither one thing nor the other. If this process goes on long enough, it will leave Slough Creek with no more real cutthroats.

Still, Yellowstone Lake appeared to many as a bastion, a place the cutthroat had to themselves. Whatever else might go wrong, the species would have this colossal refuge to fall back on. Until. . . .

One of the alien fish stocked during the early years of the park was a species of trout unlike all the others. It came from the Great Lakes, and it was introduced into Lewis Lake and Shoshone Lake, both of which lacked game fish during those early years. It was the lake trout. It is different in one crucially important way: it gets big. Very big. These are not the charming little brook trout kids catch in the park with worms. Look up photographs on the internet. They regularly get to be three feet long, and the world record was over four feet. They live a long time. A cutthroat may live for a decade, if it is very lucky. A lake trout can live nearly as long as a human.

They were no problem as long as they were safely isolated in the smaller lakes in the southern part of the park. In 1994, though, the fish biologists who work in the park got a terrible shock. Lake trout were caught in Yellowstone Lake. This addition changed everything. The relationship between lake trout and cutthroat trout that was already developing in Yellowstone Lake was like the relationship between sharks and mackerel. The lake trout made cutthroat their favorite meal. If uninterrupted, they might have destroyed the Yellowstone Lake cutthroat population entirely.

The situation was catastrophic in every way. The lake trout live in deep water and so are safe from predators. They do not spawn in streams like the cutthroat do. They do move into shallow lake water to spawn—but they do so at night when the animals and birds that might have picked them off cannot see them and are not active anyway. They were mostly safe, even from human anglers.

And that is one reason it took so long to notice them. When they were discovered in 1994, it quickly became clear that they had been there a while. Human anglers missed them because they were not fishing deep enough. The lake trout were already well established in their new home.

How had they gotten there? That is the mystery. One thing is clear: they had human help. Someone carried them from one of the southern lakes to their new home.

As the situation developed, the National Park Service responded with a series of control efforts that have evolved with the situation and intensified. Anglers are now encouraged to target the lake trout and allowed to use tackle illegal everywhere else. They are actually required—not encouraged but required—to kill them on sight. The fisherman returning to one of the marinas with a dead lake trout is treated as a conquering hero. The kitchens at the hotels will cook the fish, and the successful angler becomes a local celebrity again when the fish is served, laid out on an oversized platter, spectacularly dead. And more: the Park Service, using gillnets, has killed millions of them and has even gone so far as to unleash commercial fishing boats on them, as if they were codfish off New England. Lately, they have been dropping masses of a soy-based pellets onto known spawning areas; the pellets disintegrate, rot, and drive dissolved oxygen out of the water, annihilating the next generation of lake trout (in a manner not terribly different from the way they killed—in his 1954 debut film—Godzilla, King of the Monsters).

The response was absolutely necessary and is going as well as anyone could hope. Still, it is strange. It is just not what you expect to find in a national park. The agency charged with preserving the park is now engaged in mass fish-murder.

Looking into the mystery of how the lake trout got there in the first place, biologists were helped by an oddity of fish anatomy. Fish have, in their heads, a structure called an otolith, or ear-stone. The otolith grows as the fish grows, and on close examination, a biologist can see their growth rings, rather like the growth rings in a tree trunk. Furthermore, every lake has its own special chemistry. There are trace elements in its water that can be used as identifiers—trace elements that that lake alone has in that exact proportion—and the growth rings on otoliths preserve that special signature. When the growth ring for one year shows the chemistry of one lake, and the growth ring for the next year shows the chemistry for another, then the fish was moved that year.

The biologists Andrew Munro and Thomas McMahon, of Montana State University, Bozeman, and James Ruzycki of the National Park Service, used these facts of fish life to determine what had happened. They published their results in 2005, and the article is a remarkable thing, maybe unique in the annals of crime. What the scientists had done was forensic fish biology. Their report was like a coroner's inquest . . . on a lake.

The results were clear. The lake trout had come from Lewis Lake. That part was perhaps to be expected; Lewis Lake is a short drive up the South Entrance Road to the nearest shore of Yellowstone Lake, while the other places the trout might have come from are a formidable hike from the truck. More surprising were some of their other findings. The first transplanted fish had been moved all the way back in the mid-1980s. Furthermore, there were multiple transfers, and the number of fish moved was—given the guerrilla nature of the thing—outright enormous, numbering in the hundreds of fish.

Open questions remain: Who did it? Who transplanted the fish?

1

He is an ecological version of the Zodiac Killer: he was persistent, diabolical, malicious—and he remains entirely unknown. Was it a group? A family? Actually, it seems most likely that the villain was just an individual, a highly secretive individual, kind of like the Unabomber, only with fish. If more than one person was doing it, the secret would have had a good chance of leaking out by now. At this date, we will need a confession to identify the villain. All physical evidence is long gone, except the fish themselves.

One can guess how it might have happened. The perpetrator will have caught his limit of lake trout in Lewis Lake, then made the transfer while no one was looking, by the dark of the moon, surely. Trout are not the toughest fish, so they will not have done well sloshing around in a bucket in a motor vehicle on Yellowstone's challenging roads. Perhaps, on the first try, they all died. Perhaps he improved the process, as the Unabomber did. He might have had a fishing boat, a purpose-built fishing boat with what anglers call a live-well, for keeping fish alive until weigh-in at tournaments. Maybe the fish made the trip that way, with just barely enough space, but plenty of oxygen.

It happened again and again. Fish died on the way, but he took his time, and got better at it as he went. From the nearest spot on Lewis Lake to the nearest spot on Yellowstone Lake is seven miles, an eleven-minute drive, according to Google. Our perpetrator did not have Google; he relied on native cunning. From the boat launch ramp at Lewis Lake to the marina at Grant Village, on Yellowstone Lake, is nine and a half miles. Fifteen minutes. It so happens that those two lakes are the only ones in the park where power boats are allowed, and a power boat is the kind of vessel needed to carry a live-well. A match made in hell—but perhaps he just did it the low-tech way, with an old Coleman cooler or five-gallon buckets from Home Depot.

He had time. He appears to have had all the time in the world.

The only winners, in the end, were the lake trout, especially that first generation. Imagine them in that Home Depot bucket or, if they were lucky, in a live-well, bouncing with the potholes, surfing on the curves now to one side, now to the other, never knowing what it was all about. But if they survived . . .

If they survived being caught, then bashed around on the South Entrance Road, they entered their new home, dazed at first, huffing those first pints of Yellowstone Lake water over their gills, suffering the fish equivalent of seasickness. Then they looked around.

And they found themselves in the same position as the first humans to cross the Bering land bridge into the new world, or the first European explorers to bump into Central America.

On arrival at their new home, they found themselves in a fish paradise.

A Step into the Abyss

Yellowstone is deadly. It kills people with surprising routineness, and not just the unwary. What is most striking, though, is the absolute strangeness of its dangers. People are eaten by bears, buried by avalanches, gored by bison, poisoned by innocent-looking plants, kicked to death by moose, and so on. Perhaps most horrific, however, is Yellowstone's single most iconic hazard. There is a unique awfulness to death by hot spring.

Geysers, hot springs, fumaroles (steam vents, that is), mud pots, and the Mammoth terraces are together what are known as the "thermal features" of the park. No one knows how many there are, although a traditional guess is ten thousand. The number has a suspicious roundness to it because it is, of necessity, a guess. Thermal features change too fast to be inventoried precisely, and the park is too big and wild anyway. Among the thermal features, hot springs are the most common. They begin life as rain or snow that seeps down into the earth and becomes superheated away down among the bedrock that is itself heated by the magma underneath the park. The water then finds a crack that allows it to rise back to the surface.

Because it is often not bubbling or seething in any way— indeed, it is usually just sitting there—the water in a Yellowstone hot spring is deceptive. The steam (even that may be absent) is the visitor's only clue to how hot it is. It is frighteningly hot, frighteningly when one understands the danger. The colors of the spring provide a kind of rough-and-ready thermometer. These colors often are the result of light reflecting off the different species of microorganisms that live in the water. These microorganisms have evolved so that they are adapted to the nightmarish heat. What may be the best-known spring in the park, Grand Prismatic Spring at Midway Geyser Basin, can serve as an example. Where you see reddish-brown around the outer edges of the spring, the water is around 131°F. Moving inward toward the center, the next color is orange, indicating water around 149°F. Beyond that is a yellow band where the water is 165°F. The intense blue at the center is 189°F. Many springs exhibit this color at the center. It indicates water that is too hot to allow any life-form to survive in any numbers.

So, a spring like Grand Prismatic Spring is plenty hot enough to cook food, as native people were known to do. It is therefore plenty hot enough to kill.

The irony is inescapable. The thermal features were the single phenomenon that most impressed the founders of the park. There were other lakes in the country, and other canyons—but there was nothing quite like the geyser basins. And today, there is nothing quite like the geyser basins for providing a horrific death.

So, we were reminded when, just as we were beginning work on this book, extraordinary news came from the park. A visitor had been walking the boardwalk loop at the West Thumb Geyser Basin, on Yellowstone Lake, and spotted a black shoe in Abyss Pool. One happy thing about Yellowstone is that people do not usually throw their garbage over their shoulders; a shoe in a pool, a common enough sight everywhere else, set off alarms here. The visitor reported the shoe to a tour guide, who, investigating, got quite a surprise. The guide saw that the shoe was not just a shoe. The previous owner's foot was still inside.

Or part of it. As the former park historian, Lee Whittlesey, noted of LeRoy Piper, the bodies of those who fall into hot springs disintegrate. There was not much left in the well-named Abyss Pool, one of the deepest hot springs in the park. Investigators had found bits of another shoe there earlier in the week, and when the foot turned up, they also found what they called "fatty tissues" floating on the surface of the spring. That was it.

What had happened? And whose foot was it?

What Abyss Pool had done to the body was in line with what hot springs always do to people who fall in. There have been over twenty such deaths in the history of the park, although the figure is inexact. Some people will have simply disappeared . . . or at least we can guess that they did.

The facts of the known deaths are as gruesome as anything in the history of Yellowstone. Take the case of David Allen Kirwan and his friend Ronald Ratliff. On July 20, 1981, the two parked at the Fountain Paint Pot parking area, at the Lower Geyser Basin. Ratliff's dog bounded out of their vehicle and jumped into Celestine Pool. This is one reason the authorities require dogs stay on a leash in the park. They see a pool and want to jump in, and they have no understanding of the concept of "death by boiling."

Celestine Pool is one of the hot ones, later measured at 202°F. The dog howled, and Kirwan rushed to its aid. Here is Whittlesey's description of what followed:

> Ratliff and another bystander both saw that Kirwan was preparing to go into the spring, and the bystander yelled,

"Don't go in there!" Kirwan yelled back, "Like hell I won't!" Several more people yelled not to go in, but Kirwan took two steps into the pool then dove headfirst into the boiling water. One witness described it as a flying, swimming pool-type dive.

Kirwan actually made it to the dog, then gave up and tried to climb out. Ratliff tried to help and suffered second-degree burns to his feet in the process. Another visitor, a man named Earl Welch, took Kirwan's outstretched hand and pulled him up on the walk.

It was an ugly scene:

> Welch was suddenly overwhelmed with the feeling that he was walking with a corpse. He could see that Kirwan's entire body was badly burned, as the skin was already peeling off. It seemed to Welch that Kirwan was blind, for his eyes appeared totally white. Another man ran up and began to remove one of Kirwan's shoes, and the men watched horrified as the skin came off with it. "Don't do that!" said Welch, and Kirwan responded very tiredly, "It doesn't matter." Near the spring, rangers later found two large pieces of skin shaped like human hands.
>
> Kirwan experienced third-degree burns over 100 percent of his body including the entire head. He was then taken to Old Faithful, where a burn specialist who was coincidentally on duty could do little for him other than to pump in intravenous fluids at a high rate. Bob Carnes, a ranger who saw him at the clinic, remembers thinking that Kirwan did not have a chance for survival. "He was blind and most of his skin was coming off."

He was, at least, somehow not in pain. He died the next morning at a Salt Lake City hospital, the usual destination for the park's burn victims. People who work at Old Faithful learn to dread the sound of the helicopter ambulance, come to haul a new victim away, headed at high speed south toward the Intermountain Burn Center in Salt Lake.

In the commotion around Celestine Pool, as Kirwan stumbled out of the water, everyone forgot about the dog. He died, one hopes more quickly than Kirwan, and sank to the bottom. The dog was a large one, either a Great Dane or a mastiff, although no one was sure in the aftermath. That aftermath was surreal.

The dog began to cook in the 202°F water, and a not-widely-publicized curiosity of the geyser basins manifested itself: as happened recently at Abyss Pool, dissolved fat floated up to the surface. Because the dog had been so big, there was a good deal of it, enough to change the chemistry of the spring.

The boiling point of water is 212°F at sea level. Yellowstone is anything but sea level, so the boiling point is more like 199°F. Under the surface in a hot spring, the water is often hotter than that, but the pressure of the water overhead keeps it from boiling off into steam. The dog's fat was lighter than the surrounding water, which is why it floated to the top. Once there, its lighter weight allowed the water underneath to flash into steam. It essentially turned Celestine Pool, temporarily, into a geyser. There followed a sudden, unexpected eruption. What remained of the dog was blown through the air and out of the pool.

That was an unusually bizarre incident. Hot spring deaths more often fall into patterns. The local practice of what is known as hot potting has claimed victims. It involves finding a spring that can act as a natural Jacuzzi. There are a number of places in the park and in the immediate area, legal and otherwise, where hot springs mingle with less lethal water to make a place where it is possible to sit and happily stew. Had the owner of the foot in Abyss Pool come to grief looking for a hot tub?

It has happened repeatedly. In June 2016, for instance, twenty-three-year-old Colin Scott was touring the country, having just graduated from Pacific University in Oregon. He and his sister, Sable, visited Norris Geyser Basin. It is the hottest place in the park. Here is a strange thing about Norris, mildly strange: it is at seventy-six hundred feet above sea level, but it is so hot that the park's only species of lizard, the sagebrush lizard, does well there. It lives at Norris as if on an island. The water at Norris is also unusually acidic, although the exceptional heat and acidity probably did not matter all *that* much in the incident that followed.

The pair were looking for a place to go hot-potting. They left the boardwalk near Porkchop Geyser, which is itself a reminder of the extremes that happen at Norris: in 1989, the geyser blew itself to pieces. It looks today as if someone took it apart with dynamite. The middle of Norris Geyser Basin is not a good place to leave the boardwalk at all. The Scotts went a long way off the boardwalk, 225 yards, according to investigators. Sable filmed their trip on a cell phone. They reached a spring that was not especially large or deep: four feet wide, ten feet deep, and apparently nameless. Colin Scott reached over to check the temperature—which was measured, later, at 212°F, even hotter than Celestine Pool. He then slipped and tumbled in.

Sable did what she could, which was not much. Colin went all the way in. There is no cell service in that part of the park, so she had to hike all the way back to the museum on the other side of the highway, a long trip. When the rangers returned to the spring, they found that Scott's body was partly visible, and obviously dead. A lightning storm prevented them from recovering it, and when they returned the next day, it was gone. A park spokesman said that "In a very short order, there was a significant amount of dissolving."

That word, "dissolve," then appeared in news sites all over the world.

The focus above is on victims who were being reckless. Often, however, the death is purest accident. Among these, what happened to Andy Hecht is representative. For sheer horror, it is not possible to beat his story.

Andy was nine years old when he and his family were visiting the Upper Geyser Basin on June 28, 1970. They were approaching Crested Pool, a strikingly beautiful spring near Castle Geyser, and a few hundred yards from Old Faithful. It is today lined by railings that are substantial enough that what happened to Andy is not likely to occur today. It developed so quickly that witnesses could not entirely agree on what had happened. Here is Whittlesey's account:

> A puff of wind apparently blew the pool's hot vapor into Andy's eyes, momentarily blinding him at a turn in the walkway. Some accounts claim Andy tripped at the edge of the boardwalk, which had no guardrail. At any rate, he plunged into the pool, where the temperature was over 200 degrees Fahrenheit. Andy tried vainly to swim a couple of strokes, then was scalded to death and sank. According to two national magazines, the last glimpse his mother had of him was seeing his rigid, stark-white face, the mark of his pain and apprehension of death, sinking into the boiling water. Andy's father stated that they did not see him fall; he was behind them on the boardwalk when they heard a splash, turned around, and saw in horror that he had fallen into Crested Pool. Regardless, his body sank out of sight. Eight pounds of bone, flesh, and clothing were recovered the following day.

Incidents like these are representative in one way: they show us what water, heated in the drastic way characteristic of Yellowstone, does to the human body.

Of the above, David Kirwan's case lasted the longest, even though he only survived until the next day. He was totally immersed in a spring that was over 200°F. What happened to the skin, on every bit of his body, was what doctors call protein denaturation. Exposed to such extreme heat, the complex structures in the protein in all those skin cells were broken apart. Blood flow to the cells stopped—what doctors call coagulative necrosis—and the cells died in their millions. Think of what happens to meat when you cook it, or the whites of an egg when you boil it. That is what happened to the cells in Kirwan's skin, close to all of them, and he was actually being exposed to greater heat than you would want to subject an egg to, or a steak for that matter—and recall how his eyes turned white, like the eyes of a fish wrapped in foil in a barbecue, or the white part of a hardboiled egg. The greatest danger to burn victims is ultimately infection, but Yellowstone hot-spring injuries often do not allow the patient to get that far. Instead, all over the body, edema develops as liquid seeps from all that damaged tissue. The next step is dehydration, and shock. That is why the doctor at Old Faithful was pouring intravenous fluid into Kirwan. In a victim of this kind of extraordinary whole-body trauma, hypovolemic shock is usually the cause of death. In Kirwan's case, it may have been a mercy.

Where the shoe, and the foot, in Abyss Pool were concerned, the authorities did answer the "who" part of the mystery.

It was partly just a matter of waiting to see which car in the parking lot at the West Thumb Geyser Basin sat unclaimed. Investigators ultimately zeroed in on a Kia SUV. It belonged to a seventy-year-old Los Angeles man named Il Hun Ro. Inside the vehicle, they found Ro's wallet, complete with driver's license and $447. They also found a photo album, notebooks, and a book of poems with handwritten notes. There was no suicide note. DNA from a relative confirmed that the foot belonged to Ro.

The shoe and foot had turned up on August 16, but investigators concluded that Ro had died over two weeks earlier, on the morning of July 31. Ro had stayed at Canyon the previous night. He would have parked in the West Thumb lot early in the morning of the 31st, surely, or there would have been witnesses. West Thumb Geyser Basin is a popular stop just off the Grand Loop Road, and Abyss Pool is hemmed in on two sides by boardwalk. It, too, is a popular stop, and the dates—the end of July and the start of August—are the busiest of the Yellowstone year. That was one feature of the incident that was strange from the start. It was like finding a body in Times Square with no witnesses and no idea how it got there.

But the investigators left it at that. They announced to the news media on November 17 that the investigation had been closed. With no sign of foul play, there was no reason to continue. And with no witnesses, it was impossible to learn what had happened.

The hot springs of Yellowstone do not leave much evidence. When they kill, they cover their tracks. They even erase the victim.

Not the Chariots of the Gods, Please

Yellowstone is odd in many ways, some happier than others. One of the happiest is the way the past is not obliterated here. Elsewhere in the country, what people did only a few centuries or even a few decades ago is buried under concrete. Go try to find a Spanish colonial building in Los Angeles, or anything from Sam Houston's time in the city named for him. There are so few that the handful remaining are, in one way or another, museums.

No so Yellowstone. Here, you can see on the ground evidence left by people not just hundreds of years ago, but thousands.

When white explorers began to penetrate what is today Yellowstone National Park, in the first half of the nineteenth century, they found the area inhabited mainly by a group of Mountain Shoshone that is today known as the Sheepeaters, after their practice of making bighorn sheep a big part of their diet. When we think about Western Indians of that time, we tend to picture scenes from *Dances with Wolves*, of buffalo hunts on wide open prairie, but the life of the mountains was not like that. In July 1835, the mountain man Osborne Russell entered the future park by travelling down the Lamar River valley. He and his party encountered a band of Mountain Shoshone there. In his journal, he recorded for us a picture of life as it was lived by the native people of Yellowstone. In the Lamar valley, he found

> a group comprising 6 men 7 women and 8 or 10 children who were the only Inhabitants of this lonely and secluded spot. They were all neatly clothed in dressed deer and Sheep skins of the best quality and seemed to be perfectly contented and happy. They were rather surprised at our approach and retreated to heights where they might have a view of us without apprehending any danger, but having persuaded them of our pacific intentions we then succeeded in getting them to encamp with us. Their personal property consisted of one old butcher knife nearly worn to the back, two old shattered fusees [that is, smoothbore muskets], which had long since become useless for want of ammunition, a small stone pot, and about 30 dogs on which they carried their skins, clothing, provisions etc on their hunting excursions. They were well armed with bows and arrows pointed with obsidian. The bows were beautifully wrought from Sheep, Buffaloe and Elk horns secured with Deer and Elk sinews and ornamented with porcupine quills.

The Mountain Shoshone, in fact, are well known today for the quality of their bows. The technique by which they were made was complex and demanding, a kind of Neolithic high-tech. They were fashioned from the iconic spiraling horn of the bighorn ram from which they took their tribal moniker, softened and worked in the hot springs of the region. We, of course, have no way of knowing if any of the artisans fell in.

Other tribes lived in and near the park or have a tradition of passing through. The Crow tribe were so much a presence that their reservation included much of what is now the eastern part of the national park; today, the mountains along that eastern boundary are called the Absaroka Range, taken from the name the Crow use for themselves. The Bannock, who today live on a reservation in Idaho, passed through annually on their way to hunt buffalo on the high plains to the northeast. The most famous group that passed through did so just once. During their epic flight from the US Army, the Nez Perce spent almost two weeks in the park, entering near what is now West Yellowstone, Montana, and leaving through the wilderness up along the northeast corner, after causing some epic turmoil.

There were other tribes, and those were the native people we know the most about, going by the names they use today. Their ancestors went by different names, lost now. The earliest human groups arrived a very long time ago. Their arrival had to await the melting of the glaciers that covered the park almost completely, and to a depth, in places, of four thousand feet. Some of the park's really tall mountains, like Mount Washburn, were entirely under ice. If you could possibly have visited it, the park would have looked like Antarctica, although it would not have been as cold. As the ice ages ended, the glaciers retreated, and you can see the evidence of that retreat in some places. If you drive into Yellowstone from the north, after you leave Livingston, you motor south, up Paradise Valley. All around are marks on the landscape left as the ice melted. Only the most obvious are those long ridges of boulders and gravel that appear regularly from about the point that you pass Mallard's Rest campground and fishing access on the Yellowstone River. Those are glacial moraines, debris that the ice carried with it as it pushed north out of the mountains.

The humans went the other direction. Gradually, year by year, generation by generation, they penetrated what we know of as Yellowstone National Park. The ice was leaving the area fourteen thousand years ago, and we know people were there because they left us a few clues. What archaeologists call "fluted" points, the stone spearpoint characteristic of the earliest human groups in North America, have turned up in the northern part of the national park. They were produced by the Clovis people—hence, the name "Clovis point"—and were used as the business end of hunting spears. One such spearpoint turned up along the Old Yellowstone Trail just inside the park in 2007. Fragments of others came to light when a construction crew was building the old Gardiner post office in 1959. The man who dropped them did so maybe as much as thirteen thousand years ago. These examples were fragmentary, but other Clovis points found around North America are awesome things, the longest a point found in Washington State that was nine inches long. They were like massive stone daggers attached to spears and were used to take down the extinct giant mammals of the time, like woolly mammoths. Imagine rushing up to an elephant and jamming a piece of sharpened rock in its side. That is what they did.

From that point, humans were a part of Yellowstone, their use intensifying about three thousand years ago with the arrival of the bow and arrow, and by that point the ancient hunters were leaving evidence all over the place.

There is an old myth about them. It is usually traced back to the early park superintendent Philetus Norris. He gave his name to the geyser basin, among other things. He also wanted people to visit the park, but he lived in the era when being killed in the unfinished Indian wars was still a going proposition. He is thought to have therefore invented the claim that Native Americans had never spent much time in the park and so could not be a threat. When Norris came west to take up his superintendency in 1877, he stopped on the way at the Little Bighorn battlefield to gather the remains of a friend who died there; the battle had happened during the previous year, so potential tourists who feared violence in the West were not being unreasonable. Not to worry, Norris wrote reassuringly. The Natives were deterred, he claimed, "by a superstitious awe concerning the rumbling and hissing sulfur flames of the spouting geysers and other hot springs, which they imagined to be the wails and groans of departed Indian warriors who were suffering punishment for their earthly sins."

As noted, the Mountain Shoshone were so unconcerned by the hot springs that they used them as a place to make their bows. Far from being a place they visited only rarely, native people seem not to have been able to get enough of the place. When you know what to look for, you can see signs of them absolutely everywhere.

There are, for instance, ring sites, places where you can see, on the ground, the circles of stones that once held down the bison-hide walls of their lodges—teepees, to use the traditional word for them. Sometimes the stones surrounded wickiups, conical structures made of tree branches that served as shelter for a brief stop, or longer. Some were substantial enough that there are still, incredibly, a few of them intact, standing since the nineteenth century in unvisited corners of the park. There are hearths, places where campfires burned, still dark with ash hundreds or thousands of years later. In the Yellowstone River valley north of Gardiner, there are buffalo jumps, places where native groups built rock alignments that channeled bison toward a cliff; part of the group hazed the bison toward the cliff and forced it to stampede, while the other part waited to kill the animals when they crashed to a messy landing below the cliff. And everywhere there is toolmaking debris: chipped obsidian, chert, quartzite, and other materials left when a tool was worked. In the boundary lands along the Old Yellowstone

Trail west of Gardiner, archaeologists even found a piece of a settler's broken bottle, picked up by a native, then chipped and worked into a blade. Everywhere, just everywhere, native people left the marks of their passage.

That brings us to the unsolved mystery in this matter.

Our hope is that this book will be readable for younger teens. If you are a kid reading this, however, you will likely have to ask your grandparents about the subhead we gave this section. And they will likely roll their eyes.

Or maybe not. *Chariots of the Gods?* was a bestselling book written by a Swiss hotelier and confidence artist named Erich von Däniken. He wrote the first version of the book during quiet hours at the hotel and just after leaving jail, where he was serving a sentence for fraud. His claim was that the earth had been visited by UFO beings in the distant past, and that we can see the evidence in ancient art and architecture. The pyramids in Egypt, Stonehenge, and the statues on Easter Island, he says, were built by aliens. How else could they have come to be? One of the best known of his claims is that massive earth artworks, like the famous Nazca Lines in Peru, were landing strips for alien spacecraft. Why else would they be fully visible only from above?

The book had tremendous vogue through the 1970s, spawning a series of films, among other things. Actual archaeologists find it exasperating. They have never had much trouble sticking a pin in von Däniken's claims and blowing them up. For all the phenomena he says cannot be rationally explained, there are rational explanations, often easy ones.

Still, one hesitates to admit it, but sometimes in the park *Chariots of the Gods?* comes to mind.

For instance: one of the most eye-catching mountains in the northern part of the park is Mount Everts. It dominates the view to the east from park headquarters at Mammoth, hanging over Fort Yellowstone and the hot springs like a wall,

8,849 feet high at its summit. No trail leads to that summit; it is a bushwhack all the way, but one that locals take on when looking for a moderately challenging climb. The view to the east is mostly impenetrably dense forest. To the west—to the right, during the climb—is the face the mountain shows to the traveling public. For most of the way, a turn to the right would lead over what would almost amount to a cliff. As always, whenever climbing any Yellowstone peak, the view grows ever more compelling. Below is the Gardner River canyon. Beyond that, the valley of the Yellowstone River stretches away. Sepulcher Mountain and Electric Peak make up the southern flank of the valley. In the distance, the Yellowstone disappears into a kind of alpine jumble, dozens of peaks all blending together.

Below, though, something very strange may appear.

Directly below is a dead-flat mesa called Rifle Range Flats. In the spring, and only in the spring, it turns bright green; that terrain below is a desert, so the green will not last. As the green intensifies through June, perfectly straight lines appear. They are not there at any other time, and searching for them at their level, on Rifle Range Flats, reveals absolutely nothing. They appear like ghosts, and they disappear that way.

The lengthiest is a quarter-mile long and perfectly straight the whole way. There are others on the flat, and beyond the Gardner River there are more, although none so perfect and oddly compelling as those below. Thing is—that is the national park, down there. It was protected before it could ever be settled. There should be no perfectly straight lines, and certainly not one a quarter-mile long, appearing loud and clear, then disappearing as if it had never existed. How could it, and the others, have gotten there?

But this one is easy. As strange a sight as they are, there is an explanation. When the US Army governed Yellowstone, early in its history, the soldiers did things that would strike us as odd.

For one, they grew crops. Farther down the valley is land that was not originally part of the park; homesteaders lived there, and to the extent that they could, in a desert, they too grew crops. The straight lines are irrigation ditches, filled in now and forgotten—except when they reappear in the spring, spectral visitors from a lost age.

Some are not as easy to explain. Some have no explanation at all.

Why, for instance, is there a wall, a stone wall, in the Yellowstone River valley built apparently by ancient Americans, but for no visible purpose? Long, elaborate, utterly improbable, and looking like the Great Wall of China in miniature, it snakes up the north wall of the valley and disappears into the sage-and-cactus desert above. It stands alone in that part of the valley, a monument to . . . what? And to whom?

This is one mystery object you can see for yourself. It is easiest if you are headed north, but south can still work. As you leave the park through the North Entrance and Gardiner, Montana, you leave the park road network and find yourself on US Route 89. There are no turns to make; just drive north on 89, along the Yellowstone River. Just before the river enters the tight canyon ahead—Yankee Jim Canyon—you will see a sign done in US Forest Service brown and white, reading "National Forest River Access and Picnic Area/Yankee Jim." It is 13.5 miles from Yellowstone National Park North Entrance station.

Navigation in this part of the world is tricky. There are no street addresses. Not quite a hundred yards beyond the gravel drive leading to the Yankee Jim picnic area—again, headed north—is a power line crossing the highway at a right angle. Park there (in the dirt beside the road—there are no parking lots, either). Look at the ridgeline in front of your hood and look hard. The wall is there, running roughly north-south from just short of the road to an unguessable height on the ridge above. It is made of native rock, so it blends into the hillside in a way that probably has helped keep it an unexamined mystery.

That height is unguessable because the terrain is so awful as to make a reconnaissance too painful to attempt. The wall of the canyon faces almost perfectly southward. During the winter, it holds precious little snow, and for most of the rest of the year, it bakes. The sun is so brutal that little can grow, except a few highly drought-tolerant trees like junipers and the usual sagebrush and cactus. The rock is all volcanic scree and touching it during the summer is like touching a stovetop. The nearest water is in the river below.

So building that wall was no picnic. It required heavy labor for what must have been a long time. It was not someone's hobby or an idle task taken on a whim.

Do not confuse the wall we are here speaking of with the barrier just up the road, where a cattle guard crosses the highway and is linked up with a wooden buck-and-rail fence, also running up and down the ridge. That barrier is intended to stop bison from migrating farther up the valley, and so possibly carrying disease into the cattle ranches that fill the big valley south of Livingston (the fictional setting, by the way, for Kevin Costner's television series *Yellowstone*). The wooden rail fence does draw attention to one very odd feature of the rock wall. The wooden one is a response to a political demand, from the cattlemen in the valley beyond. It is intended to stop absolutely all bison from moving down the valley—and yet note its incompleteness. It need only run a short distance up the hill, because nature has provided a really genuinely gigantic barrier in the walls of the canyon. Why, then, does the stone wall exist when it runs parallel to a wall a thousand feet high?

Native people did build structures of a size and permanence that are much greater than we usually associate with them, in this part of the world (and the wall, if you know where to look, is visible on Google Earth). As noted, they built jumps over which they ran herds of bison; to get the herds headed in the right direction, they constructed lines of rock cairns that archaeologists call "drivelines," and these lines might extend several miles. Inside the park is a site where they created drivelines that led to a marsh inside a natural ravine, where the animals were slowed by the wet ground and so were more easily killed. The Mountain Shoshone constructed wooden sheep traps that were comparably massive.

Also inside the park, near Mammoth Hot Springs, are similar walls not unlike the one at Yankee Jim Canyon. Paul Schullery, a longtime Park Service interpreter and author of a number of books about the park, has written a description of one of them that captures well the feeling of pure surprise at the moment of discovery:

> A few years ago I was scanning the hills above a meadow near Mammoth Hot Springs. I was looking for grizzly bears, but along a low slope on one side of a small drainage that emptied out into the meadow, two parallel rows of boulders caught my eye. Ranging in size from one to several feet across, the boulders ran downhill in lines so straight and perfect that there could be no doubt they were put there by humans. They had clearly been there a very long time, but nobody, not even the archeologists and other historians I later asked, had noticed them. I took an archaeologist to see them, just to confirm my suspicion, but the purpose of the boulder lines was pretty obvious to me. Crouching behind them, a hunter would have been well concealed from elk, deer, or bison as they descended through the narrow draw and out onto the meadow on their way to the nearest standing water. I started spending time in that meadow in 1972, and I glassed those slopes countless times looking for bears, but it took me eighteen years to notice those rocks.

It is as if he had discovered a little Stonehenge in one of the park's most traveled areas, and that is what the experience of finding one of these places is like. You, along with everybody else, blunder into the thing and are amazed that you have missed it all this time. You are also, often enough, on your own when it comes to explaining what the devil it is.

Just in roughly the area of the North Entrance, there are a number of intriguingly mysterious structures. There are several rock walls like the ones at Mammoth and Yankee Jim Canyon. There are stone circles. There are cairns, piles of rock obviously arranged by human hands, their purpose obscure. The age of all these rock arrangements is obviously great, obvious because they are so thoroughly coated with undisturbed lichen.

Not so the really strange rock arrangement that appears on the shoulder of Mount Everts, in about the place from which a climber can see the local version of the Nazca Lines in the spring. It is a structure of rock sourced locally, and artfully arranged into an oval, more open to the east than the west. It looks rather like an eagle's nest, laid on the ground and made of stone rather than tree branches. What it looks very much like is a Crow vision quest structure.

The Crow call them "fasting beds," and they are an integral part of the spiritual life of the Crow tribe. Stuart Conner was a Billings, Montana, attorney and former Yellowstone ranger who studied the fasting beds of the region for years, and wrote about them:

> A vision quest in the culture of the Crow Indians is a quest for personal supernatural power. Power is usually acquired by the visitation of a guardian spirit in a dream induced by fasting, praying, and formerly by self-mutilation. The guardian spirit can be anything in nature, but traditionally was often the moon or the morning star or an animal or bird invested with supernatural power. The power is passed

to the faster by the guardian spirit, usually with instructions for making a medicine bundle, and with a medicine song and ceremonial procedures to be used to invoke the power when it is needed.

The fast lasts upward of four days and involves the opposite of comfort: the more difficult the experience, the more likely it is that the seeker will be granted a vision. The fast therefore takes place on a bed of stone. "The preferred locations," Conner continued, "are those eminences with a view across great plains or valleys, often to distant mountain ranges. . . . Most fasting beds of unknown origin in Crow Country are U-shaped or oval and just large enough for a person to sit inside cross-legged. . . . The U-shaped ones are open on the east end. I have been told by a Crow man that the opening is so positioned that nothing separates the faster from the morning star. The morning star has great supernatural power. It sometimes becomes the guardian spirit of the faster."

That describes the structure of Mount Everts perfectly, and it is pointed directly at the part of the sky where Venus rises. It is also oriented such that, during the summer solstice, the sun shines directly on the fasting bed for the greatest amount of time, given the enormous mountains all around. At the solstice, the sun disappears behind the far end of the Yellowstone River valley; the peaks at that far end are like a gunsight with the sun in its notch. At that moment, the ridge, from below, lights up the brightest green.

But, as noted above, this fasting bed has no lichen on it. It was therefore built recently . . . and that is one of its appealing features. The Crow have never abandoned this ancient practice. So a modern Crow spirit-warrior hijacked the park as his own personal supernatural channel—and more power to him.

All these things are the work of one or another of the tribes that lived here: Mountain Shoshone, Crow, or some other group. It is just difficult, sometimes, to figure out what they were doing. Except for the wall in Yankee Jim Canyon, you should not try to find any of the places described above. Something might go really amiss, something involving bears or snakes or mountain lions, leading you to come to grief in a way that might be legally actionable. It is better that some of these places remain a family secret anyway.

But here is another you can see—almost—from the car:

On Yellowstone Lake, at Bridge Bay, is a structure that no one can quite figure out. It is right next to the Grand Loop Road, 0.8 miles north of the intersection that leads to the campground and marina at Bridge Bay. If you are headed south, it is about exactly a mile from the intersection with the road to the Lake Hotel and appears at almost the exact point at which the trees along the lakeshore end and the road opens up to reveal a wide view of Yellowstone Lake (and if you are driving northbound, it appears just as that open view is ending and the road is reentering the forest). There is a long turnout next to the lake a tenth of a mile south of the mystery object. Park there and walk north to the place where the shore-side trees begin. Then look closely along the water's edge.

What you may see is a strange rearrangement of the terrain. It is only visible during a dry year, and then only during the autumn—keeping in mind that Yellowstone autumn begins earlier than it does on the calendar. If you are here, however, when the lake level is a little down, you will see a thing that looks, appropriately, like a giant fishhook, or a scale model of a pleasure boat marina. A line of rocks protrudes above the level of the water. The line runs out into the lake, then turns southward, looping around to enclose a portion of the lake about the size of a large swimming pool. The questions are: Is this thing natural? Or did humans build it, long ago?

What it does look like is a fish trap, and that is what many authorities believe it to be. Similar structures—indeed, structures that look just like this one—can be found all over the world, although such traps usually were built to make use of the tide or a river current, and there is no appreciable current here. Nevertheless, the Mountain Shoshone will have either driven or baited fish into it, then blocked the only opening—and the Shoshone are the likeliest tribe to have built this structure, since the Crow did not like fish. The species they were after was the Yellowstone cutthroat, which crowds into the shallows in the spring. We know from accounts written by early visitors that fishing on the lake was, in the park's first decades, absurdly easy and productive; we have report after report of anglers catching dozens of fish with ease. Having filled the dammed area with fish, the Shoshone either speared them or caught them with basket nets; they made a special spear for such purposes, an eight- or ten-foot-long shaft with a barbed end that they thrust downward with both hands.

Even if the structure is a natural phenomenon, as some believe, it could be made to work as a fish trap. Maybe it was half one and half the other, a natural shoal that the Mountain Shoshone modified to work as a trap. It is a problem that comes up in North American archaeology over and over: where do the limits of the "natural" end, and the human modifications begin?

Do us a favor, though: if you visit the trap, or the wall in Yankee Jim Canyon, leave the rocks alone. They have been there for a long, long time.

In later chapters, we will return to the subject of the aboriginal people of the area. They left us plenty of mysteries to ponder. For now, let us turn to an utterly inhuman force.

Our Own Interdimensional Cross-Rip

Late on the night of July 8, 1984, something extraordinary happened in the woods. No one was present. If anyone had been, they would likely have been killed outright.

UNSOLVED MYSTERIES

What happened was violent and mysterious both—but mostly violent. The destruction that resulted was like science fiction, and we have only that destruction as a clue to what happened.

The event occurred in the forest on what locals call the Norris cutoff—the road that runs from Canyon Village to the Norris Geyser Basin. It makes the middle section of the figure-eight that is the park's Grand Loop Road. The event would be even more of a mystery—if we knew about it at all—except that it happened close to the road. You can still see the area, although it has changed greatly. The National Park Service has a short boardwalk and an informational display there, explaining a little about what happened. It is 8.5 miles from the highway intersection at Canyon Village, if you are headed west; if headed east, it is 3.1 miles from the intersection at the Norris Geyser Basin. Look for a crosswalk at that point crossing the Norris cutoff road at right angles. There are parking areas on either side, which is more parking than is normally needed. Few people stop here because the passage of time has erased a great deal of the drama—but if you know what to look for, you can still see it.

On that night, July 8, 1984, there was an explosive burst of energy here. The morning sun revealed that the forest had been torn to pieces. It had been turned into a mostly vacant lot—but not entirely vacant because it was still filled with the slain. On their sides lay every tree in the forest. Walking off the pavement here, the previous day, would have revealed only a palisade of green and brown. Here grew a dense, unbroken wall of lodgepole pines. Now, an observer could look across a square mile of dark green vegetative carnage and see the forest on the far side, the view more or less unimpeded.

The view was reminiscent of those few photographs from the Tunguska event, the explosion in Siberia in 1908 that toppled millions of trees and has captured the imagination of science fiction writers ever since . . . keeping in mind that the Tunguska

39

event, in terms of the amount of land affected, was about eight hundred times larger. One can easily understand why Tunguska has proven so enduringly awe-inspiring. It is thought that a meteor exploded that night, with a force of 12 megatons of TNT, a much greater release of energy than comes even from the average thermonuclear weapon. Something like 80 million trees were knocked flat there. No wonder it also has captured the imagination of conspiracy theorists and nuts. One enduring explanation of the event is that a UFO crashed (although in the 1984 film *Ghostbusters*, Dan Aykroyd's character Ray Stantz explains Tunguska as an "interdimensional cross-rip," giving us the title for this section).

We will not be talking about UFOs here. There is no need. Still, the damage to what people began calling the "blowdown area" on the Norris Road was amazing. How had it happened?

In the 1980s and early 1990s, the most common explanation was that a tornado had touched down. The average tornado features wind in excess of a hundred miles per hour, so that would account for the clean sweep among the trees, which had been knocked down like bowling pins. The area of damage was actually smaller than tornadoes normally produce.

This was never an "official" explanation. There was no one with the authority to grant such prestige to an explanation anyway, and in the 1980s, the nation was not as thoroughly provided with weather data as it is today. Weather satellites were not then connected to your personal computer. If you are old enough to remember them, you would laugh at the idea of a 1984 computer doing such a thing. The Norris cutoff really is the middle of nowhere, though, so even today, Doppler radar would be no help. The nearest Doppler stations are in Pocatello, Idaho; Billings, Montana; and Riverton, Wyoming, and the three come together . . . to make a perfect blind spot over the middle of the park.

UNSOLVED MYSTERIES

And tornados are not common in Wyoming. Since 1950, they have averaged ten per year and have killed a grand total of two people.

They do happen, though, and three years later, there occurred another event that demonstrated in a really spectacular way what the weather could do along these lines. On July 21, 1987—almost the same exact time of year—a much greater and more violent event happened just to the southeast. It was almost unwitnessed except for some people camping in the backcountry, even though it developed in the early afternoon. It is known to historians and meteorologists (and just plain weather geeks) as the Teton-Yellowstone tornado, and it set records for sheer violence.

The tornado touched down at 1:28 p.m. in the Bridger-Teton National Forest, east of Jackson Lake in Yellowstone's sister park, Grand Teton National Park. It moved northeast, wiping out the forest as it went. A well-known University of Chicago meteorologist named Ted Fujita unlocked its secrets later. The tornado intensified rapidly and was soon a category F4, with winds between 207 and 260 mph and damage classified, by people who classify such things, as "devastating." In the area where it was at its most violent, it uprooted full-grown Engelmann spruce trees and stripped them of their bark; it even ripped up the ground itself, throwing clods of earth around like bullets. It kept moving northeast and eventually passed into Yellowstone National Park, although into an area where there was no one to witness it. It is a defining feature of Yellowstone that it is mostly composed of places where a million trees can fall in the woods and no one will hear the sound.

That is about how many trees the Teton-Yellowstone tornado knocked over and threw around, and of course killed. It cut a path a mile and a half wide and twenty-four miles long, and it would have killed anyone who got in the way. At the time,

41

it was the highest-elevation tornado ever recorded, causing damage between 8,500 and 10,000 feet above sea level.

So the Norris blowdown area (a mere 7,900 feet) might have been the result of a tornado. Lately, however, another guess has become the more common: a massive wind shear. The words "microburst" and "downburst" also come up.

Do not feel bad if you have never heard of these phenomena. They do not appear in most people's lives, if they are lucky. Wind shear is mainly of interest to pilots, and sometimes to unfortunate air travelers.

A wind shear is a sudden, radical change in the direction of the wind, and it commonly happens near a downburst. To simplify, these situations develop during thunderstorms. A column of sinking air hits the ground and spreads out in all directions. The vertical downdraft is then converted into horizontal straight-line winds. A downburst can be confused for a tornado from the damage that results, although an expert can tell them apart. The wind speeds are comparable: when a downburst hits the ground, the wind blasting away from it can reach 150 mph.

When an airplane flies into a situation like this, the results can be fatal, and not just to light aircraft; commercial airliners can be pushed right out of the sky. A famous occurrence was the crash of Delta Airlines Flight 191 on August 2, 1985. The aircraft, a great big Lockheed L-1011, was descending into Dallas/Fort Worth in worsening weather. The aircraft had its gear down and was in final approach as it flew underneath a forbidding dark cloud. On the "black box" flight recorder, recovered afterward, a crew member commented on the lightning, and the sound of rain pelting the windscreen can be heard in the background. Suddenly, the plane was struck by a violent downburst. It was almost instantly dropping fifty feet per second. The captain desperately tried to abort the landing, spooling up the engines in an effort to escape the downward blast of air, but the aircraft had been thrown into a radical descent from which it could not recover. In the cabin, only the seat belts would have kept the passengers from being tossed upward along with all the other loose stuff that was now bouncing around like thrown dice. For the passengers, the resigned boredom of a typical flight flashed instantly into terror. The downburst pushed the aircraft, still a mile from the runway, into the earth. Still intact, the plane went on a wild ride across farmland, crossed a highway, struck a vehicle (and killed the driver), and started to disintegrate. Its deranged forward motion finally ended when it struck two water tanks and exploded. There were 163 people on board. Surprisingly, 29 did survive.

Such a downburst is what may have struck the forest that night in 1984. It would have been comparably violent, or possibly a good deal worse. We can only imagine what it was like in the middle of the doomed forest; only a few luckless animals will have seen it. The normally placid forest would have felt first the rising wind, then the rain, gentle at first, then increasing, and finally pelting the trees and forest duff with rainwater and hail. The violence would have increased—but it was still normal for Yellowstone, where a sudden thunderstorm can whip itself up any time.

This one, however, was not normal. The energy intensified. Suddenly, the wind accelerated into a kind of insanity. The noise of its motion around the needles and branches of the trees rose to a howl, then a deafening howl. The trees were now their own worst enemies. Foresters talk about the "sail area" of a tree: the capacity of its crown to catch the wind like the canvas sail of a boat. Lodgepole pine roots can only hold the tree upright for so long—lodgepoles are notoriously shallow-rooted. In the end, the frenzied assault of the wind got the better of the roots, and over they went, tree after tree, crashing to earth with a sound only marginally louder than the mad howl of the wind itself.

They fell in the hundreds, leaving a great hole where there had been nothing but solid forest before. The first human witnesses arrived in the morning, to wonder what had happened. They wonder to this day.

As strange as it was, the event in its way was typical of Yellowstone. The weather is more extreme here: the snow deeper, the wind wilder, the lightning more maniacal. In this as in so many things, perfectly normal natural processes are intensified. Meteorological violence can whip itself up in minutes.

The incident had a sequel involving another colossal force of nature. The summer of 1988 is famous in Yellowstone history for the fires that blew up as the summer progressed, ultimately burning about half the park. The path each individual fire took is easily visible today: look for the swathes of bright green lodgepoles, a lighter shade than the older trees. One can even reconstruct the direction the fires took. The prevailing wind across the park runs from southwest to northeast, and it pushed the fires in that direction, too, marking out long, wide swaths of burned terrain.

One of the largest of the individual blazes was the North Fork fire, which, among other things, almost destroyed the village at Old Faithful. It covered a great deal of ground, and when it finally reached the blowdown area, it went to work. A reporter from the newspaper the *Missoulian* visited the area twelve years later, and described what had happened:

> A tornado or rogue wind blew down 660 acres of trees in 1984. The downed timber rotted and dried out for four years and when the flames of the North Fork fire hit in 1988, the fire had a happy home. Instead of burning erect lodgepole pines and moving on, the fire settled in to feast on the downed drought-dried timber, smoldering for days and searing the ground. The fire vaporized the organic matter from the soil's upper layers under rotten logs, burning as hot as 1,200 degrees Fahrenheit. . . .

Some thought the blow-down area would remain sterile, perhaps for decades.

They were wrong. When you visit the blowdown area today, you cannot see far. The wide-open vacancy left by the blowdown event has now been filled in. At the end of the short boardwalk is a wall of new trees, another of Yellowstone National Park's innumerable new, bright green lodgepole forests. All these trees started growing after the great conflagration. Like so much of the park, it resembles a Christmas tree lot—except that some of the trees are getting to be too big to put in the living room.

As in all the burned areas left by the 1988 summer of fire, the blowdown area is a typical display of a truth about the place. No matter what crazy thing you throw at Yellowstone, it always makes a comeback.

2

BATS FOR THE BELLHOPS AND OTHER STRUCTURAL SURPRISES

The UFO has landed. The old Canyon Lodge, at the Grand Canyon of the Yellowstone. SCOTT HERRING

Yellowstone has reinvented itself over and over, both the human Yellowstone and the natural one. The latter, steaming there in the background of all those photographs, has its own rules, and we have only learned a limited number of those. The main thing that landscape does is re-form itself, in much the same manner as in Ernest Hemingway's famous description of how bankruptcy happens: "Two ways. Gradually, then suddenly." The life-forms move through their natural cycles, the ground slowly erodes—and then one day, the whole thing blows up.

The human Yellowstone never sits still, either. Every generation or two, at least since it became a park, it has transformed itself into something quite unlike what came before.

It is because of this constant change, by the way, that a large minority (and sometimes a majority) of comments about the park are negative. Always, it is believed to have fallen away from some former perfection that it possessed in a golden age that might or might not ever have existed. A great deal depends on perception.

It began life, or at least its most recent life, as hell on earth, a thing resembling the inside of a nuclear bomb blast. The violence of the most recent Yellowstone caldera eruptions cannot be exaggerated. Consider this: when Mount St. Helens exploded in 1980, covering much of the West with ash, it ejected between one-quarter and one-half of a cubic mile of volcanic rock. What we now call Yellowstone blew up two million years ago and ejected six hundred cubic miles. In effect, Yellowstone was Mount St. Helens multiplied over five thousand times, each St. Helens erupting at once. And it kept exploding over and over and will do it again eventually.

Then it changed and became the exact opposite. For millennia, it sat beneath thousands of feet of ice, crushed like a daisy under a boulder. Whatever the area was like before, it took on much of its present physical shape during those thousands of years. The river valleys were scoured out, then filled back up with glacial debris. The higher peaks in ranges like the Beartooth Mountains were dramatically reshaped. Places like Hayden Valley were filled with glacial till. The rough edges left by the volcano hardly stood a chance.

The ice departed, and the park changed again, to become, among other things, a home and pantry for native tribes. The now-nameless ancestors of tribes like the Crow and the Shoshone lived here for uncounted generations—actually, for about three hundred generations, give or take a few dozen.

The pace of change accelerated when the place became a government park. It was at first a mere curiosity. It was afterward a military reservation visited mainly by two sorts of people: wealthy easterners and frontier drifters. In time, it became a destination for people touring the West by railroad. After the Second World War, automobiles arrived in really large numbers, and the crowds increased. Today, it is a destination for people from literally the entire world, and the crowds increase still. It is hard to say what it might become next, but it would be good if the crowds quit doing that.

During its time as a park—and really, since the ice receded—people have left their mark, the marks accumulating and often confusing the people who have come later. Inside the park, there are six large, developed areas: Canyon, Tower/ Roosevelt, Mammoth, Old Faithful, Grant Village, and the cluster of structures on the northwest corner of Yellowstone Lake between Bridge Bay and Fishing Bridge. Except for Grant Village, which was mostly developed at once, these areas were put together one or two buildings at a time, or sometimes a bunch, every development partly erased every generation and rebuilt according to the latest fashion. Since fashions change, the result is a clash that we do not notice only because we see it all the time.

Old Faithful is probably the most mismatched of the group. Imagine a room in a private house. It has patterned wallpaper from the Victorian era, Art Deco lamps from the 1920s, plastic furniture from the 1950s, harvest gold shag carpet from the 1970s, *Flashdance* posters from the 1980s, and a 98-inch flat screen TV from today. That is Old Faithful, where every era in the human history of the park is represented, and often not well.

But often superbly, and we would not want it otherwise.

If the villages in the national park were uniform in their design, then the uniformity would have resulted from the buildings all being put up at the same time, and that means they would all meet the standards of beauty of that one time, and we would have inevitably changed our minds the instant they were done but would have found ourselves stuck with them. Imagine if Old Faithful had been demolished and entirely rebuilt in 1971. We would then harvest gold *everything*, with avocado green trim.

The variety reflects the life lived here. Along with the buildings, traditions have accumulated among the people who work in the park, and even among those who only visit. Some date back to the early years. Some are dangerous, some silly, some profound. As with the buildings, there is regularly no rhyme or reason.

That is part of the charm.

When Did a UFO Land at Canyon Village?

In 1957, and it has been there ever since.

How else can you explain why the old Canyon Lodge looks like that?

But there is an explanation. During the early years of the park, businesses like hotels and restaurants were housed in the most extraordinary miscellany of "buildings." They were often tents, and some of the structures were more like shacks. With the arrival of the railroad, a succession of much larger hotels were constructed, until those early generations finally had hotels that could properly be called "grand." Three still exist: the Mammoth Hotel, the Lake Hotel, and the Old Faithful Inn.

Of these, the Old Faithful Inn is likely the most famous, and it is surely the most distinctive. Built in the winter of 1903–1904, it is a messenger from another era. Amazingly, like Honest Abe's childhood cabin, it is mostly built of locally sourced logs. It is certainly the largest log hotel in the world, and it's maybe the largest log structure, period.

It is an early example of what came to be called the "National Park Service rustic" style. Beginning at an early date, planners and architects building in the national parks sought to produce structures that blended in with the natural environment. They developed a style that rejected the industrial cities of the outside world. The result was architecture that was handmade by master craftsmen but was irregular and asymmetrical in the way that any log cabin would be.

There are innumerable examples of National Park Service rustic buildings in Yellowstone; because it is the oldest park, Yellowstone is one of the places where the style came into existence. These buildings are as important and impressive a feature of the place as the geysers and the canyon. One you might miss, if you do not look for it, is the Roosevelt Lodge. You might miss it because it is in the least-visited corner of the park, far to the northeast. Furthermore, it is at the end of a side road and not even visible from the Grand Loop. The isolation is part of the appeal. The lodge is the centerpiece of what is now called the Roosevelt Lodge Historic District. There are dozens of structures here from the first half of the twentieth century, many done in the "logs-out" style. Sit on one of the rocking chairs on the lodge porch in the evening and watch the colors change on the mountains to the north, and you will appreciate where the name "rustic" comes from. The experience is the very opposite of the postmodern outside world.

That was not the end of the story. The United States emerged from the Second World War with the only large industrial economy in the world that had not been wrecked. Detroit converted from manufacturing weapons to manufacturing gigantic cars, and the automotive culture of the 1950s began to bloom. The Eisenhower administration built the interstate highway system. Suburbs, fast-food, drive-in theaters, NASCAR, and a whole library of automotive-themed music and other art followed.

Perhaps inevitably, the national parks were swept up in the enthusiasm. It is commonly asserted that the national parks were neglected during the Great Depression and the war, and that they were "falling apart" by the 1950s, but "falling apart" is impossible to quantify. The parks got free construction labor from the New Deal, and hardly anyone visited the parks during the war, anyway. Perhaps it was just bureaucratic empire-building. At any rate, in January 1956, the director of the National Park Service, Conrad Wirth, gave a special presentation to President Eisenhower. "Here is the attendance picture," he said, "358 thousand visitors in 1916—21 million in 1941—50 million last year—and by 1966, the parks will have at least 80 million visitors." The parks, he warned, were going to be wiped out by an automotive tsunami. Wirth was giving the presentation to unveil his fix: Mission 66, a master plan to rebuild the parks and make them automobile friendly. It would begin that year, in 1956, and finish in 1966, the fiftieth anniversary of the establishment of the Park Service.

The planners let go of the National Park Service rustic style with both hands. They substituted what designers call midcentury modern. It is the kind of architecture you see in the Tomorrowland section of Disneyland, what the author Bill Bryson terms "soaring 1960s Jetsons-style architecture."

It looked very strange in the national parks, and it still does.

It was widely regarded as a mistake almost the minute it was done. In his unlikely bestseller *Desert Solitaire*, the novelist and

BATS FOR THE BELLHOPS AND OTHER STRUCTURAL SURPRISES

essayist Edward Abbey wrote a famous attack on what he called the "sinister Master Plan" that is probably better known today than the original plan. The buildings have been coming down ever since, but now a peculiar thing has happened. They are now rare enough, and old enough, that people have developed a fondness for those that remain.

To see an example, do this: when you finish looking at the Roosevelt Lodge (named for a camping trip Theodore Roosevelt made nearby), drive back down the hill and a few hundred feet to the west, and look at the service station. People rarely give such structures much attention, but this one was built in the early 1960s as part of the master plan, and it is a perfect expression of the midcentury modern aesthetic. Look, and you will see how strange it is.

Note the amazing contrast with the Roosevelt Lodge Historic District. These days, the Park Service makes every effort to keep businesses off the Grand Loop, yet here this one is, on a patch of barren gravel fifty feet from the Loop, obscured not at all by the roadside weeds. The entire front face of the station is plate glass set in burnished aluminum, more glass than in a dozen other Roosevelt area structures combined. The roof of the building extends without a break to form a canopy over the pumps, the whole, canting at about fifteen degrees, much higher in front than in back. The Space Age has arrived in Wyoming. The station is a glassy fuselage suspended beneath a mighty airfoil, a Flying Wing poised to lift off and go bomb the Soviet Union with free road maps and quality customer service.

There are Mission 66 structures at every location and they can usually be spotted for what they are by that aesthetic. It is strongest at Canyon Village.

To see it requires only a minor side excursion during a visit to the Grand Canyon of the Yellowstone. At Canyon Junction, turn (or continue) eastbound, onto North Rim Drive. Just past the gas station—itself a Mission 66 structure—make the first right turn into the parking and shopping area. The big Park Service visitor center there is new, but otherwise, almost all the buildings that surround the parking lot are Mission 66 structures. A giveaway is the flat, or nearly flat, roofs, a distinctive feature of midcentury modern design. If you arrive at Canyon in the spring, you might also note the snow on the ground in the shade and on the north sides of buildings. After a snowy year, the drifts may be four or five feet deep. You might note them—but the designers of those roofs did not. Roofs in snow country are not normally designed to catch the snow.

Other distinctive qualities of the era are the glassy front walls and the use of barely disguised I-beams as decorative features. Again, it is the opposite of the rustic aesthetic. Here is the forward-looking confidence of the 1950s captured in architecture. Technology had won the Second World War and delivered the nation into this period of outlandish prosperity. Turning our backs on the past was fashionable.

The use of I-beams as ornamentation reached its extreme at the old lodge, on the east side of the parking lot. Here is where we began this section, with the structure that, UFO-like, spreads its landing struts in a gesture of steely welcome toward the parking lot and the very motor vehicle technology that gave birth to Mission 66.

As noted, the structures are now rare enough and the era distant enough that people have come to find a charm in them that was absent before. The lodge is operated by the hotel concessionaire, Xanterra. The nearby general store, also a Mission 66 building, is run by a separate concessionaire, Delaware North. Between them, they teamed up to make lemonade out of lemons. Having inherited buildings from the 1950s, they refurbished them to target the nation's more-or-less permanent nostalgia for the 1950s. The store, for instance, features a 1950s-style diner. It has *always* featured a 1950s diner, but the décor now calls attention to the datedness that used to be a problem.

The lodge has been restored to something close to the way it was when it was opened in 1957 (confusingly, at Canyon, the word "lodge" regularly refers to two different structures—the UFO in the main village area and a large, new hotel further to the east). The original lodge is now a collection of restaurants that fills the old building. The people who did the restoration knocked out interior partitions, revealing an expansiveness in the building that the walls had hidden. Where possible, they recreated the original décor. The building as a whole now looks as it did when it was new. It looks, that is, rather like an airport terminal in a midsize city, one built in the 1950s.

Go inside and dig the nifty starburst light fixtures, which match more or less exactly the originals from the Eisenhower era. Dig the very nifty question-mark-shaped bar. The restorers knew, however, not to take it too far. Find some of the photographs of the original building that were taken when it was new. They are available online. Here is soaring Jetsons-style architecture taken to its extreme.

It is now immensely charming—and at the same time, you will likely find yourself asking a question of yourself that generations of park visitors have asked:

"What were they thinking?"

Bats for the Bellhops

As a summer day slides toward evening, you may notice an odd sight. The sun has disappeared behind the hills to the west. The sky there turns pink, and bands of light may streak across the horizon like distant spotlights. If you are out strolling around, say, in the Upper Geyser Basin, you will see, then hear, then feel the mosquitoes, although this is not the worst place in the park for bugs.

But there, in the air just above your head, is a blur, a dark blur. It is not a bird; it is getting too late in the day for that, and the way this thing is flying is . . . not right. It seems clumsy, almost, as if the creature were still learning to fly. It flies the way Snoopy's cartoon friend Woodstock used to. That impression is strengthened greatly when an alarming thing happens: one of the black shapes flies right at your head but veers upward at the last possible second. For the briefest instant, you see the shape clearly, outlined against the now-purple sky. It makes you think, oddly, of Halloween decorations.

Your guess is correct. Those are bats.

There is a tendency to be immediately alarmed, but you should resist the temptation. The bats in Yellowstone are not out to bite you and would only have an opportunity to do so under bizarre circumstances. Vampire bats do not live anywhere near Yellowstone; they are very much a warm weather animal (they may sometimes turn up in the southernmost part of Texas). The danger of getting rabies from a bat has been much publicized, but we need to avoid allowing ourselves to be terrified by stuff on the internet. In 2021, an Illinois man awoke in the middle of the night with a bat on his neck; he refused treatment, and a month later, he died of rabies. Terrifying, no?

No. His was the first death from rabies in the whole United States for *three years*. It was the first human case of rabies in Illinois since 1954. You are much, much more likely to be eaten by a shark or stung to death by bees. You are immensely more likely to be killed by ants.

They are not, to be sure, flying hamsters. Do not pick them up and pet them and put them in a Habitrail. Otherwise, the thing to do is regard the bats as another of the park's interesting animals.

Bats are, in truth, really amazing animals. They are the only mammal that is capable of birdlike flight—flight, that is, in which their wings are flapping. In this, they are different from flying squirrels, which are really gliding squirrels, despite what we saw in the old cartoon about Bullwinkle's friend Rocket J. Squirrel, who flew around like, well, a rocket. This killer adaptation is one reason there are so many different kinds of bats, living almost everywhere on the planet.

While some species of bats eat fruit, the ones in the park eat insects, using sound waves to home in on them in rather the same way a submarine uses sound waves to find other vessels without revealing its periscope (although the term for the submarine's sound gear is "sonar," while for a bat, the word is "echolocation"). Because they are warm-blooded and are so vigorously active, bats have to eat insects in spectacular quantities, and they have the happy habit of eating insects we humans especially hate. They can eat as many as twelve hundred mosquitoes an hour. A nursing mother will eat her own body weight in bugs in a single night—in fact, she must, because of the demands nursing places on her body.

People tend to look at bats and see them as flying rodents, but bats share almost nothing in common with rats and mice. Whereas the rodents we get in our houses are adapted to have offspring in extravagant numbers, a bat mother may have only one pup per year (and "pup" is the term for them). The mother recognizes the pup's smell and voice and can find it in a colony that may number thousands. Because they have only one pup at a time, they put a great deal of care into it, same as we do. Bats can live as much as thirty years. Rats and mice do not do that, either.

Having only one pup at a time has also made their populations vulnerable. Bats elsewhere in the country have been victimized by a fungal disease called white-nose syndrome. In spite of the name, it is not funny in the slightest: it is named for the visible white fungal growth that develops especially on their muzzles. Bats hibernate during the winter, or go into torpor, and the fungus attacks them then, moving from bat to bat through their closely packed colonies. It seems to irritate them, causing them to move around during the winter—and so starve to death, having run out of fat reserves before the spring brings their insect larder back to life.

Bats were not intensely studied in the park before white-nose syndrome appeared elsewhere in the country (the fungus causing it is thought to be an exotic, from Europe). It has not made it to the park yet, but scientists are now trying to establish a baseline understanding of the park's bats so that they will know what has changed if the syndrome does appear. They have identified thirteen species in the park, with appealingly goofy names like "big brown bat," "Townsend's big-eared bat," "hoary bat," "pallid bat," and so on. During the summer, they come together in roosts to have their young (the scientists call that a "maternity colony," by contrast with the place where they hibernate during the winter, which they refer to using the Roman-sounding term "hibernaculum"). They like mines and caves for this purpose, but Yellowstone does not have as many of those as other parks do. The bats instead roost in buildings. The park authorities try to keep them out, but realistically—well, look at how many buildings there are in the park, and look at how large some of them are. Keeping such a small, persistent, numerous animals out is like trying to keep any animal out. You fail. You always fail.

That leads us to the title for this section.

If you are strolling around at Old Faithful just after sunset and you do notice the bats, see what might be happening over at the Old Faithful Inn. You will want to do this after the sun has set, but well before the sky reaches full dark. If the timing works out this way, you can stroll there after an eruption of Old Faithful Geyser, and the sidewalk that surrounds the geyser amphitheater is a good viewpoint. Look upward toward the wood shake roof of the Inn. Do you see motion? A great deal of it? If you do, it may take the form of a dark stream, like the smoke from the funnels of ships in old films, ships that burned coal. Look closely. What you are probably seeing is the evening bat flight.

The bats live in the Inn in some numbers, in the empty spaces below the roof gables and all the other miscellaneous unused and unvisited spaces above the ceilings. One of the little-known facts about the Inn is that the bellmen live there. The rest of the employees live in large dormitories here and there around the area, but the folks who show you to your room have their own peculiar space up in the rafters. They are in many ways park aristocracy—the tip income alone sets them apart. Their home is certainly peculiar. There are enough bats living in the vicinity that the bellmen long ago named it Bats' Alley.

(Aristocrats, indeed. The name is, among other things, pretty obviously a reference to T. S. Eliot's *The Waste Land*, to the lines "I think we are in rats' alley / Where the dead men lost their bones." The people who work in the park are an oddly erudite bunch.)

It is not just the Old Faithful Inn. Any large structure may be full of bats, and the small ones, too. At the Lake Hotel, the front desk crew may keep a large fishing net in the front office or behind the check-in counter, the kind of angler's net that might be used to boat lake trout out on Yellowstone Lake. It is needed for those occasions when the bats get inside. This can be quite a spectacle. If you are staying at the Lake Hotel and hear screaming erupt somewhere down the hallway, it will be a bat inside a guest room that is the cause. An employee—they can be quite blasé about this—will take the fishing net toward the source of the screams. You can think of it as a kind of echolocation, although usually the screams are loud enough that there is no mystery about where they are coming from. The employee will net the bat, take it outside, and set it loose. They keep the net for this purpose because if they do not, a scene may develop like a friend saw at the Lake Hotel once: an employee was chasing a bat down the hall with a broom used as a goad, trying to herd the bat toward a door. Working in Yellowstone regularly involves strange tasks.

Anyone finding all this frightening or offensive should really go elsewhere for a vacation. In Yellowstone, the animals have the right of way.

The employees are, however, trained to be coy about this phenomenon. I experienced this gentle evasiveness myself when I was trying to learn more about the bats in the larger buildings. I spoke to a man who worked at an information desk in one of the park businesses. People who are given that job are always the cream of the crop. This fellow was about sixty, with a trim gray beard and a winning attitude. He looked like Sean Connery in *The Hunt for Red October*. I assumed I would get some solid information here.

"What can you tell me about the bats in the attic?" I asked.

His eyes registered alarm. He smiled a thin smile and began speaking: "Founded in 1872, Yellowstone is the first national park in the world."

I suspect I rolled my eyes. "Yes, I know you're not supposed to talk about it. But I know they're there. Do they ever get inside here during the day?"

He continued, still smiling, sort of, but with a distressed look on his face. "Yellowstone was founded to preserve its geothermal areas, which contain half the geysers in the world."

I suspect I now frowned. "Look," I said, patiently, "I used to work in the park. I know they told you not to talk about the bats. But your secret is safe with me."

His facial expression could now be described as sickly—and yet he pressed on: "In addition to its geysers, visitors come to see wildlife in the world's most intact temperate ecosystem."

And so on. I have exaggerated a little, but not much. He was not supposed to talk about it.

BATS FOR THE BELLHOPS AND OTHER STRUCTURAL SURPRISES

He was told not to, however, because it was a subject that would inevitably come up. So look around outside, just as the light is beginning to fade. During the summer, you are almost guaranteed to see a number of bats. However, whatever information you can get about Bats' Alley and other bat-culture aspects of park life will require some work.

Bears for the Bellhops, Too

Most of the other animals in the park leave the structures alone. They want nothing to do with the human masses. There is, however, one big exception.

Very big.

Consider what happened at the Lake Lodge one winter.

If you have ever worked in a kitchen, you may be aware that the worst task in a place like that is cleaning the grease trap. What happens is that bits of food sink to the bottom of the trap, and being food, those bits rot. The grease layer over the food waste holds the smell in—until that unlucky employee gets to clean the trap, at which point the odor of rot is released. People commonly gag and retch when they reach the bottom.

Inside the Lake Lodge is a large cafeteria (Wylie's Canteen is the formal name). It is an informal place where they sell plenty of fried food through the summer. When it comes time to shut down for the winter, one of the tasks is, naturally, emptying the grease trap. The prospect was so forbidding that one year—this is said to have happened in the 1970s—the manager decided to skip that step, to just cover the thing and hope for the best. Once the building was boarded up and the heaters were off, the cold would solidify the grease and lock in that special richness.

So they left it there and closed up the building . . . but it turned out that the local wildlife was not inclined to cooperate.

The Lake Lodge winter-keeper was the one who found it. He was making his rounds of the area and noticed something amiss at the lodge. What was amiss was the building itself. It was missing part of its wall—because a bear had caught a whiff of the grease and had given in to the temptation. The bear ate the grease after first removing the wall.

They do things like that. There are, in Yellowstone, two kinds of bears. In the past, the more common one was the black bear, *Ursus americanus*, the smaller and less aggressive of the two. Smokey the Bear is a black bear; so was the 1960s TV star Gentle Ben. The larger and more aggressive bear is the grizzly, with the wonderful name *Ursus arctos horribilis*. They are sometimes difficult to tell apart, although if one is killing you, that is probably a grizzly. Grizzlies are much larger than black bears; in Yellowstone, a black bear male might weigh something in the vicinity of 200 pounds, while a male grizzly can reach 700. The black bears can be dangerous, but the grizzly is the one to really watch out for. When someone is seriously injured by a bear in the park, a grizzly will normally have been responsible, and it happens on average about once a year. People are quite literally eaten by grizzlies, if the bear manages to have undisturbed access to the body for a while after making the kill.

The bear who disassembled the wall of the Lake Lodge was participating in a grand old Yellowstone tradition. Since the very beginning, hotels and the bears have been an item. The animals come to visit, and in the past, it has been difficult to get them to leave.

Theodore Roosevelt noticed the relationship, at an early date in the history of the park. He visited Yellowstone in 1903, arriving in April, so early in the spring that when he and his party traveled into the interior of the park, they rode over the deep snow by horse-drawn sleigh. The bears, he discovered, were almost all still hibernating. "I was sorry not to see the bears, for the effect of protection upon bear life in the Yellowstone has been one of the phenomena of natural history," he wrote later, and continued:

BATS FOR THE BELLHOPS AND OTHER STRUCTURAL SURPRISES

Not only have they grown to realize that they are safe, but, being natural scavengers and foul feeders, they have come to recognize the garbage heaps of the hotels as their special sources of food supply. Throughout the summer months they come to all the hotels in numbers, usually appearing in the late afternoon or evening, and they have become as indifferent to the presence of men as the deer themselves—some of them very much more indifferent. They have now taken their place among the recognized sights of the park, and the tourists are nearly as much interested in them as in the geysers.

It was amusing to read the proclamations addressed to the tourists by the park management, in which they were solemnly warned that the bears were really wild animals, and that they must on no account be either fed or teased. It is curious to think that the descendants of the great grizzlies which were the dread of the early explorers and hunters should now be semi-domesticated creatures, boldly hanging around crowded hotels for the sake of what they can pick up, and quite harmless so long as any reasonable precaution is exercised. . . .

At times the bears get so bold that they take to making inroads on the kitchen. One completely terrorized a Chinese cook. It would drive him off and then feast upon whatever was left behind. When a bear begins to act in this way or to show surliness it is sometimes necessary to shoot it. Other bears are tamed until they will feed out of the hand and will come at once if called. Not only have some of the soldiers and scouts tamed bears in this fashion, but occasionally a chambermaid or waiter girl at one of the hotels has thus developed a bear as a pet.

With the bears, as here, you get comedy and terror in equal proportions, and it has always been that way. Here is Billy Hofer, Yellowstone's premier naturalist during the early years, and President Roosevelt's guide during his visit. He was writing in the outdoor sports journal *Forest and Stream* in 1905 (the "Lake Outlet" is the old name for what we call Fishing Bridge):

> I saw one man this summer who said he had been hurt by a bear. I asked him how. He had a bad cut on his forehead. He said he and several others were watching the bears eating slops at the Lake Outlet. A female grizzly with two cubs was not very friendly. The cubs came toward the crowd and the old one came too. The crowd broke and ran. Some went up trees. He ran against a tree, striking his head against a dry limb. This knocked him out. His friend said the bear came within ten feet of him, then went back. When he came to his friend helped him to camp, dressed his cut, and this was the way he was hurt by a bear.

Today, the Park Service operates a fleet of garbage trucks that are the linchpin of an elaborate garbage-gathering operation. Those trash cans you see that are built like a tank are designed to resist the assault even of a grizzly. The maintenance crews empty those cans before the trash gets a chance to rot, and the contents of the garbage trucks is landfilled outside the park. A significant amount is recycled.

Nothing like that happened in the early decades of the park. The hotels and restaurants especially had a problem getting rid of garbage, and the bears were looked on as an efficient means of disposal. Roosevelt called them "scavengers and foul feeders," but they are really opportunists, eating whatever comes along. That is how they end up eating tourists, and it is also why they do love garbage. Long before Roosevelt's visit, the hotel kitchens had adopted a practice of dumping their waste in the same places, and the bears knew where and when that happened. Watching them became a popular pastime, and for many years the rangers played along. People watched from bleachers erected at a dump near Canyon, the bleachers erected specifically for the purpose of watching the bears eat refuse on a kind of stage below. At Old Faithful, garbage was dumped on a stand labeled "Lunch Counter—For Bears Only." While the bears (both kinds) fed on the rubbish, a ranger would deliver a talk about them, often while sitting on a horse. Somehow, the horses learned to tolerate this very strange situation.

In truth, the rangers came soon enough to see the travesty of it. During the Second World War, when gasoline and tires were tightly rationed, visits to the park fell dramatically, and the Park Service used this breather as an opportunity to end this wildly popular pastime.

Still, there was the garbage, being issued from the hands of visitors and employees in massive quantities (these days, it is something between eight and nine million pounds a year, most of it in the short period of good weather during the summer). It went to landfills inside the park, where the bears, mostly grizzlies, visited nightly. Meanwhile, on the road, the black bears stopped traffic. This tradition also dated back to the early years of the park, and they originally stopped stagecoaches. The black bears—females with cubs seemed to specialize in it—plopped down beside the road and begged. The term in the park for what resulted was a "bear jam," and the jams got longer and longer as more automobiles visited the park. Almost unbelievable behavior resulted. People put their children on the bears' backs to get photographs of the kids taking a bear-back ride. People smeared jelly on their children's faces to get photographs of the bears licking it off. People fed the bears a horrifying range of delicacies that included such treats as lit firecrackers.

Again, the rangers were perfectly aware that the situation was increasingly intolerable. This time, it was not war but a cultural shift that enabled them to put a stop to it. During the 1960s and early 1970s, both people in government service and at least some of the public itself came to regard nature differently. Yellowstone, they decided, should not be run like an amusement park. It should be as natural as possible. This change enabled the park's managers to at last chase the roadside bears back into the woods and stop the public trying to feed them. The latter task took years and years, but today, few people look for junk-food-addicted bears alongside the road.

The park landfills were closed, too, but not before providing my favorite hotel + bear story. A traditional activity of hook-and-bullet magazines and sporting goods manufacturers is the effort to find a bear repellent for hunters and anglers. We today have pepper spray, but for decades, the outdoor industry sought a repellent in vain. Toward the end of the landfill era, they hit upon the idea of using paradichlorobenzene. That is the active ingredient in mothballs. People use it also as a repellent for animals like squirrels, and some bright spark had the idea of scaling it up to target bears.

It so happened that the hotels stored a great deal of cloth in various forms while the operations were closed, which was much of the year. They therefore used mothballs in great quantities. In the spring, when the cloth came out for the new season, those great quantities went to the landfill.

It also so happened that the landfills were frequented not just by bears. Wildlife biologists went there, too. The concentration of bears in one place presented a rare opportunity to get a close look at these difficult-to-observe animals, dozens of them all at once. The bear biologists would park their cars at the edge of the landfills and watch, tape recorders and notebooks ready at hand.

The bears came down. They sniffed over the mothballs. The biologists looked on in increased interest. Would paradichlorobenzene work as a repellent?

The bears did respond. The mothballs affected their behavior immediately.

The bears ate them.

BATS FOR THE BELLHOPS AND OTHER STRUCTURAL SURPRISES

And Other Structural Surprises

As we have noted, buildings have been accumulating in Yellowstone since the beginning, and no overall plan has ever governed that accumulation—which, as we have also noted, is all for the best. The very oldest of them is in the park, although it is certainly showing its age.

Between Old Faithful and Madison, at the Lower Geyser Basin, a short road leaves the Grand Loop and follows the Firehole River, running generally southwest. It ends at what locals call the freight road trailhead. The trail that begins here follows an old freight road—closed to motor vehicles, but open to bicycles—until it crosses the Firehole River. To one side is the trail for Sentinel Meadows and the Queen's Laundry. It leads, among other places, to a travertine mound next to Queen's Laundry Spring. The structure you will see there, atop the mound, is nothing much to look at now. The early park superintendent Philetus Norris built it in 1881 as a bathhouse; during that time, the thermal water in the area was not as hot as it is elsewhere, and tourists soaked in the springs (which is both illegal and dangerous today). The structure is just two rooms, with no roof, the walls done in Lincoln-Log fashion with V-notches in the wood. It was never finished. It is, however, thought to be the very oldest building still in existence put up by the government for public use in a national park—any national park anywhere.

That it still exists at all is a bit of characteristic Yellowstone strangeness. It would have disintegrated—untreated wood does not last long here—but the logs are being "silicified," to use the geologists' term. The white stuff covering the ground here, and in the thermal areas up and down the Firehole valley, is geyserite. It is a kind of silica. The silica seeps into the voids in the wood, and essentially turns it to stone. The bathhouse is, if slowly, turning into a fossil right in front of us.

The other old structures in the park, many of them, are a good deal more handsome, and certainly better maintained.

The fact that they are old means that they have developed eccentricities over the years. Some of the eccentricities were there from an early date, if not from the start.

Take the Mammoth Hotel, for instance, a wonderful old grand hotel built originally in 1883, then substantially reconstructed in 1913 and again in 1936. The reconstruction, in both cases, was overseen by Robert Reamer, the architect responsible for the Old Faithful Inn, and the man who may have had more impact on the human face of the park than any other. Off the main lobby is a room that spends most of its time as a kind of sprawling lounge (it has its own bar), and is occasionally a conference room, one with a view of the Mammoth area and the landscape beyond to distract conference-goers. It is called the Map Room because of the extraordinary piece of art that adorns its north wall.

The local historians Ruth and Leslie Quinn explain further: the "Map Room owes its name to a stunning map of the United States as it existed in 1936. Measuring 17'2" by 10'4" and containing 2,544 pieces of wood, the meticulous craftsmanship has been restored to its original beauty by the National Park Service Conservation Laboratory." The map was designed by Reamer himself during the 1936 reconstruction of the hotel. The idea was suggested by the widow of Harry Child, the hotel company president. The Quinns continue:

> With no precedent to base the design upon, Reamer pored over all the maps he could find in the Seattle Public Library. The largest and best map available was only three feet by six feet, so it was photostated in sections to bring it to the desired size. America's forty-eight states, an eagle, and a compass were delineated by the use of different woods that originated in nine countries. To achieve the proper grading and balance for the various states, fifteen varieties of wood were chosen. The main auto roads, such as the

> Yellowstone Trail and the Lincoln Highway, and the lines
> of the major railroads were created using rubber strips in
> red & blue. State capitols, major cities, and railroad hubs
> were highlighted.

(We can trust Ruth and Leslie Quinn because they have been working as park tour guides, and training tour guides, for literally decades.)

In Reamer's map, Alaska and Hawaii are absent because they were not states in the 1930s. There are no interstate highways because they did not exist, either, and there are only a few national parks. The map includes surprisingly small towns— La Jolla, California, and Anceney, Montana—because the Child family lived in both places.

Here is the really strange part: even after all that effort, the map contains a crucial mistake.

As the Quinns explain, "One state capital is incorrect. The *dot* is in the right place, but the painter changed it to the wrong name. Can you find it?"

No effort has ever been made to fix the mistake, or likely ever will, because it has become the center of a running Easter egg hunt involving the hotel staff and the public. This is another place where the employees have been encouraged to be not at all forthcoming, in a playful way. The staff will tell you that a capital is incorrect—but then never say which. No one will ever say which. Note that the Quinns do not say, either.

The real challenge is to find the mistake *without using the internet.* I have been trying since the 1990s. I am still trying.

Reamer also had a hand in the magnificently rambling Lake Hotel; it was built originally in 1891 but redesigned, again by Reamer, in 1903. He was a busy man. It is such a delightful place that you may end up visiting it several times, or even many times, before you notice that there is something odd about the whole layout.

2

As you drive up toward the hotel, the entrance road deposits you first into either the main parking lot or a second overflow lot. You park and approach the colossal white-and-yellow hotel. Here is where things seem . . . *off*, somehow. The old-fashioned streetlights are appealing, but why the screened area to the right? Peek through the wooden screening, and you will see that it is a kind of a maintenance yard, with delivery trucks and propane storage. Keep going, and you enter the hotel itself—but through a doorway with nothing special about it. Surely a big, fancy Colonial Revival grand hotel would want to welcome its visitors with something other than what looks like the fire escape—and why is the main entrance next to the back door of the *kitchen*?

It gets stranger when you at last wander past the front desk, the art exhibits, and the sunroom with its grandfather clock and grand piano and string quartet, and eventually exit the door toward the lake and find yourself out "back." Here, looking up and around, you will see a three-story portico, the kind the Romans might build, complete with a colonnade done with classic Ionic columns. Walking away from the structure, you will see big matching porticos and other entranceways, all grand. To go much farther requires a boat, but it is worth the effort. Take a tour boat ride from Bridge Bay, and you will see the hotel is visible from far across the lake, its bright yellow the only artificial object in view, once you have gone far enough. It looks best from the water because that is the way it is pointed.

It is only when you get the *really* distant view, from space, that you see what has happened. Look at it on Google Maps. Close to the spot where the Mountain Shoshone fish trap is located, note how the Grand Loop Road, colored in yellow, veers away from the lake. Notice also the second route that runs right along the lake. Note how it runs between the Lake Hotel and the lake. Yes, for many years, that was *the* road, and now it is not, the Grand Loop having been rerouted inland.

BATS FOR THE BELLHOPS AND OTHER STRUCTURAL SURPRISES

Much of the Lake Village area is thus pointed the wrong way. It explains why there is a store, ranger station, and now-closed service station pointed at the lake itself, all otherwise high and dry and far from the main route that the vehicle traffic follows. These structures were all on the highway, and now they are not.

The Lake Hotel, one of the grand ladies of the park, is presenting her backside to the world.

Perhaps oddest, in a fun way, is the Old Faithful Inn. Robert Reamer's masterpiece, it is both a work of the highest architectural accomplishment and a thing profoundly strange. After all, look at it: it is the world's largest log cabin. It is the log cabin on the syrup bottle done up as if it were ambitious for a place in the Manhattan skyline. It is a cute little ski-resort VRBO that has lost its mind.

It was built between June 1903 and June 1904. That means most of the construction went on during the brutal Yellowstone winter, which sounds odd, but construction crews of that time built structures like that in the winter because the logs could be skidded over the snow and ice. One of the local scientists has set himself the unofficial task of finding the stumps. No one knows where they are. The thing to look for is trees that were cut when they were not growing, which an expert can spot. The volcanic rock that went to make up the massive central fireplace is supposed to have come from Black Sand Basin. A surprising proportion of the building was thus sourced locally. Today, that might be regarded as an exploitation of the national park for commercial ends (bad), but it suited Reamer's purpose of constructing a hotel that looked as if it had grown here (good). In this question, most people today are more than willing to take Reamer's side.

Everything about the Inn is superlative. That central chimney weighs five hundred tons and stands eighty-five feet tall. The structure as a whole is said to contain ten thousand logs, but there is no way to check the claim. You may wonder how a log cabin can be seven stories tall and still stand up. The answer is actually inside some of the logs you see running straight up and down. Look closely. You will see that some are split from top to bottom. Find something steel like a butter knife, slide it inside the crack, and tap (don't worry—it can take the strain). You will be surprised by the sound. It is not a knock; it is a metallic ping. Inside those logs, Reamer hid the steel I-beams that support the structure.

The original hotel is that which is closest to the lobby. Some of the rooms there are available to the public furnished the way they were when the building was new; the rooms, to say the least, look nothing like Motel 6. Reamer returned to add wings in 1913 and 1927, and he returned once more to design the Bear Pit lounge in 1936. He had to wait until the later 1930s to do it because Prohibition had to end first. Reamer commissioned a Chicago artist named Walter Oehrle to etch scenes of misbehaving bears into glass to decorate the space behind the bar. The lounge was moved in the early 1960s, and the panels disappeared—but then turned up in storage during another renovation in the 1980s. You can see them now behind the bar where Reamer intended them to be. Parts of the original Inn—older than those panels by decades—are still to be found around the lobby, including much of the lobby furniture, the candelabra-lights mounted on the walls there, the wrought iron around the fireplace, and the brass clock above. Also original is everyone's favorite, the massive medieval-style front door with massive medieval-style latch, still painted bright red and clattering ominously, as it did when Theodore Roosevelt was president and a room at the Inn with a bath down the hall could be had for four dollars a night.

One of the stranger features of the building is in the upper reaches of that A-frame lobby. During a visit to Old Faithful, you might do the following. First, do not visit the

BATS FOR THE BELLHOPS AND OTHER STRUCTURAL SURPRISES

Inn immediately after an eruption of Old Faithful Geyser. If you do, you will not be happy. Immediately after an eruption (or perhaps five minutes after), the people who were in that massive crowd around the geyser visit the lobby of the Old Faithful Inn all at once. Times Square on New Year's Eve is quiet and sedate compared to the lobby after an eruption. Instead, go in between eruptions, or better still go in the early evening when the guests are settled into their rooms, diners are waiting for a table to open at the dining room, families sit at the furniture writing postcards or playing board games, and a pianist plays the grand piano. You will then be experiencing the Inn in a manner pretty close to what Reamer intended. Then go out into the middle of the lobby floor and have a look up and around.

You will hurt your neck doing so but look anyway. You will see two balconies with people moving around in them. If you climb to the first, you will find yourself on a railed landing that overlooks the lobby on all four sides. It is a favorite place for families to relax at the end of the day, and for the adults, the hotel company operates a bar in one corner. A door leads out onto a platform with a view of Old Faithful and Geyser Hill. A second balcony above, L shaped and running along two walls, is less heavily visited. That is as high as you can climb. At the second balcony, you will be stopped by a locked gate. What stretches away above you is the climb up the Crow's Nest, the collective term for the long run of stairs that snake upward to what looks, from below, like a child's playhouse. The structure at the top is the Treehouse.

The stairs are actually scary just to look at, and are said, by employees of the Inn, to creak ominously as you ascend into the upper realm. The Treehouse itself is such an eccentric feature to have—even in an already highly eccentric hotel—that it seems unsurprising to learn it is supposed to have been a fulfillment of a childhood fantasy nurtured by Reamer himself. It is indeed

2

a kind of playhouse, one hanging in midair 76½ feet up, as far from the lobby floor as it can get without leaving the building.

There is more structure above. The stairs continue, to emerge into the open air on the side of the Inn roof. A final flight climbs to what might be called the summit ridge. Here is what is termed the Widow's Walk, a platform sitting astride the peak of the Inn's main A-frame roof. Here are the flagpoles visible from below.

The poles fly the flags of Idaho, Wyoming, and Montana—the states that share Yellowstone National Park—and the flag of the United States. Four red and white pennants fill out the eight flagpoles, a gesture toward tradition: the eight flagpoles originally flew bright streamers. The flags are the responsibility of the crew of bellmen, who daily climb the dizzying, creaking stairs to raise and then lower the flags. Former Inn employees report that in past decades, the task was a punishment for bad performance; a trip to the summit, in addition to the fear factor, removed the miscreant from his regular job (remember what we said about the tips) for however long it took to get the task over. The flags serve one other important function locally. On the day that the Inn closes for the year, the flags are lowered early. The area employees are a bedraggled few who have weathered the summer and have lasted well into the local autumn. In the vernacular of the park, these employees are "survivors." They watch the flagpoles intently that day, normally a day in the second week of October. When the flags come down, the survivors know the local season is truly over. Some will labor on at Old Faithful until early November, but the village becomes a ghost town.

Flag duty is no longer the punishment it was. The Inn will take reservations from the general public of people who want to make the climb. One guest is selected for each day of the summer, and the reservations go quickly.

BATS FOR THE BELLHOPS AND OTHER STRUCTURAL SURPRISES

It was stranger still—in a pleasant way—during the early years of the Inn. In the evening, the lobby floor would be cleared for dancing, and an orchestra would climb all the way to the Treehouse and perform there, the canted walls of the Inn roof bouncing the sound downward. On the other landings, spectators would watch—all the balconies were open at the time, not just the bottom two. On the Widow's Walk, in the open air above, a US Navy searchlight had been installed. When Old Faithful erupted after dark, the searchlight lit it up like a Christmas tree. That seems a very strange thing today, when the goal is generally to operate the national parks so that they are as "natural" as possible, but that kind of thing was common in parks during the early days. It is reminiscent of the Firefall in Yosemite Valley, where hot coals were dumped off Glacier Point to make what appeared to be a glowing waterfall, while the crowd below sang the "Indian Love Song" and "America the Beautiful." In Yellowstone, for that matter, the roads were regularly impassible during that era because cars were stopped to feed junk food to the bears. The searchlight was removed in 1948, but people were feeding the bears beside the roads right up into the 1970s.

Access to the Crow's Nest is restricted today because of the 1959 Hebgen Lake earthquake, a massive event to which we will return later. It was so violent that it twisted the support timbers enough that it is today judged safe for only a few people at a time.

But there are always plenty of volunteers. People look up, and they want to make the climb; they daydream about it, sharing Reamer's childhood reverie.

If you are one of the lucky few selected, you climb the creaking stairs, led by one of the bellmen. In the Treehouse, you hang above the lobby, certain death there below, suspended with nothing but the thickness of the wood to hold you up, and the over-a-century-old bolts in the ceiling keeping Reamer's fantasy-house dizzily suspended, seven stories up.

Everything about the Old Faithful Inn loudly declares the skill of the master craftsmen who built it, and the eccentric genius who dreamed it up. So fear not . . . although you will still be plenty afraid.

3

Weird and Wonderful Wolves

One of the new stars of the show: a Yellowstone wolf howling. GETTY IMAGES—
MARK MILLER PHOTOS

For generations, the one animal people thought of when the topic of Yellowstone National Park came up was the bear. Bears along the roads greeted them year after year, until they entered the national consciousness, so that a television show on a national network about Jellystone Park naturally made a star of a happy-go-lucky bear misappropriating tourist picnic baskets.

Starting in the 1990s, that changed. The bears had to make way for a new kind of animal celebrity.

There are multiple species of wild canines in the park. "Canid" is the word scientists use for these animals, all related— fairly closely—to our domestic dogs. The coyote used to be the most common, and even during a brief visit, seeing one is not too difficult. They turn up almost everywhere, but as with any animal, they are easier to spot in places where the forest is less dense. There, they pop up just trotting along the side of the road, mostly uninterested in the humans and their machines. Much less common is the red fox, which is also harder to see because they are nocturnal and prefer forests. Coyotes are less nocturnal and prefer open areas like sagebrush flats; researchers think these differences have evolved as a way to minimize competition between the two species. The practical effect is that the coyote is one animal on your Yellowstone to-see list that you will probably check off.

But you do not need to come to Yellowstone to see either of them. Both get along so well living alongside humans that they regularly wear out their welcome. Foxes have made themselves at home in cities all over the world. They are, for instance, a common sight in cities in Great Britain, one estimate putting the number living in London at an amazing ten thousand. As for the coyotes here in North America, you may have heard a pack of them yapping and howling right outside the window of your suburban or urban home, wherever that may be. Persecution of other big predators during the nineteenth and twentieth centuries opened ecological space that the coyote avidly filled.

WEIRD AND WONDERFUL WOLVES

The coyotes of cities like Los Angeles have become infamous. In the foothills of the city, dogs and cats are no longer safe outside at night. They share the hills with a survivor, a predator that is too crafty and adaptable to be suppressed, and many Angelenos no longer find that yapping and howling much fun.

The distinctive red fur with black socks will help you identify a fox, while a coyote is most often colored tan and gray. The most important thing to understand about both is that they are not large. Coyotes are comparable in size to the family dog, although you would not otherwise mix them up. They weigh 25 to 35 pounds and stand as high as 20 inches at the shoulder. Foxes are much smaller, weighing between 10 and 12 pounds.

They share the park with another canid that is not small at all.

The gray wolf is both a newcomer to the park and a longtime resident. Wolves have lived in what is now Yellowstone National Park for the local equivalent of "forever"—they were likely here from the time the glaciers receded. The settlers who came west in the nineteenth century to farm and ranch hated wolves with a passion, and the US government was entirely on their side. Both settlers and government agents killed wolves in their thousands, until they were almost entirely gone from the lower forty-eight states. The last wolves in Yellowstone National Park were killed in 1926. There were sightings of individual animals, and a few lone wanderers surely passed through, but there was no reproducing population. They were effectively gone for decades.

In the 1970s, though, gray wolves were added to the federal list of endangered species, and according to the Endangered Species Act, the feds were required to take action to restore them. After years of controversy, in 1995, thirty-one wolves were captured in Canada, where there had always been plenty (the capture followed the delivery of a charming letter exchanged between the governments of the two countries, basically saying, "Dear Canada, as per our previous discussion, please give us some wolves. Sincerely, the United States"). The animals were shipped south and placed in special "acclimation pens" in the park. The thought was that they would find their new surroundings alien, and being great travelers, they would run for home. When the pens were at last opened, however, no such problem developed. They took to Yellowstone National Park as if they had been born there.

One might guess that they were also delighted. They were the first predators of their size and awesome efficiency to live in this place in the better part of a century, and the park was full of food for them. Their population expanded beyond what anyone had thought might happen except in the most optimistic guesses. They quickly filled the park and began to overflow its boundaries. Today, the descendants of those reintroduced wolves are radiating out around the western United States. They have lately made it as far as California, where the chances are good they will find the Sierra Nevada as inviting as their forebears found Yellowstone.

You will need a little luck to see one, but not too much. They, too, are nocturnal but are active in the early morning and around sundown. As we will see, there are places in the park where they are easier to spot, and their habit of traveling in groups helps, too.

And as noted, they are not small. The one thing people notice about them, on first seeing one, is their sheer, awesome size. The larger ones weigh 130 pounds. Yes, they are related to your family dog—but the family resemblance only goes so far.

In early 2022, there were just under a hundred wolves in the park, organized into eight packs. The numbers fluctuate, and the packs change regularly as well. Nevertheless, they have returned to stay.

They were full of surprises. One unexpected event followed another, until we have come to expect the unexpected from them. Nevertheless, when Yellowstone regulars tell each other the latest news about the wolves, the comment that follows is often, "Wow . . . that's strange."

What have they done to shake up our expectations? And what might they still do?

The Loneliness of the Long-Distance Runner

One major surprise was that those first reintroduced wolves did not all disappear.

No one really knew what to expect when the wolves were shipped south from Canada. One guess most observers and scientists would have agreed with was that the wolves would make themselves scarce. When the acclimation pens were opened, the hope was simply that they would not run back to Alberta, or at least run toward Alberta and be mowed down on Interstate 90 or shot by a yokel (a serious felony). They were otherwise expected to radiate out into the vast, roadless wilderness areas that make up so much of the park. The national park itself is 2.2 million acres. Surely, once the pens were opened, they would hightail it out into that big empty space—empty of humans, at least. There was plenty there for a wolf to eat.

Consider what happened with the Crystal Creek pack. It was named for their acclimation pen along Crystal Creek, which flows down to join the Lamar River at the Northeast Entrance Road. If you are driving toward the Northeast Entrance, you can see the general area where the Crystal Creek acclimation pen was; although Crystal Creek itself is small and might or might not be marked on whatever map you are using, it happens to enter the Lamar River from the south at just the point where the highway crosses the Lamar on the big new highway bridge. That stretch of wet-looking ground, with willows and other shrub-like plants growing together in a snaking line down the ridge to the south, is Crystal Creek, and somewhere up there is the spot where the Crystal Creek wolves got their start, explorers in their own New World.

The great surprise was simply that the Crystal Creek wolves did not leave the Lamar Valley. They did all the things wolves do. They killed and ate elk. They killed coyotes. Wolves cannot tolerate a competing canid in their area; they pounce immediately, and when a wolf catches up with a coyote, the coyote dies—it is a highly uneven match. They "interacted" with grizzly bears, as the wildlife biologists put it, which is a little like saying the US and Soviet armies "interacted" during the Cold War; grizzlies and wolves do not get along either. They dug dens. They did not have pups, but almost every other kind of activity a wolf can engage in played out in that valley, and it happened in front of thousands and thousands of park visitors.

Here, we need to understand a peculiar feature of Yellowstone National Park. Most of the famous locales, like the lake, the canyon, and the major geyser basins in the Firehole River valley, are all between roughly seven and eight thousand feet above sea level. When locals talk about this part of the park, they speak of "the interior," or sometimes "the plateau." The northern part of the park is different. If you are driving north from Norris toward Mammoth, you enter this northern section when you cross the Gardner River, but the change becomes more obvious as you leave Swan Lake Flat and drive through Kingman Pass, which some maps label the Golden Gate. If you are driving from Canyon toward Tower/Roosevelt, you enter this section by making the long, grueling descent from Dunraven Pass. If you come into the park from Cooke City/Silver Gate and drive through the Northeast Entrance, you will be descending almost all the way. In each case, as you drive, your elevation above sea level is falling, often dramatically. If you enter through Gardiner, Montana, and the North Entrance, you are already there.

You are now in an area that, as you look around, is noticeably different, even if you do not know all that much about the outdoors. The most striking difference from the interior of the park is the lack of trees. If you drive the long set of roads between Mammoth and Cooke City, you will watch as the forests seem to recede. The soil here is different, and the climate, and so, therefore, are the plant communities. Here are fewer conifer forests and more open meadows and sagebrush. Grazing animals like it because the open areas allow sunlight to grow more of the kind of low vegetation they need to eat (elk and bison cannot eat trees). But the key word is "open." Here, you can see quite literally for miles.

Locals call it the northern range, and it is the best place for you to look for wolves during your visit—and for bears, too, and for almost every kind of grazing animal. Its mere existence, combined with the return of the wolves, has changed human life in the park in far-reaching ways.

Because of those views, you can see everything the animals do, and the presence of all those grazing animals means that among them are plenty of wolves. The Crystal Creek pack started a trend that first summer after the reintroduction. They were the first group to take to the open and feast on the elk in the full view of every human on the road.

It has had effects good and bad on the community of the park. The winter used to be a sleepy time in places like Gardiner and Mammoth, but because the wolves do not hibernate, and indeed have a wonderful time as the weather begins to kill the weaker grazing animals, a wolf-tourism complex has developed. Gardiner can be almost hectic at times in the winter, and the locals do not necessarily like it.

There has also developed an extraordinary sociological phenomenon. The park has always had what are locally called "geyser gazers," people who fall in love with the geyser basins and live at Old Faithful year-round, making the greatest sacrifices to stay out there all the time, trying to get a better feel for what is happening underground. We now also have "wolf watchers."

You will see them on the northern range, sometimes fifty at a time, parked in the larger turnouts and all generally looking in the same direction. They are there because the wolves—usually more than one—are in view. The things that look like small bazookas, mounted on tripods, are spotting scopes. Some of their spotting scopes may be worth about as much as your car.

You may not find them easy to talk to. They are a canid *Cosa Nostra*—as cliquish, that is, as the mob. They are seriously eccentric people, although not dangerous, I assure you. Their expertise, when it comes to wolves, is also as great as that of anyone in the world, academic biologists included. It comes from looking at them all the time, in those long sight lines on the northern range.

One other feature of wolf life has made it possible to watch them all the time: they live in a pack (that is the official term for it). This is the reason that, when one turns up, there are usually more, and sometimes all the animals in the group are there, too. Research in Yellowstone has settled on 11.8 as the average number of wolves in a pack, although the number goes up and down regularly, and it only takes two to make a pack. The average number is higher in Yellowstone than elsewhere, one would guess because of the abundance of food for them here, and some Yellowstone wolf packs have grown to enormous sizes. The Druid pack holds the record for Yellowstone, and maybe the world. Packs are named for landmarks in their territories; the Druids took their name from Druid Peak, which rises above the Lamar River valley. Another northern range pack, they displaced the Crystals and became the new stars. At its largest, the pack numbered thirty-seven.

At the core of the pack are the largest and strongest animals. Wildlife biologists call them "alphas," for the first letter of the Greek alphabet. You may hear it argued that there is no such thing, but that is hogwash; there is always a single male and female who are in charge, by virtue of the simple fact that there is always one of each that is biggest and healthiest. They alone reproduce, and they mate for life, one of the appealing features of wolf society for everyone who watches them. In a normal year, these two have a single litter of pups in a den excavated in the earth, often into the side of a hill, and near water. The pups are born in the spring, and the rest of the pack brings them food until the pups are seven or eight months old, at which point they start traveling with the pack.

There may come a point, however, when a crisis is reached. At about the age of one or two, the young wolf faces a choice. He or she (both sexes do this) will be allowed to mate only if an alpha dies, or if the animal strikes out on his or her own. When they do this, the scientists call them dispersing males or dispersing females. If the literal lone wolf finds another of the opposite sex, he or she can form a new pack. The drive to succeed in the quest is powerful, and among the results are some of the most extraordinary stories ever to emerge about these extraordinary animals.

Take the tale of Limpy, for instance. The government keeps track of wolves by giving them a number, followed by a letter to designate their sex, so the alphas of the original Crystal Creek pack, for instance, were 4M and 5F; the numbers are sequential, and now run up into the thousands. Some wolves have been so captivating or memorable, however, that they are given an unofficial second name by the people who watch them. One such was Limpy, sometimes more gently known as Hoppy, wolf number 253M, if that matters. He was named for a distinctive rolling walk that apparently resulted from an injury he sustained when he was very young. It made him the easiest wolf to spot in the group; even a novice watcher could make him out. It made him a favorite.

And then he disappeared.

Limpy was a Druid, and the alpha of the pack was another celebrity wolf, 21M. In spite of his injury, Limpy grew to be an animal so strong that he might have become alpha himself. However, 21M would have to make way, and 21M was indestructible. One day, the park wolf biologists noticed the signal from the radio collar Limpy was wearing had gone silent. Author Nate Blakeslee, in his book *American Wolf*, picks up the story:

> Six weeks later a coyote trapper checking his snares in the hills outside a town in Utah found he'd caught something far too large to be a coyote. There hadn't been a confirmed wolf sighting in the state in over seventy years, but the trapper knew one when he saw one, even if the rancher he was working for initially didn't believe him. The wolf he'd caught was still alive and wearing a research collar. Word quickly reached Yellowstone: Limpy had been found— almost three hundred miles from the Lamar Valley.
>
> Rather than carry him all the way back to Yellowstone, officials with the Fish and Wildlife Service decided to release him in Grand Teton National Park, about 125 miles north of where he was captured. A few packs had already been established in Grand Teton by dispersing Yellowstone wolves, but it still offered plenty of opportunities for an ambitious young wolf looking for his own territory. Limpy, however, had his own agenda. Eleven days after he was dropped off in the far northern end of the park, his signal was picked up east of Yellowstone Lake, some forty miles away. He was headed home. On December 20, Limpy was back with his clan in the Lamar Valley. In a little over two months, he had completed a remarkable round-trip of more than a thousand miles.
>
> It was the kind of story newspaper editors loved, and Limpy's homecoming saga was reported far and wide. But he didn't stay in the park for long. He spent the next few years roaming southwestern Wyoming, until researchers eventually lost track of him.

WEIRD AND WONDERFUL WOLVES

Limpy's adventure, the one that took him to Utah, was not the greatest journey a Yellowstone wolf has made. That record may belong to another wolf, one that turned up at the Grand Canyon—but not the Grand Canyon of the Yellowstone. The other one.

A woman shooting photographs in 2014 at Grand Canyon National Park in Arizona caught an image of a canine that did not fit expectations. Other sightings followed, and eventually, wildlife biologists were able to get a sample of the animal's scat—its droppings, in this case her droppings. The *Salt Lake Tribune* reported the results:

> No one else was cleaning up after the large canine hanging around the North Kaibab National Forest near the Grand Canyon so Fish and Wildlife Service biologists did.
>
> The result was the confirmation of the first Rocky Mountain gray wolf—fully protected under the Endangered Species Act—in Arizona for more than seven decades.
>
> Many speculated that the animal was a hybrid wolf/dog, but now that it has been confirmed as a female gray wolf some wonder if it is the same wolf that spent time in Utah's Uinta Mountains in late August to mid-September.
>
> The scat of the Grand Canyon wolf was . . . sent to the University of Idaho's Laboratory for Ecological, Evolutionary and Conservation Genetics. "The DNA results indicate this wolf traveled at least 450 miles from an area in the northern Rocky Mountains to northern Arizona," Benjamin Tuggle, Southwest Regional Director for the Fish and Wildlife Service said in a news release. "Wolves, particularly young wolves, can be quite nomadic, dispersing great distances across the landscape. Such behavior is not unusual for juveniles as they travel to find food or another mate."

Her story was written up in a large newspaper because the Grand Canyon wolf was already a celebrity. A worldwide contest among schoolchildren resulted in a name for her: she became Echo. Before that, she had been 914F, and she was a Yellowstone wolf. She had been collared early that year near Cody, Wyoming.

She was now much sought after, but unfortunately disappeared on another long run, this time to the north. Whenever wolves venture on these odysseys, they do so at the risk of their lives. In a widely reproduced story, Reuters reported the outcome:

> A gray wolf killed last year by a Utah hunter was "Echo," a female that had garnered international attention after roaming from Wyoming to become the first of the protected animals seen at the Grand Canyon in Arizona in 70 years, U.S. wildlife managers said on Wednesday.
>
> News that the lone wolf spotted last fall near the north rim of the Grand Canyon was the same animal later killed in Utah by a hunter who said he mistook it for a coyote ignited outrage among wildlife advocates.
>
> "It's tragic that Echo traveled over 500 miles . . . only to be cut down by an incredibly irresponsible coyote hunter," said Bethany Cotton, wildlife program director for WildEarth Guardians.
>
> Authorities have not released the name of the coyote hunter, who in December reported to Utah wildlife officers that he had accidentally shot and killed a radio-collared wolf near the border with Arizona.

They did not release the name because he would have been in some danger. On some news sites, this story was accompanied by a photo of Echo howling. Her name was here sadly ironic, an outcome the schoolkids surely did not intend: the howl could only echo and echo and never be answered, because there were no other wolves at Grand Canyon National Park, although it is a good bet that they will be back. Even if they have to come all the way from Greater Yellowstone, these "dispersing" youngsters have surprised us over and over.

Back in 2004, seemingly out of nowhere—unless you know what they are capable of—a female wolf turned up dead very close to Denver, apparently struck by a vehicle on Interstate 70, and because the animal was dead, scientists were able to determine quickly that it was a Yellowstone wolf. This one had traveled not quite 500 miles—assuming animals travel the route recommended by Google Maps. She had surely run farther than that.

It was the beginning of a long and inevitable run of appearances by Yellowstone wolves in Colorado. A total of six individual animals turned up there between 2004 and 2019. The other inevitable outcome occurred in 2021, as the Associated Press reported:

> Colorado's first litter of gray wolf pups since the 1940s has grown to include six pups.
>
> Colorado Parks and Wildlife said Thursday that staff spotted the pups living in a den with two collared wolves known as John and Jane in northern Colorado, KCNC-TV reports.
>
> The agency first announced June 9 that staff had spotted three pups in the pack.
>
> Gray wolves were hunted, trapped and poisoned into extermination in Colorado in the 1940s.
>
> Officials last year confirmed the presence of the small pack of wolves in northwestern Colorado after a number of sightings since 2019. The animals were believed to have come down from Wyoming's Yellowstone National Park.

People in Colorado were surprised, but Yellowstone people were not. Wolves do these things. It is normal for them to make journeys like those in the stories you hear about the dog lost on a picnic who crosses the country to get home.

An open question, however, is *how*. How do they do it? It is a secret of theirs. We can sometimes see which way they go, but even that is a hit-and-miss affair. Note that both Limpy and Echo wore radio collars—but the collars were dead. Even the routes they followed are unknown, and the strategies and everyday trials of their journeys are not available to us at all.

Think of what they had to do—but you will have to think hard because what they did was both mundane and epic, and it was light-years away from our everyday experience of the world. Think of the obstacles. A wolf leaving Yellowstone can stay in national forests well down into Wyoming—but the wolf does not know anything about the arbitrary boundaries we stamp on the landscape. Let us use that first Colorado wolf as an example. She ultimately had no choice but to descend out of the Northern Rockies and down onto the high plains. There she would have found fences . . . and how many in the course of her travels? Hundreds, perhaps? How many were made of barbed wire? She would now have been running across ranches and farms, where the ranchers and ranch-hands and farmers and farmhands all had rifles in their pickups and every reason to shoot what would have looked to them like a coyote. Country people tend to shoot coyotes on sight. There were traps intended for coyotes, too. There were lights on the horizon at night, towns and small cities that would have represented a potentially fatal temptation. The glow of Laramie, Fort Collins, and finally Boulder and Denver would have been visible to her from a long way, even up in the mountains, but she could pick up high mountains again, down by what we know of as the border between Wyoming and Colorado. Before that, there was Interstate 80 to be crossed, unavoidably, and rail lines and smaller highways and uncountable roads. Still, on and on she ran, howling at night, hoping always for a response.

And so the Yellowstone wolves run up and down and back and forth across the western United States and become media darlings in the process. When will they reach Yosemite? One of their descendants may already be there. Who knows?

They are certainly on their way.

The Unsinkable Mollies

The animals we consider to be intelligent are often those that live in groups with what scientists call a "dominance hierarchy." Dolphins, elephants, gorillas, chimpanzees, canids—all live in groups where some animals are in charge, and some are not. Humans, of course, live that way, too, and part of the connection we feel with these animals is a kind of sympathy.

Why would animals that live in such groups be more intelligent? They have to be. Consider what may be the most complex of all: that which develops among chimpanzees. Male chimpanzees form a strict dominance hierarchy. They enforce the hierarchy not with violence, usually—although that option is always there, and a healthy adult male chimpanzee is powerful and highly dangerous. Usually, aggressive displays are enough to enforce the order. Chimps form coalitions and engage in what can only be called politics. When they are hunting, groups will set fairly elaborate ambushes, with a division of labor. Communication is elaborate, too. The ultimate challenge to the male hierarchy is what can only be called warfare. Chimps are territorial and patrol the borders of their territory in what infantrymen would recognize as squads. When they encounter their neighboring group, they attack. The attacks are not mere demonstrations. They kill. They may expand their territory, and troops may even fight their neighbors to extermination.

Note how much there is for a chimpanzee to remember. To survive and thrive living such a life, you have to remember who threatened you, who did you a favor, who joined your coalition, who left it, who is perhaps unreliable, who gave you food, who kept you from eating, who failed in his role in the last hunt, who endangered everyone by screwing up during the last fight with the enemy, and so on, and on. A very large brain is a necessity.

Life among the canids is similar. If you have a family dog, chances are you regard him or her as smart. You may have a dumb dog, and maybe even have fun at the dog's expense—but what you are doing there is measuring the dog against smarter dogs you have known. Dogs are intelligent. Think about it: they will lie. That is, they tell falsehoods. Yes, they do. Have you ever seen one, although unhurt, pretend to walk with a limp to get your sympathy?

A great deal of the affection and connection people feel for the Yellowstone wolves—and it is a powerful feeling—comes of this shared intelligence. They are so much like us, in so many ways.

The connection people feel with the wolves is also sentimental, and so many will object to this assertion: among the things we share with them is combat, and what can only be called war.

What else to call it? Some readers will argue that the violence between packs is of course not war. They will object that the packs are not nations or states, that the violence is not organized, that the animals are not divided up into armies with ranks and accepted ways of confronting the enemy, that there is no leadership with a strategy and war aims. That is all true, sort of. The wolf packs do have a common ancestry and an identity; it is very much possible for them to see the matter as us versus them. They have territory, and they do defend it. The territory expands and contracts with their ability to defend it. They do not tolerate outsiders, killing them on sight. What the relationship between packs does resemble is the kind of permanent low-level warfare that exists between tribal societies.

No one disputes that the wolves kill each other. This is not a matter just of rumor or storytelling; scientists have studied the issue at some length. Yellowstone has become the world's premier laboratory for this kind of research because of the simple fact that there are plenty of wolves here now, that they are mostly protected from people with guns, and that they live in that northern range we talked about earlier. Whatever they do, they do it right out in the open. Living in those airy spaces across the northern part of the park means that scientists can see their every move.

Wolves can be economical, even conservative, in their approach to killing. When hunting for food, they do not necessarily pile on like a gang-tackle in a football game, or a rugby scrum, which is what we usually imagine them doing. Instead, they may run alongside a fleeing prey animal and nip carefully, artfully at the neck. If they can open the carotid artery on, say, an elk or moose, they can then stand back and let the animal bleed until it is no longer a threat (a healthy elk or moose can kick a wolf to death). When hunting others of their own kind, they may exert the full force behind those teeth of theirs. One sees a great deal of speculation about that bite force, most of it baloney, but this much seems defensible: being bitten by a wolf would be comparable to being bitten by a fair-sized shark.

An important study of aggression between packs of Yellowstone wolves was published in 2015. It was quite an effort: the researchers assembled their data from observations taken over sixteen years, starting with the reintroduction year of 1995. They "documented 121 interpack aggressive interactions"— acts of war, we might call them, although the researchers certainly do not. When a pack decides to fight another, what enables it to win? Answering this question, some of what the researchers found was in line with what we would expect: the larger pack defeated the smaller one, and the pack with more males in it was more likely to win. One major finding, however, required explanation: the pack with the older animals was more likely to succeed. "Through their experience," they concluded, "older wolves may be better able to assess the fighting ability of opponents before an interaction takes place (through howling communication or scent-mark investigation) and subsequently decide to engage a pack they feel they can defeat or avoid packs they feel outcompete their own." Older wolves, that is, know when to fight and when to run, literally.

One of the researchers was Kira Cassidy, a scientist with the Yellowstone Wolf Project. She has continued to work on this issue, and more recently wrote a description of one of the encounters that taught her and her fellow scientists what made for a winning pack. It is an eyewitness account of one of nature's most gripping displays of sheer ferocity:

It was 10 a.m. but the mid-morning sun was just barely cresting the eastern ridge. I'd been alternately huddling for warmth in my layers of down and stomping around the small dirt trailhead trying to keep feeling in my toes for over two hours. Watching as the western slopes lit and warmed, I beheld nature's visual timepiece, anticipating the blanket of sunlight edging temperatures into positive degrees.

I was tracking the Slough Creek wolf pack by listening for pings on the radio receiver, indicating one of the collared wolves was nearby. Finally, I saw them travelling up out of the Yellowstone River corridor, their thick winter coats shedding river ice, keeping them a lot warmer than me and definitely not worrying themselves over the speed of the sunrise that morning.

The seven figures followed in each other's footsteps, noses to the ground. They gathered around one area, and judging by their quickly rising tails and hackles, it was the fresh scent of rival wolves. The alpha male took off running to the north; the five pack females and a yearling male following quickly. Intrigued by the wolves' behavior, I tuned the receiver to test the signals for other packs. Sure enough, loud beeps from a Druid Peak pack wolf rang out—they must be close by, too. I looked back in the scope and watched the Slough Creek pack running hard now, the dark black alpha male in the lead. Scanning ahead of them about 400 meters I saw five members of the Druid Peak pack. They glanced at each other and began their own charge, tails like flags, straight at their opponents.

The distance closed rapidly and all of a sudden it was chaos. The Slough alpha male slammed his body into a Druid wolf but when another grabbed his neck and shook violently, he broke loose and ran out of the fray. The Slough females followed the male's wake but finding themselves in the midst of four huge male Druid wolves, tucked tails and ran. Two of the Sloughs turned around and hopped briefly onto their hind legs, trying to figure out who was a pack mate and who was not. The Druid wolves stayed in a solitary unit, chasing and spreading out the Slough wolves for several minutes, keeping them from joining together. As the commotion died down, the Slough wolves started to bark-howl from all angles. They were lost and separated, not sure where to go for fear of running into the Druids again. Eventually the tension dissipated and the Druids relaxed. The Sloughs wandered in several small groups, separated by miles of mountainside.

Even though the Sloughs outnumbered the Druids, they had lost; completely displaced from the fight location—firmly in Slough Creek pack territory.

The Druids, however, had more male wolves, and more experience.

Some packs show more aggression than others; some, indeed, make it a habit. When the subject of aggressiveness comes up, talk will eventually, inevitably turn to the Mollies.

As we have seen, most packs are named for a landmark in their territory. An exception is the Mollies pack, named for Mollie Beattie, the head of the US Fish and Wildlife Service during the reintroduction; she died young of brain cancer in 1996, and the pack was named in her honor. The pack, in its earliest form, included some of the original reintroduced wolves; it is today the oldest pack in the park. That it is so might be surprising, because the pack occupies an area that is not as easy to live in as the northern range. Their home territory is the Pelican Valley, an area north of Yellowstone Lake. If your visit takes you either east or west on the East Entrance Road, you will cross the bottom end of the valley when you drive over Pelican Creek, just before it enters Yellowstone Lake about a mile from the village at Fishing Bridge. Look up the creek valley, and you are looking toward the home of the Mollies pack.

It looks idyllic enough, but it has a serious drawback: elk, the favored food of the Yellowstone wolf, migrate out of the valley during the winter. Elk are members of the deer family, and while they are a good deal larger than the mule deer you will see in places like Gardiner and scattered throughout the park, they are of a size wolves can cope with. A Yellowstone cow elk might weigh 500 pounds, and bulls perhaps 700, depending on their age. Younger animals, obviously, are smaller. Still, a common way for a wolf to die is from a well-aimed kick delivered by an elk. It is a major hazard of the rugged life they lead.

Everyone in the park community who was following the affairs of the wolves was surprised, then, to learn what the Mollies were doing. They developed a kind of specialty. They began taking on, and killing, bison. Not just calves. Full-grown bison.

And they can weigh an actual ton.

They are the largest animals in North America. Seen from up close—from inside a car, the only safe place to be when one of these beasts is near—a bison seems less like an animal than some monstrous *thing*, a piece of the geology, a boulder perhaps, that has somehow gotten up and started walking around. The head alone is larger than plenty of wolves, and heavier than some people; it is a kind of battering ram, with a pair of nasty horns thrown in. When a bison walks, the head bobs up and down like an oilfield pumpjack. The noises they make are a menacing grumble—again, as if the geology had come to life. They are profoundly dangerous.

Not just to wolves. Look on YouTube for videos of people who have gotten too close to bison in Yellowstone. They are thrown through the air like rag dolls, flying end over end over end. According to an interesting report published in 2019 in the journal *Human-Wildlife Interactions*, bison are the most dangerous animal in the park, injuring more people than any other. "Bison injured 56 people and killed 2 people in Yellowstone National Park from 1978 to 1992 and injured 25 people from 2000 to 2015," according to the report, put together by Michael Conover, a wildlife biologist at Utah State. "Eighty percent of victims were approaching the bison when attacked and half were trying to take a photograph. Of the 25 injured people, 10 people were thrown into the air, 9 were head-butted, and 6 were gored; almost half (48%) required hospitalization."

So, the news that a wolf pack was killing these main battle tanks of the wilderness was surprising. It was a trace less surprising to learn that it was the Mollies doing it.

They have always been aggressive, even though the pack came into being as the result of a retreat. Early in the history of the reintroduction, they were the Crystal Creek pack, named for the location of their acclimation pen; they had been the Petite Lake pack, in Alberta, Canada. The new Druid pack, in the process of taking over the Lamar River valley, drove the Crystals out and all the way south to the remote and inhospitable Pelican Valley. The Crystals kept that name until the year 2000, when their alpha female, the last of the original Crystal Creek wolves, disappeared, presumed dead. That is when they were renamed to honor Mollie Beattie.

They developed certain . . . tendencies. Their behavior fell into a pattern. During the winter, when the elk left Pelican Valley, they would journey north to the Lamar River country. For a human, it would be a dreadful struggle, but for a wolf, the trip is nothing much: twenty miles north through deep snow and the rawest wilderness to finish atop Specimen Ridge, with its commanding view of a wolf's version of the Promised Land. Below them, from the ridge, the Lamar River drainage spread forth, with its big herds of grazing animals.

They started making the journey around the year when they were given their new name, and soon made a habit of it. In 2004, they achieved a consummation. The long-running alpha female of the Druid pack was 42F, mate to 21M, probably the two most famous wolves of the early reintroduction era, indeed probably the most famous wolves in the world, at that time. By 2004, 42F was getting on in years. She was matriarch of the pack that had, long ago, thrown the Crystals out of Lamar Valley, so it made a kind of poetic sense when, in February 2004, the Mollies, descendants of the Crystals, celebrated their annual arrival in the Lamar country by killing 42F.

The Mollies came for the elk, not the vengeance. Still, it calls attention to a truth about the wolves. As we have seen, they have an avid fan base, and one reason is that the lives the wolves lead do resemble Renaissance drama—Shakespeare, that is. The alpha animals are the king and queen. They ascend to the throne, often enough, through assassination (42F is thought to have become alpha that way). They must always fear the Hamlet who might kill them in their turn. In this scenario, the Mollies are the nobles driven into exile unjustly, returned to seek blood-red *revenge*.

The most famous occasion of Mollie mayhem occurred in winter 2011–2012, when they departed their valley and left a trail of dead rivals in their path. They killed the alpha male of the Mary Mountain pack. They killed the alpha male of the Agate pack. Arriving in the Lamar country, they ran into the Blacktail pack, themselves out of their territory, to their regret this day. The Mollies sent them fleeing, with one of their members dead on the field. They penetrated farther into the Lamar drainage and stayed longer than they ever had at that date because of the weather: there was, ironically, too *little* snow in the Pelican Valley. When they target bison, they need deep snow to slow them down and exhaust them.

In general, snow is the wolves' friend. At the time of year when other animals are stressed, wolves come into their own.

Once in the Lamar drainage, there followed a series of battles between the usual residents of the valley and the Mollies. The centerpiece of this campaign was the confrontation between the Mollies and the Lamar pack, led by the most famous wolf of all, Oh-Six, a female born during that year who gathered a devoted following among wolf watchers and casual tourists alike. In his "biography" of Oh-Six, *American Wolf*, Nate Blakeslee refers to the affair as the "Rampage of the Mollies." He describes one of the opening encounters, as observed by Laurie Lyman, a longtime fixture among the wolf watchers. The two packs collided unexpectedly:

> If O-Six was ever going to stand and fight, this was the time to do it.
>
> Her answer came in the form of a bellicose howl, which the rest of her pack lustily joined. There would be no retreat. When the Mollies heard the challenge, they jumped to their feet and raced down the hill with tails raised, still spread out in a long line like a cavalry charge. The Lamars moved steadily uphill to meet them, spreading out until the rival packs faced each other in two almost perfectly matched lines, each advancing on the other.
>
> Just before the lines met, however, the Lamars panicked and broke ranks, fleeing in every direction. The charging Mollies were upon them almost immediately. A

black Lamar pup was caught and dragged down, and soon eight snarling wolves were around him in a circle so tight that Laurie couldn't see him at all. She had watched wolves kill coyotes in just this way: all you saw from a distance were the raised tails and straining haunches of the attackers, but you could imagine all too easily what was happening at the bottom of the pile. It was usually over in a few seconds. The pup was almost twice the size of a coyote, but he was still in serious trouble.

After perhaps a minute the attackers left the pup lying in the snow and headed off en masse to pursue other Lamars careening through the trees. Laurie could hear bark-howling coming from all over the ridge as the splintered Lamars ran for their lives.

The black pup in fact survived, only to be killed later in the prolonged struggle between the packs that year. Before they were done with their annual trip out of the Pelican Valley, the Mollies would have killed nine wolves. They eventually retreated. Oh-Six and the Lamars kept possession of the valley. But they paid a price.

It was this relentlessly aggressive group that taught itself to kill bison. Likely they would never have tried—and also would never have succeeded—had they not possessed this trait. Blakeslee also describes how they execute such kills, referring to a rare videotape, actually unique, taken in Pelican Valley. The video is so rare, in fact, that it is *not* on YouTube. It shows "fourteen Mollies attacking a bison at least ten times their size. In the heat of the battle, they leaped onto the fleeing bull's back, holding on to his flesh with their teeth until the bison flung them through the air, swinging his massive head in an effort to hook them on the way down." Research done in the park, on the Mollies (published by the Public Library of Science in 2014), looked at this gang-swarm behavior. Animals that hunt in groups normally keep their numbers low, between two and five; more than that, and the hunters end up wasting effort. Not so the Mollies, when attacking bison. The researchers found that they had their greatest success with a mob numbering between nine and thirteen.

The nature of their prey of course demands it. Two wolves against a bison would only be suicide.

"Bison are herd animals," Blakeslee continues, "but the Mollies had learned that their solidarity held out only as long as the footing was good. Again and again they drove their quarry into deep snow and set upon him, until eventually, after nine hours, the bull succumbed, and the wolves had their prize."

The Mollies brought this strange skill to the Lamar during this eventful winter of 2011–2012. Because the Lamar Valley is so open, they were filmed in action by George Bumann, a local guide who was teaching a class on the Yellowstone wolves. This one, you can see on YouTube. In it, we again see the gang-swarm strategy. Blakeslee spoke to multiple witnesses, and describes the encounter from more angles than the film can manage:

> On February 12, two groups of Mollies took on a herd of bison in a snowy meadow below Jasper Bench. One faction, twelve wolves strong, chased a string of adult bison out of the trees and onto the valley floor. The panicked bison— unaccustomed to such bold and reckless attacks—ran for their lives, struggling to break trail in the deep snow. A second squad of Mollies, consisting mostly of yearlings, went up the hillside and made contact with a calf, only to be driven back by its nearby mother. When the yearlings high on the hillside saw that their comrades on the valley floor had managed to take one of the bison down, they came sliding down the absurdly steep hill with reckless abandon, pivoting this way and that, tumbling head over heels, reaching the bottom by sliding on their rears.

3

In short order all nineteen Mollies were around the downed behemoth, and together they made it disappear. Not since the heyday of the Druids, when thirty-seven wolves stalked this same landscape, had the Lamar Valley seen a force like this.

Wolves have always eaten bison, but before the Mollies, we expected them to stick to the calves, which normally weigh less than a single adult wolf. At the time the Mollies became a pack, one of the only studies of this matter was one that had been conducted at Wood Buffalo National Park in Canada in the 1980s, and what the researchers found was not surprising. The wolves there tried to pick off the calves, but if the adults stuck together and presented a united front—like a Roman legion facing the barbarians—the wolves were stymied.

Now, we have to think differently. One of the open, and fun, questions of wildlife biology is how greatly the two— wolves and bison—influenced each other's development as species. Before the wolf reintroduction, the bison . . . just never quite made *sense*. Watching them lumber around a place like Old Faithful, delicately nibbling dandelions, left you scratching your head. Their bodies always seemed like overkill. If all they did was galumph around and occasionally toss a tourist, what need was there to be built like a John Deere bulldozer? The challenges of that life did not appear to demand anything like such a response.

Now, it is much easier to see why they are like that. Park visitors—human park visitors—are not the creatures with whom they normally live.

One reason we have this newfound wisdom is that there are many more bison in the lower forty-eight now, and many more wolves. There will be more bloodcurdling videos, and for as long as they last, as a pack, the Mollies are likely to be the stars.

WEIRD AND WONDERFUL WOLVES

We Should Listen to the Fairy-Tale Things

Back in 2009, there occurred an incident that shocked outsiders. People who live in and around the park were less surprised; among them, a more common reaction was the thought that it should have happened sooner.

A yearling male wolf, 729M of the Gibbon Meadow pack, turned up at the Midway Geyser Basin in March 2009 and, as the spring progressed, was seen more and more often around the Biscuit Basin area, and the village at Old Faithful. He napped on the porches of the employee housing. He chased bicycles, and at least once chased a motorcycle. He began to regularly approach people at Biscuit Basin, showing absolutely no fear of humans. He also approached cars. It looked like what older rangers remember the bears doing, in the old days when bears were allowed to beg along the road. The word they use for it is "panhandling."

In general, he behaved—endearingly—like Two Socks, the wolf that Lieutenant Dunbar dances with in *Dances with Wolves.* The rangers reacted by shooting him.

They did so, however, after watching him closely for two weeks and hazing him away from public areas. In such situations, they use shell crackers, explosive rounds fired from a shotgun, intended only to frighten. They also use the kind of nonlethal deterrents police departments use to disperse rioters: bean bag rounds and rubber bullets. The wolf, however, kept coming back, and the rangers at last decided he was "habituated," to use the term wildlife professionals have adopted for this situation. It refers to the habits of the wolf: the habituated animal has become used to people. The real problem with 729M was that he had come to associate people with food.

It happened again in 2011. Wolf 812M was a Mollie who also came to associate people with food. He was hazed away on seven occasions, rangers going so far as to hit him repeatedly with paintballs and spray him with bear spray, but as with

729M, he kept coming back. This incident took a turn toward the ominous when 812M came after a man who was just off the East Entrance Road. Bystanders on the road filmed him (the video is still on YouTube) as the wolf circled the man and approached over and over and over. The man can be heard on the video yelling at the absolute top of his lungs and, when the wolf would not relent, swinging with a heavy stick he turned up on the ground. The wolf *still* would not relent. He was not small, either. The rangers eventually killed him, too, and during the necropsy, found that he weighed 110 pounds.

When these incidents happened, the press releases talked about visitor safety—the animals were removed, that is, to keep the public from harm. We do not generally think too closely about what that means. What it means is this: the habituated wolf has come to associate people with food. The thought is that one day, having come to associate people with food, they will look on people *as* food.

In North America, it has not happened very often. Captive wolves occasionally attack (people keep them as pets, and it backfires sometimes). Wolves can also have rabies. An Inuit child died after being bitten by a rabid wolf in Alaska in 1943, and an Inuit hunter died of the same cause in 1942, but even deaths from rabid wolves are rare.

Incidents of wolves actually preying on humans have been, in North America, just as rare (a great deal rarer than, for instance, shark attacks). In 2010, snowmobilers near the remote town of Chignik Lake, Alaska, came upon the body of Candice Berner, a thirty-two-year-old teacher who had been out jogging when she was attacked by wolves. It was a case of outright predation, and there was no doubt about what had happened.

Because it was March, the details of the event were written in the snow, and in great detail. Berner was a petite woman, under five feet tall, and some thought her size might have led the wolves to choose her over some other victim—but while the events were written in the snow, the wolves' thoughts were not. The Alaska Department of Fish and Game (DFG) made a thorough investigation. What they found were signs of a protracted struggle (one can only imagine what was going through the troopers' minds as they looked through all this). Multiple sets of wolf tracks appeared 250 feet from the place where they presume she was killed. She was running, and so were the animals; it appeared to the troopers that the animals had to run to catch up with her. They found a mitten 200 feet away from the death site, and another mitten 63 feet away. One of the mittens had a thumb torn off, so the assumption had to be that there was a literal running fight.

Forty feet from the spot where she was killed, the troopers found a depression in the snow with blood in it, with the wolf tracks converging on the depression, so it was here that they first knocked her down and injured her seriously. The same thing happened again ten feet farther on, but from here, the evidence of the tracks changed. Berner had been running along a road, but here, she left it and moved downhill; at this second depression, she had been struggling and then crawled away. Then the tracks changed again, and it was clear she was no longer crawling. Instead, the wolves were pulling her downhill, away from the road, and she was small enough that they could do so without much trouble. Here, there was a great deal of blood, so she was now severely injured. The wolves pulled her to a point where the wardens found a wide patch of melted snow with blood in it. The troopers decided this was where she died. The wolves dragged her body at least twice afterward, but there were no further signs of struggle.

The Alaska DFG troopers killed wolves in the area and used DNA to tie the killing to at least one of them, and possibly more. From the tracks found at the scene, it was clear that more than one wolf was involved. For some reason, the pack had simply decided to treat Berner as they would a moose or a caribou. If she *had* been a moose or a caribou, the signs of struggle and death written in the snow would not have been radically different.

A similar incident happened in 2005, when twenty-two-year-old Kenton Carnegie was attacked, killed, and partly eaten at the mining camp of Points North Landing, Saskatchewan, and this incident is especially interesting to people concerned with the Yellowstone wolves. The wolves in the Carnegie case were habituated; they were eating garbage from the camp and had approached people in the area. Ten months before Carnegie's death, a lone wolf attacked one of the miners. Then, on November 8, 2005, Carnegie left to go for a walk and did not come back. When searchers found his body, it was surrounded by wolf tracks; when the body was being recovered, witnesses saw two sets of eyes glowing in the woods nearby, and howling echoed in the distance. Carnegie had been partly eaten: the pathologist, after the autopsy, reported that 25 to 30 percent of his body mass was gone, from his midsection to his thigh. As with Candice Berner, this was a case of outright predation.

Unfortunately, the kind of careful investigation that the Alaska DFG performed for Berner did not happen here, for various reasons. Some suspicion remains that the culprit may have been a bear. Fatal attacks by bears are a good deal more common than fatal attacks by wolves. However, the tracks argue otherwise.

And that is it. There are more records of attacks earlier in history, but those records are often sketchy, regularly not even naming the victim. The Berner and Carnegie attacks are the only recent fatal incidents involving wild wolves actually hunting people with the intent of eating them.

I have been speaking, however, of North America. The Old World is a different matter altogether. There, we find records of thousands and thousands of incidents, and in these incidents, the wolves were not fooling around. They were hunting. They killed their human victims because humans were an item in their regular diet.

It makes sense. Look at the art, literature, legends, and mythology of Europe and Asia. They produced the Norse gods Sköll and Hati, two giant wolves who are the bringers of chaos and destruction, consuming the sun and moon at the end of the world. And Fenrir, another Norse god, a monstrous wolf who is the evil child of Loki. And Ahriman, the evil spirit of ancient Persia, who created the wolf out of sheer malevolence. And the demonic wolf of Celtic mythology, Gwyllgi, whose key feature is his glowing red eyes. And Cailleach, the evil old hag of Scottish folktales, who brings winter and death, and comes riding on a wolf. And the werewolves who turn up in folktales all over Europe.

We could continue. Evil wolves survive in the fairy tales we still tell our own children. In sanitized versions of her story, Little Red Riding Hood's grandmother is locked in a closet, and the girl is frightened only by the wolf. In the older versions, they are both devoured. The hunter who saves them has to kill the wolf and split him open to get them out. The first two of the Three Little Pigs, of course, are killed and eaten. The wolf is, after all, big and bad.

These stories were the creations of people who dealt with wolves daily and hated them. They detested them for their habit of killing their livestock, and they feared them for their habit of eating the people.

They did eat people, often. For guidance in this matter, we can be thankful to John Linnell, a wildlife biologist at the Norwegian Institute for Nature Research. Linnell led a team of seventeen other researchers in a massive effort to comb historical efforts and get at the truth. Their book-length report, *The Fear of Wolves*, was published in Norway in 2002.

What did they find? Plenty of stories of wolf attacks that did not sound real. For instance, the charming story told and believed in Norway of the soldier Anders Solli, who was walking home on Christmas Eve, 1612, when he was attacked by a wolf. He killed it with his sword and went on his way. The rest of the wolf pack paused to eat their slain pack-mate, then attacked Anders again. He discovered that the blood of the first wolf had frozen, and so his sword was stuck in its scabbard. The wolves ate him entirely, leaving only his sword, his skis, and for some reason, his right hand. This story is told and believed all over Norway—and all over the rest of Scandinavia, where it is said to have happened to different soldiers with different names. The researchers heard also the story of the family traveling by horse-drawn sleigh through a wintry countryside. Chased by wolves, the family, to save itself, throws its youngest child overboard. The wolves pause to eat the child, and the rest of the family is saved. This story is told and believed all over Scandinavia and Russia (and in the United States, a version shows up in Willa Cather's novel *My Ántonia*). It happened everywhere and nowhere. Along with the story of Anders Solli and his inedible right hand, it is what we would call an urban legend. The researchers also heard the story of two children killed by wolves in Scotland—at a date when wolves had been extinct there for eighty years. They heard the story of the shepherd in Iran who drove off some wolves attacking his sheep, and then sat down and died, possibly of a heart attack—and was recorded as having been "killed by wolves."

Amid all that, they found plenty of real cases. "The majority of attacks," the researchers write, "concern wolves with rabies." It was at one time a terror, and is no more:

> Although wolves do not serve as a reservoir for rabies, they can catch it from other species. It appears that wolves develop an exceptionally severe "furious" phase and can bite a large number of people (>30) in a single attack. We have found records from Italy, France, Finland,

WEIRD AND WONDERFUL WOLVES

Germany, Poland, Slovakia, Spain, the Baltic States, Russia, Iran, Kazakhstan, Afghanistan, China, India, and North America. The earliest record we found of such an attack was from 1557 in Germany, and the most recent was from Latvia in 2001. Up until the development of post-exposure treatments (first developed by Pasteur in the 1890s and refined in the 1950s) bites from rabid wolves were almost always fatal. Treatments are presently so good that the majority of victims now survive.

Then there are the other stories, true stories in which the wolves do not have the excuse that they are possessed by a virus.

In a single county in Poland, in the single year of 1819, nineteen people were recorded as having been killed by wolves.

In an episode remembered in history as "the Wolf of Gysinge," during a three-month period in 1820–1821, a single wolf in Gysinge, Sweden, attacked thirty-one people. Almost all were children between the ages of three and a half and fifteen. Of these, twelve were killed, and many of them were partly consumed.

Finland is well-represented in this unfortunate roll-call, even though it is a lightly populated nation of extensive wilderness— or perhaps for those very reasons. In Kaukola in 1831–1832, eight children and one woman were killed by a single wolf. In Kivennapa between 1839 and 1850, what was thought to be a single wolf killed one adult and twenty children; we have the ages for only four of the children, who were between six and eight years old. In a series of incidents remembered as "the Wolves of Turku," between 1879 and 1882, possibly as many as thirty-five children were killed by a single pair of wolves; finding the pair eventually involved the local, then the national government. There were even calls to bring in the army, and professional hunters came from Russia and Lithuania. In the end, they got the pair, and the attacks stopped.

Russia is famous for its wolves; its wolf population is thought to be the largest in the world, and yet Russia seems to have gotten off lightly. The most famous episodes occurred in Kirov and Vladimir, beginning amid the disruption caused by the Second World War. In Vladimir, there were ten fatal attacks, with the victims mainly children. In Kirov, twenty-two children died.

France produced what may be the most famous series of wolf attacks in history. It is remembered as *La Bête du Gévaudan*, the Beast of Gévaudan, as if the thing responsible were a single supernatural creature, a European version of Sasquatch or the Yeti. It was, in fact, a pack of wolves. Gévaudan was a province in the rugged Massif Central highlands of south-central France. Between June 1764 and June 1767, there were as many as 210 attacks there, with perhaps 113 killed, maybe fewer, maybe more, and a number of them were eaten. The victims, as so often, were mostly women and children; it was they who, like Little Bo-Peep, were the traditional shepherds in the countryside. A garish mythology arose about the attackers (or attacker—was it perhaps, people thought then, just a single monster or werewolf?). *La Bête* was able to walk on its hind legs. Its hide was bulletproof. It liked to decapitate its victims and drink their blood. A local boy was said to have contracted a fever after the beast merely looked him in the eyes. It mocked the dogs and hunters that pursued it. There were a great many of the latter because the attacks became a national *cause célèbre*. Even the king, Louis XV, became involved. Linnell summarizes the affair:

> Enormous resources were used to try and kill the wolves—including the army, several nobles and royal huntsmen. A large proportion of the local population was conscripted to take part in the hunt. Many wolves were killed, but the attacks continued until a wolf was killed in autumn 1765. This wolf was very large and was identified as being that responsible for attacking people from a series

of scars inflicted by people who had defended themselves. However, after a brief pause the attacks resumed again and continued until June 1767 when a second especially large wolf was killed, this time with human remains in the stomach.

Then, the attacks at last stopped. Why has nothing like this happened in North America? It may have at some point in the unrecorded past. In fact, given that humans and wolves have lived side by side here for maybe thirteen thousand years, it has surely happened. We just do not know about it.

It also seems inevitable that it will happen again. An ominous quality of the cases recounted above (a small slice of the whole record, leaving out the thousands killed in India and the rest of Asia) is the way individuals and packs develop a *habit* of killing people. Packs, as we saw with the Mollies, do develop a culture. What happened at Gévaudan, we can guess, is that the local wolves found it easy and rewarding to kill the shepherd instead of the sheep, and being intelligent, they remembered and so continued doing it. They developed a culture of manslaughter.

This may all seem like a dangerous topic, given the political precariousness of wolves in the United States. There are plenty of people in the Western United States who would like to see them wiped out. However, we owe it to the wolves to at least think about the worst-case scenario, because when wolf experts get together, in private, they admit it is probably inevitable. Eventually, people will be attacked.

Therefore, when park people heard about the shooting of the two habituated wolves—first 729M in 2009, then 812M, the rogue Mollie, in 2011—they did not necessarily get angry. Instead, they nodded. Some people objected, but most did not. It made sense, and it still seems like the right thing to have done. If we ever have a fatal wolf encounter in the park, the chances are good it will involve a habituated wolf.

That is one lesson to take from events like the death of Kenton Carnegie at that mining camp in Saskatchewan. If those wolves had not been feeding on the camp garbage, would he ever have met them? Would they even have been in the area? And did the proximity of humans in their everyday life teach the wolves that they need not fear these clumsy, bipedal creatures who run so very slowly?

So never feed wolves, obviously. Let them remain wild animals, away off in the distance (the Park Service rule is that the distance should be at least 100 yards). Having read the information above, you may no longer be eager to walk up to one anyway.

It is also true that modern Americans are not vulnerable the way the peasants of Gévaudan were. One quality we do not share with the people of the Old World who were terrorized by wolves for thousands of years is that they were relatively poor. Before at least the nineteenth century, in no country did large numbers of rural people own firearms. Modern Americans have so many firearms that no one knows the actual number to the nearest ten million. They also mostly live close to other people in well-lighted towns and cities, and no one leaves home without a phone. The lonely peasant girl with only a shepherd's crook to defend herself was easy prey, but the modern cowboy in his pickup truck—not so much.

Even in the park, where people generally do not carry guns into the backcountry, nearly everyone has bear spray. The word "spray" calls to mind hairspray or Right Guard Sport, but bear spray is actually a serious weapon. It is 8.1 ounces of almost unbelievably noxious capsaicin, under extreme pressure. Test-firing a can for the first time is an astounding experience. An orange chemical cone explodes out with a ripping noise and an actual kick. The chemical reaches out twenty or thirty feet. It will stop anything with eyes and lungs.

So, enjoy your view of *La Bête du Wyoming*, from a safe distance . . . and keep a close eye, all the while, on the kids.

4

NORTHERN NUTTINESS

The absolute end of the road. The North Entrance Road, and beyond, the river that destroyed it, the Gardner. SCOTT HERRING

4

As we have seen, Yellowstone is not just the national park. Greater Yellowstone extends over maybe twenty-two million acres, depending on who you talk to. Some people think it extends well up into Canada.

So, when you drive out one of the national park entrances, you are not really leaving, not for a long while. This is especially the case in the north. When you make the trip down from Mammoth and drive through the North Entrance, you will find yourself on US Route 89. For five miles, all the terrain you see on the other side of the Yellowstone River is the national park. Depending on your route, you will be in the Greater Yellowstone Ecosystem, or on the edge of it, for hours.

It was from this direction that the first generations of tourists entered the park, hauled here by the railroad. Gardiner, Montana, the town on the North Entrance, is therefore almost the oldest of the towns around the park, and certainly the oldest looking. But Gardiner is a strange place. It is part government-service company town, part rural ranching-and-farming hub, part Old Montana frontier village, and part tourist trap of violently aggressive tackiness.

It has always been a strange place. One of the residential "streets" (it is not paved) is 5th Street. Ask one of the locals what they call it in private. The name is obscene—not pornographic, but merely gross.

And here is a story of old Gardiner. The cemetery is just outside town on the south side of the Yellowstone River. We will return there in a later section of this chapter. If you look to the west, from the cemetery, you may notice an odd sight: if the sun is beginning to set, the hills there may be shimmering. That is glass, broken glass, in vast quantities. What you are seeing is the town dump, the old town dump from the early years of the town and the park. It extends to the west for perhaps a quarter mile, perhaps farther. It was in use for a long time.

Walk out among the remains and study the odds and ends on the ground. You may begin to wonder why some of the glass and metal is deformed. At length, a solution occurs: it is partly melted. There were fires here, so long ago that soot and anything organic are long gone, leaving just the glass and metal.

Then the solution gets clearer. People used to burn their garbage. In fact, it was the responsible thing to do, what we would think of as the "environmentally sensitive" thing to do. If you were a good citizen, you bothered to burn your garbage. If you were a slob, you just let it blow around and draw in the bears.

Climb to the top of one of those hills, though, and look down toward the river, to the north. If the view is open enough, what you will see is the old railroad bed. Right down there, for generations, people from all over the country, and indeed the world, rolled up to Gardiner station, their gateway to Yellowstone National Park. The dump—its boundaries were always vague—extends down almost to the railbed.

So, for generations, people arriving in Wonderland were greeted by the sight and smell of burning garbage.

From that, let us turn to an event that took place here along the northern boundary that started as a disaster and led to a strange new beauty.

And All the High Mountains Under the Entire Heavens Were Covered

The communities around the park, and the businesses inside, had a rough time in 2020. They were just getting ready for the new summer season when the federal government shut down the park because of the COVID-19 pandemic. The two entrances that lead into Wyoming were opened on May 18, and the remaining three Montana entrances opened on June 1. The park then got back to a rocky version of normal.

4

Still, the disruption was considerable. Businesses inside the park are operated by large corporations that have some capital reserve, but the small businesses outside the national park had to make do. Employees were let go, then they were hired back in a hurry. Since employees in the area come to the park for the summer from literally all over the world, this process was not easy.

At first, it did not matter that much because the park remained sleepy. On May 31, a park visitor took an extraordinary video. In it, a young grizzly bear attacked a cow bison. It did not go so well for the grizzly, because the two animals were of comparable size, and the bear—wildlife scientists would call him a "subadult"—did not appear to know what he was doing. The two grappled with each other like wrestlers in the Olympics, or for that matter wrestlers at WrestleMania. It went on for five minutes, and they were still going at each other when they at last began to move out of range of the camera.

The extraordinary thing about the incident was the setting. The encounter began next to the parking lot at the Fairy Falls trailhead, just up the Firehole River from Midway Geyser Basin. The Grand Loop Road, mostly empty, was visible in the background. The two animals, unaware of whatever small audience they had, wrestled right across the steel highway bridge that carries hikers on the Fairy Falls trail. The fight finally spilled into the Firehole River itself. But Midway Geyser Basin, steaming in the background, is normally one of the park's busy places, and Old Faithful itself is only five miles away. They should have had an audience of hundreds, maybe thousands—but in a normal year, the whole incident would never have happened to begin with. It is comparable to a pair of big wild animals locked in a death match in the middle of Disneyland. With no humans around, however, the wildlife had reverted to the way they used the Firehole valley before the tourists came.

It did not last. Visitation was down for the year 2020 but began to rebound at the end of the summer, and the next year was a challenge in a different way. It was as if everyone had decided to come at once. August 2021 set a record at 921,844 "recreation visits" (so even more, when we count the people and vehicles entering on business, a significant number). July had been even better, or worse, as the case may be: it was not just the busiest July on record, but it was the only month in park history, to that date, in which more than a million visited in a single month (before 1948, the period of the postwar boom, the number was less than a million in an entire year, and it passed two million only in 1965). During 2020, 3.8 million people visited. In 2021, it was over 4.8 million. "Historically, we had twenty years between each additional million visitors and there was plenty of time to adjust," Cam Sholly, Yellowstone's superintendent, told *The Guardian*. "But getting that increase in just a twelve-month period made it hard to react fast enough."

So, the government and businesses and area residents were battening down the hatches and stripping for battle before summer 2022. During the spring, all those thousands of summer employees started driving in, and flying in. Quite a few come from East Asia now, and they have come from Europe for a long time (the hotel employees wear their home state or country on their name tags, and if all the employees at a specific location are from, say, Colombia or Thailand, that is because the hotel recruiter stopped there). The assumption, of course, was that the maximum number would be needed, and then some. Almost all of them were either in the park or in training on June 13.

That was the lucky day: June 13.

It had been a cold and wet spring already, the kind of year when a visit to the park interior—the lake, the canyon, or the geyser basins—tends to be interrupted in the afternoon when the sky turns black and the rain starts falling. This year, the rain wanted to last all day, and at the more elevated locations, it turned to snow. On the north side of buildings, the snowdrifts from the previous winter lingered. The mountains—the Absarokas, the Gallatins, the distant Tetons—were still bright white. All this was normal. Every few years, Yellowstone has such a spring. The locals actually like it, and certainly prefer it to the punishing droughts the region regularly dishes out.

Then came June 12. An atmospheric river parked itself over the western United States, running from Oregon to Manitoba and sending a constant stream of rain off the Pacific, across the coastal mountains, across the Great Basin, and directly over Greater Yellowstone. On the computer, satellite images captured it and showed it working. The river would not budge; it flowed hour after hour, all day and far into the night.

Both locals and vacationers woke up the next day to discover that whatever plans they had were now scratched.

The rain, they learned, had been warm enough that it hit all that snow and accelerated the melting that was already happening (because despite appearances, winter was in fact over, and summer was just a week away). It became a one-two punch: the rainwater and the snowmelt combined to create a great mass of water hanging in the upper reaches of the park. When it came down, it did so with violence. The focus of that violence was the northern part of the park, and the Yellowstone River valley beyond.

If we combine rainwater with snowmelt, then in a single day, locations across the northern part of Yellowstone got between seven and a half and nine and a half inches of precipitation. It was not a one-hundred-year flood; it was a five-hundred-year flood. The water surged downward into the creeks and rivers. In places where they could spread out, they did so, but in the mountains, a watercourse is often confined by the surrounding heights, and in those places, interesting things happened.

Northern Nuttiness

In the Lamar Valley—the center of the wolf watcher's world, under ordinary circumstances—the Lamar River left its banks and filled much of the valley. Downstream, however, it enters Lamar Canyon, where the walls of the mountains on either side squeezed the overloaded river and left it no options. At the tightest spots, standing waves developed, impossible to estimate: Twenty feet high? Thirty? Forty? The roar was like an international airport, and something had to give. What gave was, among other things, the canyon wall underneath the road. The next day, the asphalt was still there next to a brand-new hundred-foot drop made of raw, unstable earth. The drop started about two inches from the edge of the asphalt. No one would be driving that road for a while.

But no one could for very far anyway. Upstream, normally gentle Soda Butte Creek got up and tore the road to pieces. Slough Creek and Pebble Creek flooded the campgrounds that line their banks. Normally, Pebble Creek can be crossed literally on foot, but now it spread out and took over, and from above, it spilled out to make a brown triangle like the delta of a much larger river. At Roosevelt, Lost Creek, which can normally be jumped across in a single step, washed out the area behind the lodge. All up and down the Northeast Entrance Road corridor, the littlest watercourses were demanding attention, and the larger ones looked like the Mekong. The largest of them, the Lamar, looked like those rivers in Tibet when the snow in the Himalaya melts during the spring. One needed exotic analogies to make it make sense. The only thing in North America that quite works is the Colorado River inside the Grand Canyon, in those places where the rapids are Class V.

All over the park, people were stranded. The rivers were, among other things, flowing around and through the vault toilets that are everywhere in the park, and the national forests that surround it. The water was not to be consumed. Things were going haywire everywhere, so haywire and so extensively that it was hard to say what-all was wrong. The Park Service fairly quickly decided to evacuate the park. Ten thousand people streamed out those entrances that could still be driven.

The year 2022 was the 150th anniversary of the park, but that kind of got forgotten.

Outside the park, just beyond the Northeast Entrance, the towns of Cooke City and Silvergate were completely isolated, and farther up the road, Red Lodge had flooded. There was, however, no great threat to life and limb. The essence of the situation was simple: greater Yellowstone is in the mountains. In the mountains, the roads all follow big rivers because that is where the terrain is gentlest. The millennia of erosion caused by the water, and the glaciers before them, saw to that. Now, the rivers got up and did what they do. They were in charge, and they were reminding us all what a mass of water can do with gravity pulling it relentlessly downward. Literally nothing could stand in its way, not even the mountains themselves.

The Yellowstone River, where it exits the park and runs past Gardiner, had been rising and getting ever more brown for some days. The river filled also with larger and larger pieces of driftwood, until, on June 12, during the final storm, entire trunks were headed downriver, one after another in an endless train. These were old, dead trees that had floated loose far above, in the national park, and been conveyed here by water that was flowing higher and faster than it had in over a century (Gardiner had last seen high water like this in 1918). It was God's own lumbering operation, the wood ultimately piling itself into mountains of soggy timber far downstream.

The next day, Gardiner residents awoke to find that the Yellowstone River had taken over their lives.

The river was now filled with entire forests of vegetation, and some of it was bright green and still living. Whole living trees were pounding downstream in the general direction of the Gulf of Mexico, although they would only get there if reduced to their constituent molecules. They were at least going to get a good start on that. Some of the tree trunks were now sixty feet and more long, giant old-growth spruce and fir that charged downstream with their massive roots going first, battering rams looking for something to batter. There were standing waves from one shore to the other, and the water was a brown horror. It was all entirely "natural," but it was impossible to look at that water and not think of sewage, which, as Gardiner people discovered as the day went on, was not entirely wrong.

The town was full of people, far more than actually live here, all milling around aimlessly and making videos of the river. They were stuck. There were only two ways out of town— by helicopter and by foot. Two automotive routes connect Gardiner to the outside world: a driver leaves either through the park or north into Montana on US Route 89. The park was closed. The road in that direction was impassible anyway, and so was 89. It was flooded in Livingston, and the highway bridge across the Yellowstone River to the north was now full of holes.

But the real problem, it developed, was in Yankee Jim Canyon, eighteen miles downriver. Here, the Yellowstone, and the glaciers before it, had chewed a gunsight pass through the massive, jagged ridge that crosses the river and the highway at right angles. The river is at 5,300 feet above sea level; that ridge is so high and otherwise impenetrable that Dome Mountain, at 8,596 feet and standing directly overhead to the north, is actually one of the low spots. The water slammed into that barrier and backed up. It formed a temporary reservoir of sorts, and the highway was now underneath.

How much water was hitting that barrier? The US Geological Survey got lucky with its river flow sensor, attached to the bridge at Corwin Springs, seven miles downstream from Gardiner. It survived the battering and kept recording data, measuring the flow in CFS, cubic feet per second. On June 13, the USGS later reported, "The height of the water in the Yellowstone River at the Corwin Springs gage reached almost 14 feet—about 2.5 feet higher than the previous record flood event in June 1918. Discharge peaked at approximately 50,000 CFS . . . which was much greater than the previous peak flow of about 32,000 CFS from 1918 and in the late 1990s. This data indicate that the amount of water that was flowing through the gage in the four days between June 11th and June 15th (more than 70 billion gallons) would fill more than one hundred thousand Olympic swimming pools! If a football field would have walls on all sides, those walls would have to be three miles high to hold all that water."

It should probably have been more destructive than it actually was. Houses down the valley, on the floodplain, were immersed, their basements and first stories filled with mud. Gardiner residents, their number now greatly increased, were told not to drink the water, then to not even brush their teeth or take a shower. A helicopter was ferrying people out in a small way. The pilot told the news media that he had carried out forty people, including two women who were, he said, "very pregnant." The local Boy Scout troop opened an aid center where they handed out bottled water by the pallet-load, and the Super 8 set up cots in its conference room. The town had become a well-heeled refugee camp.

Later that day, the refugees gathered on 89 to watch where, down below, the river was about to claim another victim. Just above the normal level of the water stood a bunkhouse owned by the National Park Service and kept as housing for its employees in the area. Picture an average apartment building, but one in a fabulous location—until this day. The river cut away the earth underneath until, at last, the building slid into the water like a ship being launched and sailed away. All that was left behind were a pair of big propane bottles, looking like lost footballs. The bunkhouse stayed afloat a long time, but ultimately plowed into the Corwin Springs bridge and exploded. For the next few days, local social media sites and Facebook pages had messages that read something like "If you find my backpack in the river down the valley somewhere, call me."

But if Pebble Creek, Soda Butte Creek, the Lamar River, the Yellowstone River, and all the others were acting up, the Gardner River had gone stark raving mad.

The Gardner rises in the Gallatin Range, then gathers momentum in its own valley, Gardner's Hole, named for mountain man John Gardner (or Gardiner—the town and the river are spelled differently as a result of a long string of endearingly silly errors). It drops quickly, making a long half-circle around Mammoth Hot Springs to ultimately charge downhill and join the Yellowstone River at the town of Gardiner. In the process, it flows through terrain over which the glaciers, when they retreated, dropped a mix of everything from boulders to microscopic grains of mud. The mud has a special quality to it. It is the stickiest, gooiest mud in the region. Walking over it when it is wet is like walking through puddles of Elmer's glue. It is really uniquely horrible.

The wet spring had already swollen the river until it was just a white and brown roar. It picked up that mud and transported it down into the Yellowstone, playing a key role in turning the larger river brown, too (it is normally fetching shades of green and blue). Now, as the Gardner filled with more water than it had carried since long before the park existed, it got up and moved around. A river like that naturally forms meanders. As the river curves, the water on the outside edge of the curve moves faster than the inside edge. The faster water erodes the bank, while the slower water, because it is slow, drops the sediment it is carrying. The meander, as it erodes, makes the river itself move. The river is like a snake slithering, always changing shape, the meanders getting ever farther away from the hypothetical center.

As it filled with more and ever more water, however, the Gardner became less like a snake than a chainsaw. It sawed at the

4

banks with ever greater violence, ripping away the banks—and along the banks ran the road.

The result was no surprise. Everyone knew the road would one day be destroyed; the people who built it originally, back in the early days of the park, had gone for scenery over common sense. The Park Service had in place contingency plans to move it. The water merely called our bluff.

The river chewed entire forests away. Full-grown trees sailed down and into the Yellowstone like sailboats with green spinnakers. Boulders that had been in the same spot for a century up and disappeared. Landmarks vanished. Stair-step rapids were blasted away. And all things human were in big trouble.

The road descends from Mammoth through foothills, reaching the level of the water at the famous Boiling River, a spot where the hot water from Mammoth made a natural Jacuzzi known the world over. It was now very much off-limits, and underwater anyway. When the high water receded, it was revealed that the Gardner had dumped rocks and sediment all over the traditional Boiling River hot-potting area, shutting it down, perhaps for good.

Just downstream, the water began its rude treatment of the road. In any place where the current was meandering, the asphalt was first nibbled, then chewed, then ripped away completely, torn to bits, and distributed to improbable distances downstream. Concrete flood control sluices that had underlain the road were picked up and thrown, bodily. In places where the road had made hairpins, as it did often, it was lined by the most serious kind of guardrail. The steel guardrail, and the massive timbers it was bolted to, was now liberated when the ground underneath disappeared; the steel was then twisted like twine, into comical shapes that hung in the air where the shoulder of the road had been, roughly, very roughly. The steel and timber now dangled in space, twenty or thirty feet up.

The real destruction started at what is known locally as the 45th Parallel Turnout. There, the Gardner decided it wanted to run east a bit. Destroying the road was just the start; a chunk of asphalt the length of a football field disappeared as if it had never existed. But the Gardner kept going. It started to eat into the side of Mount Everts. It ate until a wide slice, something over a hundred feet high, was gone and carried away downriver.

So, it continued. For about a mile, the river meandered ever more violently, whipping back and forth, destroying six separate chunks of road, and undermining a highway bridge as well. The hiking bridge at Rescue Creek was not just undermined: it was transformed into a ship, and then a shipwreck. It turned up after the flood some distance downstream. Even in areas where it was not destroying human stuff, the water was scouring the bed of the river and chewing away at the flanks of Mount Everts on one side, and Sepulcher Mountain on the other.

No one was going to be entering the national park through the North Entrance any time soon.

When the Yellowstone River receded, the trapped tourists were able to escape through a dewatered Yankee Jim Canyon, which presented the odd spectacle of a high desert with its sage and cactus all covered in gooey mud. When these tourists were gone, no one came to take their place. The summer season was over for Gardiner. By the 15th of June, you could stand in the middle of Route 89 and see not a single vehicle for miles in either direction. You could stand there and wait for one, and not be in any danger. Nor would one appear, for a half hour at a time. So went much of the rest of the town's summer. It was yet another write-off. The Park Service called in contractors who, at great speed, paved the old stagecoach road that runs from Gardiner to Mammoth. It opened in October. The former North Entrance Road was gone for good.

But the Gardner River . . .

4

When the river at last settled down, some weeks later, the terrain that resulted from its insane antics was unrecognizable. The Gardner is famous among anglers, who know—or knew—its every nook and cranny. That landscape had been erased. In places, the river had chewed down to the bedrock.

Walking up the riverbank, or on the sections of road that are still there to be walked on, is a voyage of discovery. Here and there are cobble-sized pieces of the road, round now, often with yellow paint from the centerline. The paint seems to have kept some of these pieces of the road from being reduced to bits of soil. Here, there, and everywhere are lengths of sewage line tossed around like a child's pick-up sticks. Mammoth Hot Springs had not had a sewage plant of its own; those pipes scattered all over the new riverbed had carried Mammoth sewage to the treatment plant in Gardiner. When the crisis had happened, the Park Service Maintenance Division had alertly and quickly routed sewage into Depression-era wastewater ponds at Mammoth, old but still serviceable (the most important employees in Yellowstone are the NPS Maintenance Division, the people who do things like protect us from sewage, and no one will ever change my mind). Those comically manhandled sewage pipes did explain for the locals, at last, why the water was supposed to be dangerous.

As of the date at which I am writing, in mid-2023, it is not clear what will happen to the earthly remains of the former North Entrance Road. The Park Service superintendent's office has said they would like to remove it. I wish they would not. It is an amazing lesson in practical geology. The Gardner, normally not a violent creature, reminded us of its awesome latent power, which reappears all over again every year. It takes its power from the park snowpack, hanging there high above, and only the caprices of climate and weather keep all that water from coming down in a rush.

The river canyon itself is not going anywhere. Exploring it is an astounding experience. As of now, you have it to yourself.

Virtually no one fishes it because everyone has to walk the whole distance now. We are learning how deep is the devotion of the individual angler, now that all the anglers have to park the rented Escalade back in Gardiner. Many, and in places all, of the streamside trees are gone. Most of the Gardner River is in Wyoming, while the trees are now in Montana, and dead at that. They will, one day, be in Louisiana and points south. The canyon walls are in places unstable; later in the summer, 2022, they were prone to crumble merely when hit by the wind.

But the strangest thing about it is that it is all strikingly beautiful.

The stream is now lined by countless millions of rocks, all of them smoothed mainly by making a great deal of the trip here inside glaciers. Many, perhaps most, do not belong exactly here, geologically; they are from other mountain ranges, often the Beartooth Mountains, to the east. When you see a piece of hard, light-colored rock, that may be granite from the Beartooths. It is far from home.

All those millions of rocks are in every color imaginable. Furthermore, your experience of the whole environment is different, compared to the way it was before. Most people saw that canyon at thirty-five miles per hour, never stopping, even over a period of years, or decades, or a lifetime. Now, you have no choice but to look at every inch, because except where the road survived, travel is slow over those rocks. The sides of hills have been sliced open as if with a knife, revealing, in their stratified lines of sediment, the course of events at the end of the Ice Age, or, in places, a good deal earlier. In one spot, a seam of coal was exposed; I discovered it myself, and I am the only one who knows it is there. A geologist can have a literal field day.

And here is a feature of the place that is unique: for the first time in Yellowstone, ever, you can be an explorer setting foot on virgin ground. There is no other part of the park where this experience can be had. Every part of it has had feet set on it over and over. In 1887, a New York newspaper sent a well-known Arctic explorer to mush through the park in winter, "exploring" it. The exploration was a bust, but what matters here is the comment on it made by Billy Hofer, the park's premier guide during its first half-century. "There is much humbug about the whole thing," he wrote, in the outdoor journal *Forest and Stream*. "As well talk of 'exploring' Central Park, New York, as the National Park. The National Park is a well-known country; everything worth seeing is mapped out and described in reports and geological surveys, guidebooks and newspaper letters." And he wrote this passage just fifteen years after the park was established, when perhaps five thousand people visited in the whole year.

If Billy could come back in 2023, we would have something new to show him.

More Northern Exposure: A Tour of Yellowstone's Own Badlands

If you leave the park through the North Entrance, you will ultimately drive through the Roosevelt Arch; if you are headed into the park from the north, this is how you will arrive. The cornerstone was laid by Theodore Roosevelt when he visited the park in 1903 (his guide, by the way, was Billy Hofer). It was through this arch that most visitors entered, during the final heyday of the railroads. The Northern Pacific hauled them up the Yellowstone valley and deposited them in front of the arch, where stagecoaches picked them up and hauled them through TR's arch and up the earlier version of the north entrance road. Arch Park, Gardiner's small-town park, is surrounded by the loop road on which the stagecoaches ran. The brown structure next to the park, which is now the town's municipal building, was the railroad depot.

Beyond it is the Gardiner school. The football field is more often overrun by elk or bison than athletes. A little farther still is a larger building belonging to the National Park Service. It houses the park archive, and yes, they did need a building that size. Stuff has been accumulating for a century and a half.

Beyond that is a strange little thing: beyond that is the Old Yellowstone Trail.

Few people are even aware it exists. The first five miles are inside Yellowstone National Park, one of the most famous tourist destinations on the globe, but it is not on any list of destinations to visit. It is not that it is kept a secret; you could not keep something like that a secret. It is just unpaved and dusty, and there are no famous sights. It is, however, a way to see some of the stranger sights in the Yellowstone River valley.

Finding it is easy: if you just keep driving west, you have no choice but to enter it. The only turns are into the parking for the archive, which is a dead end, and into one of the park's gravel pits, and even deader end. The river is otherwise in the way; the only direction a driver can go without getting stuck, or wet, is west. At some point, you pass into the park, although where the line is, no one can say for sure. A tradition states that the iron fence that divides the town of Gardiner from the empty sagebrush to the south is the boundary, but it does not seem to be in the right place. An old tradition among Gardiner bar-flies states that the boundary was right along the sidewalk in front of the old Blue Goose Saloon, so that the National Park rangers could arrest any drunk they wished to there, but that is not true, either: the rangers can arrest people in town anywhere they want to. They are officially deputized because Gardiner does not have a police force of its own. The Blue Goose burned down, which may be all for the best.

The landscape is surely spectacular. The peaks above you are Sepulcher Mountain and Electric Peak. Sepulcher Mountain is the darker one; it gets its name from those exposures of rock jutting up from the summit, which looked like tombstones to the people who named it (they are actually stacks of volcanic rock, and the largest one is maybe fifty feet tall). Electric Peak is the mountain that will regularly have snow on it during the warm months. It got its name from an early party of climbers who summited in a storm and found their hair literally standing straight up on their heads. It is a feature of the peak that has not changed. Climbers like to say they have, while on the summit in a thunderstorm, felt their ice axes hum.

The terrain below is sometimes called the boundary lands, although it has no official name. It is Yellowstone National Park's very own badland. You half expect to see Clint Eastwood ride over one of the hills and hear the music from *The Good, the Bad and the Ugly*. There was even an Old West gunfight here, a real one, as we will see later.

The land here is what ecologists call a "cold desert." It receives little more than ten inches of precipitation in a normal year. One of the dominant plants is prickly pear cactus, and rattlesnakes live in the area. At the start of the road, back by the Roosevelt Arch, your view to the south is of a strange, hummocky landscape composed of short hills piled one on top of the other, all the way up to the forests under the mountains. This is the landslide zone. At the time of the last ice age, a glacier filled this valley up to the level of the mountain peaks, although the very top of Sepulcher was free of ice. As the ice flowed down the valley, it trapped soil and debris up against the northern face of Sepulcher. As the ice melted, the debris slumped downward, and the hummocky zone beneath Sepulcher is that debris today. It is a highly unstable landscape; when water hits it, the soil dissolves and flows downward like concrete dumped out of a cement truck. It is composed of that horrible glacial mud I referred to earlier. You do not want to be up there in the rain because you will be several inches taller after a few steps, and the mud on each foot will weigh five pounds. It is, at least, a way to lose weight, provided you can wash that stuff off before you get on a scale again. It likes your feet and wants to stay there.

Arid or not, the animals like it here. Elk are almost always in the area somewhere, especially during the fall when they enter the rut, their period of frenzied romance, when each mature bull bugles regularly, gathering together a harem of cows and fighting any bull big enough to challenge him. While on the Old Yellowstone Trail, stop the car engine and listen for them, if it is the right time of year. They can be anywhere in the vicinity of the road, although they also have that fondness I noted for the school football field. So do the bison, which will regularly pass through in large numbers during the winter.

Any time of year, you may find here an animal that you might have missed elsewhere: the pronghorn antelope. They are easy to see in this area, maybe because they do not mind the aridity; they are uniquely capable of tolerating periods without water (they get water from their food, and that is enough for them). Look for a tan-colored animal with white accents on its rump, belly, and neck. Look also for the curved black horns on the males; the female horn is usually only a bump.

Yellowstone is a place of extremes, and here we have them. The bison is the largest animal in North America, and those pronghorn antelope are the fastest. They can run 60 mph, although they do it only when in serious danger. The males also spit at each other, which is an extraordinary spectacle. People who have traveled, roughing it, in the Middle East say that pronghorns spit like camels. It is part hiss, part expectoration, and part a kind of bark.

The Old Yellowstone Trail winds through the hummocky landslide zone, climbing, then eventually descending, at which point the view opens out. You may then notice oddly unnatural lines on the landscape. Here is a strange thing about the whole place: it was not part of the original Yellowstone National Park. In fact, it was not part of the park until it was added in the late 1920s and early 1930s. Before that, it was homesteaded; some of the earliest settlers in this part of Montana lived along the road.

There are—as we will see in a later chapter—graves scattered all over the area, and not just in the Gardiner cemetery, although if you want to see an authentic Montana Boot Hill, it is beside the road at about exactly a mile from the Roosevelt Arch. Keep in mind that it is still in use, even though it is normally deserted.

The boundary lands were never a friendly place to live, though. When you see ghostly lines across the landscape, those are often the irrigation ditches by which these people scratched out a living. It was a desperate business. All up and down the valley are ditches cut into those hills to the south, running at the same elevation east-west. Those trenches captured what little snowmelt they could and channeled that wretched take into linked irrigation ditches; residents of Gardiner town hauled water for themselves in enormous wooden barrels strapped to horse-drawn wagons, which could only work in small quantities. Nowhere at this end of the valley has anyone used, in any important way, windmills. That was the case a hundred years ago, and you will not see them today, either. The reason is the wind: it will blow like a hurricane for a little while in the afternoon, but the rest of the time, it is too fickle to rely on. It is all ironic in what must have been a spectacularly irritating way because one of the big rivers of western North America is *right there*—but too far down to be of any use. Today, electric pumps can move water around, but a late-nineteenth-century settler had to just look at the Yellowstone River and put up with it. The boundary lands are dry and dusty now, and they were then, too.

As you descend from the landslide zone and onto more level ground, and the view opens up, most of the lines you see will have belonged to the Henderson homestead. It is gone now, but it was here that the real, actual Old West gunplay happened.

You reach that exact point where the Old Yellowstone Trail crosses Landslide Creek (you will probably need a GPS to find it, and Google Maps has it labeled correctly). In the summer of 1877, during the Nez Perce war, the tribe crossed Yellowstone

National Park in their flight from the US Army. While they were doing so, they sent small parties of young men ahead as a nineteenth-century version of what soldiers would call a reconnaissance in force. One such group of eighteen mounted warriors rode through Mammoth Hot Springs, down the canyon, and across the landslide zone, aiming at the Henderson ranch.

The ranch had been established in 1871 by James Henderson, and in 1877 it was being run by his son Sterling. He was at the ranch with a friend as the warriors approached.

Find Landslide Creek, and you are in the middle of the action. The Nez Perce almost got the drop on Henderson and his friend, and you can immediately see how: among the hills in the landslide zone, the eighteen warriors and their horses simply disappeared. They had to leave those hills eventually, though, and at that point, Sterling Henderson saw them. He and his friend grabbed guns and ammunition belts and ran to join three other friends who were fishing in the Yellowstone River.

The warriors were delighted with the ranch because one thing they were after was horses, and the Hendersons had a corral full. They were retrieving them when Henderson and his four friends opened fire. The five settlers were among the boulders on the north side of the road, a defensive position from which they would not be evicted easily. There followed a gun battle, the bullets passing back and forth over the road. Neither side was able to get the upper hand, so at length, the Nez Perce rode off with the Henderson livestock, after having set fire to the homestead.

They were in a hurry because—like a scene from a very old-fashioned movie—the cavalry were coming. Company E of the Seventh Cavalry, accompanied by forty-two Crow scouts, arrived in time to take back some of the captured horses. The force was led by Lieutenant Gustavus Doane, to whom we will return shortly. The cavalrymen had seen the smoke rising from the burning ranch. No one was killed or hurt in the encounter, but that was not for want of trying. Once back at Mammoth, the warriors encountered a tourist, and shot him dead. Forward elements of the Seventh Cavalry found the body, still warm, lying in the doorway of a cabin.

This whole encounter is an example of a common phenomenon, here in the boundary lands: all around here, the land is alive with Yellowstone past, but scarcely anyone knows it.

As you drive the road, you may notice a long, straight embankment to the north, in places with old concrete culverts through it. That is the route of the railroad, the one that brought visitors to the station next to the Roosevelt Arch. Only the embankment remains. During the Golden Age of railroading, a company like the Northern Pacific could build a line at great speed, and tear it down at great speed, too. The ties, spikes, and rails are gone because they were worth money; they were stripped out and shipped away when the automobile took over the job of hauling people here. Gardiner was the second town to host the railroad stop. The original end of the line was at Cinnabar, a town that disappeared so completely that when archaeologists from the University of Montana excavated it in 2007, it was as if they had found a pharaoh's tomb.

Yet the people of Cinnabar were latecomers. Native tribes used this valley for thousands of years. There are the remains, in a number of places, of their villages. Along the river are fire rings, still gray with ash. At a point about three and a half miles from the Roosevelt Arch, the Old Yellowstone Trail makes a turn and runs around a ridgeline, just off the road to the north. The ridgeline is cut, north to south, by a series of notches, like the slices along the top of a loaf of French bread. Those same archaeologists who excavated Cinnabar surveyed this ridge. They came to speculate that native people used those notches in the ridge as a way of channeling game animals toward waiting hunters. We do not, however, know which native people did this, because they were doing it for such a long time. Here, the University of Montana team found an astoundingly rare thing: a fragment of a fluted point, the kind of spearpoint that late Ice Age hunters used to bring down their largest prey. The ridge was in use as a hunting trap for thousands of years.

If you are headed north on the Old Yellowstone Trail, you will leave the national park when you cross Reese Creek, about four and a half miles from the Roosevelt Arch. Just a little over a mile from Reese Creek, you will see a sight that is a strange local secret. Look to the south—to the left, that is, or to the right, if you are headed toward Gardiner. Notice the dome-shaped—*things*, is all they are at first, some of them partial, some with a door on the front. They look a little like the old-fashioned beehive that is the state symbol of Utah, and in fact, the people who worked them called them beehive ovens. They are not what you expect. They are coke ovens, masonry structures in which workers would shovel coal, then set it on fire and let it cook. The end product was, among other things, coke, a clean-burning fuel used to make copper and steel. Ovens like these pop up in surprising places; there are huge numbers, for instance, in now-dense forest in Alabama. They sprang up like mushrooms around local coal mines as heavy industry grew in the later years of the 1800s.

What you are seeing is a remnant. There were originally 225 of them, operating around the clock. What is now an utterly rural Montana countryside, with national park and national forest all around, was, around the start of the twentieth century, an industrial hub, almost an industrial wasteland.

All around you, here, was a town called Electric. Ahead, on the road, your GPS should show you a sketchy side-track called Aldridge Road. Up in the canyon, above, there existed a boomtown for fifteen years—not a gold or silver camp, but a town built around coal mines. The coal was discovered in the 1860s, but the construction of the railroad made it suddenly profitable to dig the stuff, make coke out of it, and ship the coke north to the smelters in Butte and Anaconda. In the town of Electric, also, was the power plant for the mines, and hence the name of the town. The mountain by that name, above, was a happy coincidence if you could see it. In the saloon here (but there were saloons all over), Calamity Jane was a regular customer. So, in addition to the burning garbage in Gardiner, the Yellowstone-bound tourist also passed through this—a Big Sky version of the New Jersey Turnpike.

The operation was massive. There is still coal up around the former townsite of Aldridge, and you can even see smears of it staining the hillside gray, back by Reese Creek (from the national park boundary, look across Beattie Gulch Road; the ridge up ahead was mined for coal in a small way). The mining might have continued. It just became more economical for heavy industry to use electricity made at the hydroelectric dams that were becoming more common, and in 1910 the coal company shut the mines. The town immediately started to erode. Today, even the ruins are starting to disappear. Probably the most lasting monument to the town will be the massive tailings dump that makes an artificial bulge, visible from space, into Aldridge Lake.

We think of Yellowstone as delicate, and it is—but given time, it swallows the works of man and passes on its way, scarcely noticing we were ever there. In another hundred years, the traces of Aldridge and Electric will disappear completely. Only archaeologists will know they are there, and they might or might not care.

From the coke ovens and Aldridge Road, you will have an excellent view of our final stop on this tour of the badlands: the Devil's Slide.

That is the *highly* strange mountain dead ahead with the utterly unnatural-looking red streak from top to bottom. It got its name in August 1870, when an important early exploring party, the Washburn-Langford-Doane Expedition, passed by on its way to tour what would soon become the park (Gustavus Doane provided the military escort, the same Gustavus Doane who would return in 1877 to confront the Nez Perce a little upriver). In a popular article that ran in *Scribner's Monthly* in 1871, Nathaniel Langford told the story of the naming. He was deeply impressed by the sight, but wished the party had been more economical in its use of names invoking hell:

> We had seen many of the capricious works wrought by erosion upon the friable rocks of Montana, but never before upon so majestic a scale. Here an entire mountainside, by wind and water, had been removed, leaving as the evidence of their protracted toil these vertical projections, which, but for their immensity, might as readily be mistaken for works of art as of nature. Their smooth sides, uniform width and height, and great length, considered in connection with the causes which had wrought their insulation, excited our wonder and admiration. . . . For some reason, best understood by himself, one of our companions gave to these rocks the name of the "Devil's Slide." The suggestion was unfortunate, as, with more reason perhaps, but with no better taste, we frequently had occasion to appropriate other portions of the person of his Satanic Majesty, or of his dominion, in signification of the varied marvels we met with.

The mountain itself is Cinnabar Mountain, and the red streak appears to have been mistaken for cinnabar, a red ore of mercury. What you are seeing, we know today, is an ancient seafloor. As the mountains were built, it was turned on its side, and the layers eroded at different rates. The red is iron. Yes, your guess is correct: what you are seeing there is rust. Oddly, that streak can be climbed, at least by elk. They do not just do it on a dare.

Entire herds climb it, and even seem to use it as a convenient and safe route of migration.

We have only scratched the surface, in our tour. Everywhere in this area, the strangest things can be found. Here is another, one that requires a good deal of explaining:

As If Floods and Fires Weren't Bad Enough . . .

As you drive toward Yellowstone National Park on Route 89, or as you drive away on the same road, you will likely notice an odd sight. Just north of Corwin Springs, between eight and nine miles from Gardiner, you will see, on the far side of the Yellowstone River, a building with a long blue roof and a tower at the end. It looks, from a distance, like a New England church steeple, or a traditional clock tower, either of which would be an odd sight in maximum-rural Montana (a fun feature of this part of the country is that people frequently do not care what time it is). What makes it still more odd is that the steeple has a bright, golden roof. It jumps right out at you because it is the only thing like it in this part of the world.

What that is, is King Arthur's Court . . . and thereby hangs a tale.

What you are seeing, over there, is a small part of a large property, the Royal Teton Ranch. It once belonged to Malcolm Forbes, the publisher of *Forbes* magazine. It was acquired, along with a great deal of the surrounding land, in the 1980s by newcomers from California: the Church Universal and Triumphant.

This organization is what professors of religious studies would call a "New Age movement" spiritual group, and more specifically an "ascended master" group. It is actually a much older thing, a modified séance spiritualism. This kind of belief system can be traced back at least as far as 1848, when the Fox sisters of upstate New York, Maggie and Kate, revealed that they could act as mediums for departed spirits. The spirits communicated by means of raps on furniture or walls, and the Fox sisters were much in demand. Long after their initial period of fame, the sisters revealed they had created the raps by cracking their toe joints. They had done it at first as a joke, but the joke had gotten well out of hand, and their revelation had no impact on the burgeoning séance industry.

If we were living, say, a hundred years ago or maybe a little more, you and I would both know people who had been to séances, and maybe believed deeply in what they had seen there. The "medium," the person running the séance, would call on the spirits while the clients held hands, typically seated around a table, and almost always in a darkened room. The medium might go into a trance. Then the spirits would reveal themselves in some way. You will have seen it in old movies (and in a famous Bugs Bunny cartoon, in which Bugs goes into a "transom") because it was wildly popular, even though the whole thing had been shown to be fraudulent over and over. The magician Harry Houdini became famous in his day for unmasking them. Wracked by grief after his mother died, he went to séances and was appalled to discover that the mediums were just magicians, and not very good ones. He went to séance after séance and, at the moment the departed manifested, he jumped up and exposed the trick: the cheesecloth ghost, the secret wires and gramophone, the accomplice in the closet. For some reason, he kept getting invited (and afterward, sued).

New Age leaders today have dropped the raps and simplified the process by having the medium become inhabited by the departed spirit, who thus gains the use of a living set of hands and vocal cords. Today, this process is called "channeling." This is why they are "ascended master" organizations: the ascended masters are spirits of the formerly living who are now (to quote literature published by the Church Universal and Triumphant) "'Immortal, God-free beings' who have mastered the circumstances of their lives by victoriously passing all of

4

their tests and trials on earth." The most important ascended master for the Church is the eighteenth century French aristocrat Comte de Saint Germain, a man with an interesting résumé: he has been reincarnated as High Priest of Atlantis, Merlin, Christopher Columbus, Roger Bacon, Francis Bacon, and others. He has his hands full. Again, a sample from the Church literature:

> Through the heights and depths of the ages that have ensued, Saint Germain has ingeniously used the Seventh Ray momentum of his causal body to secure freedom for keepers of the flame who have kept alive "coals" from the violet flame altar of his Atlantean temple. He has extolled and exemplified freedom of the mind and spirit. Endowing the four sacred freedoms with an identity of their own, he has championed our freedom from state interference, kangaroo courts, or popular ridicule in matters ranging from scientific investigation to the healing arts to the spiritual quest.

Saint Germain spoke to the living through Elizabeth Clare Prophet, one of the founders of the Church, and its most important leader. She was known to her followers as Guru Ma. It was she who led the Church to this backwater in Montana, in part as a place to hide.

The Church—locals call it simply "CUT," pronounced, simply, "cut"—has borrowed its theology from dozens of sources, the most important being Theosophy and its offshoot, an organization called the I AM Activity Movement, which pioneered the channeling of ascended masters. At the center of both I AM and CUT are what they call "decrees," usually, or "affirmations." A former member of CUT, Joseph Szimhart, wrote an explanation of these matters that has about it the kind of understanding only a former believer can possess. Decrees can be thought of as "ritual techniques," although the ritual is going to strike an outsider as pretty strange. For the believer, they will not only cure diseases, but "also improve and perfect the political, economic, and environmental forces that plague mankind." Decrees, Szimhart explains, are a kind of "repetitive prayer. Similar to the chant of mantras in Buddhist and Hindu sects, I AM and CUT decrees are generally chanted in a rapid staccato and sound much like an auctioneer's delivery. CUT claims that decrees, or the *Science of the Spoken Word* (in CUT's book by that title), are 'the most powerful force in the universe.'" They also invented a "science" of colors associated with these chants. "For example, chanting a particular phrase about health while visualizing a green 'ray' would enhance the power of that affirmation or decree." Furthermore, "these decrees would be more effective if chanted loudly, more rapidly, and repeated in groups—the larger the group, the better. If nothing else, the act of decreeing out loud induces trance through high-arousal self-hypnosis. The I AM and CUT also extended the decrees to cover political goals."

Church members, in the 1980s and early 1990s, were thus like any other New Age group. They were able to believe anything; make a claim, and make it in the right New Age language, and they would believe it. The problem with that sort of thinking, of course, is that it leaves the believers wide open to manipulation by their leaders who can do with them what they please.

The Church thus had a paranoiac and millennial streak, as Guru Ma's reference to "state interference" and "kangaroo courts" may suggest, and they got it from Guru Ma herself. When CUT bought the Royal Teton Ranch, they set about making the place self-sufficient, and on an industrial scale. All this happened in the vicinity of that building with the golden roof, on the other side of the Yellowstone River. They worked with a sense of urgency: Guru Ma's ascended masters had told her that on April 23, 1990, the Soviet Union would launch a massive nuclear strike on the United States.

As that date approached, they were ready for anything, or at least they thought they were. They had one other quality in common with lots of California New Age people: they were not good at working with their hands, hence the catastrophe that followed.

In part because of the catastrophe, CUT was on everyone's mind locally, back then. Yellowstone's chief law enforcement ranger in the early 1990s was Dan Sholly, father of Cam Sholly, present superintendent of the park. In a memoir published in 1991, he commented on the group's behavior. The chief of security for the church "had been arrested for purchasing $100,000 worth of assault weapons illegally. And they had been building their bomb shelters." Some of the bomb shelters were small, "But the one in the Mol Heron Creek drainage was the main shelter complex." Mol Heron Creek runs past the building with the golden roof. "With the capacity to hold 756 people underground, it was an elaborate conglomeration of huge, corrugated metal rooms, aboveground grain storage silos, an animal corral, and 35 buried fuel storage tanks capable of holding 630,000 gallons of diesel and gasoline and 10 to 12 other tanks holding 300,000 gallons of propane." In April 1990, what Sholly referred to as an "abomination" occurred: the storage tanks began to leak. The tanks lost thirty-one thousand gallons of unleaded gasoline and diesel, part of which ended up in Mol Heron Creek, one of only three cutthroat trout spawning streams in Paradise Valley. And through this whole period, CUT was planning on sinking a geothermal well on its property, which would very probably have killed the geyser basins in the national park.

Ask not why rural Montanans hate California.

To get a taste of what worship is like in an organization like this, and what life was like during what adherents remember as the "shelter cycle," here is a "decree" that Joseph Szimhart saved from the period when CUT was scrambling to complete the bomb shelters in time to save themselves from the nuclear strike Guru Ma had foreseen. "Keepers of the Flame"—church members, that is—were told to include it in their daily devotions. South Glastonbury was an annex to the Royal Teton Ranch, farther down the Yellowstone River valley. It was also to be made nuclear-bomb-proof:

Call for the Victory of the Twin Pillars Shelter,
In the Name of the *I AM THAT I AM*, Elohim, Saint Germain, Portia, Guru Ma, Lanello, Padma Smabhava, Kuan Yin, and the five Dhyani Buddhas.
In the Name *I AM THAT I AM SANAT KUMARA*, Gautama Buddha, Lord Maitreya, Jesus Christ,
Om Vairochana Akshobhya Ratnasambhava Amitabha Amoghasiddhi Om,
In the name of my Mighty I AM Presence, my Holy Christ Self and Three-fold Flame, I call to Beloved Ray-O-Light, Mighty Hercules . . . God of Gold . . . El Morya . . . Mother Mary [more than 30 sacred names are invoked in this decree] . . . for the absolute God-victory of our Twin Pillars Shelter in South Glastonbury.
I call for the binding of all opposition and supply, our completion of the project on time and ahead of time, and for the cutting free of souls needed to physically complete the shelter!
In the name of Christ I call to you Beloved Hercules for: the proper fitting blast doors, full tanks of diesel and ethanol fuel, spare parts for all life support systems lasting 7 years, bicycles installed for back-up, a complete tool room well-equipped, 7 years of nutritious and varied food for everyone, the septic system in place . . . EMP protection . . . radiation monitor . . . $80,000 to meet all our needs for material and wages. . . .

[The decree insert covers a letter-sized, single-spaced, typed page and ends with the following]:
We claim the Victory of the Twin Pillars Shelter now according to God's Will! Always Victory! Amen.

For the group, the month between mid-March and mid-April 1990 was frenzied. On March 15, Szimhart recalls, Guru Ma set off the alarms prematurely. They were still working on the big shelter. They were not finished yet, but on March 15, Guru Ma told everyone "to go into the shelters—this was no longer a drill. Bombs were coming! Hundreds more entered smaller shelters, both in the area and some as far away as Idaho. Prophet also warned members of 'astral plane' aliens (invisible to normal sight) in a huge spacecraft that hovered over the property. These aliens, 150,000 strong, stood ready to enslave the Light-bearers and humanity after the nuclear destruction."

It was a scene that tested their faith: "Underground, the frenzied CUT members and their children shouted out their decrees to end the threat, while they found toilets and other basic shelter accommodations non-functional. A bucket brigade took waste to the surface. Nothing abnormal happened aboveground, so on March 16, every one of them climbed out to the daylight. The ranch was started up again, electricity and water utilities were turned on, and members were expected to act normally, as if this had been just another drill."

There was such a ruckus, in fact, that even the *Washington Post* noticed. On March 17, the newspaper reported on CUT members fleeing toward Montana from all over the continent. They were selling property, liquidating retirement accounts, buying a year's worth of heart medicine all at once, and stripping the local stores in southwestern Montana of all survival gear. The reporter asked the church vice president, Guru Ma's husband at the time, about rumors that the group was going into the bomb shelters immediately. He called the rumors "preposterous." He continued: "The shelters will be used only if there is a nuclear war. Why would anyone want to live underground if they didn't have to?" In fact, they already had been.

On April 23, 1990 . . . nothing happened, or almost nothing. Namibia was admitted to the United Nations on April 23, 1990; *Time* magazine was published that day, with Vice President Dan Quayle on the cover. Nothing much else. How could an organization survive a flop that bad?

They of course do all the time. A famous study of this kind of thing is a book published all the way back in 1956, *When Prophecy Fails*. In it, three social psychologists, Leon Festinger, Henry Riecken, and Stanley Schachter, described their infiltration of a religious group that called themselves the Seekers. The group was a UFO cult, but one otherwise strikingly similar to CUT. One of their leaders, Dorothy Martin, channeled communications from advanced aliens of the planet Clarion. The aliens told her that much of the earth would be destroyed in a flood on December 21, 1954. What happened when the prophecy failed? Festinger, Riecken, and Schachter found a pattern that held for other such groups. The people who were less devoted to a sect like this might drift away, but the people who were most zealous would, perversely, become more zealous still. They would seek an outlet in spreading the word, bringing in new believers as a way of confirming their own belief. "When people are committed to a belief and a course of action," they wrote, "clear disconfirming evidence may simply result in deepened conviction and increased proselyting. . . . If more and more people can be persuaded that the system of belief is correct, then clearly it must after all be correct."

So it was with CUT. When their prophecy failed, Ma explained the date was actually the start of a "Dark Cycle" of disaster and mayhem lasting twelve years. People did drift off, however, and while CUT survived the failed prophecy, it could not survive what happened a few years later: Guru Ma, still only in her mid-fifties, developed Alzheimer's disease.

The group entered a calmer, still-prosperous twilight in which it lives still. The dissolution of the Soviet Union was, Guru Ma said, a "smokescreen," but given the near-complete demise of world communism, it was hard to keep up what was essentially a Cold War paranoia. Alzheimer's developed soon after. Guru Ma lingered on, as Alzheimer's patients do, finally dying in 2009. She had transferred leadership of the organization in 1996 to a Belgian business administrator named Gilbert Cleirbaut, who was not even a minister in the church. His job was to run CUT as a business. Splinter groups started leaving in the mid-1990s. The fuel spill could not be hushed up; CUT was responsible for the cleanup, which cost, the *High Country News* reported, nearly $1 million.

The organization found itself so strapped for cash that it had to sell, or place under conservation easements, over half of the Royal Teton Ranch. It let most of the ranch employees go. It had originally planned a town of one thousand on the ranch but wrote it off and gave up on the geothermal well, too.

Some splinter groups still exist, numbering between a hundred and two hundred members. But there also still exists a core of the original Church Universal and Triumphant, centered around the little development with the chapel called King Arthur's Court (Arthur would be an ascended master, I believe, although it is hard to keep track of this sort of thing). You can pay them a visit, by crossing the bridge at Corwin Springs. The new Yellowstone Hot Springs there belongs to CUT. After you cross the river and reach the Old Yellowstone Trail, a turn to the left takes you past a cul-de-sac called Ranch Office Road. It appears just before you reenter Yellowstone National Park. Here is one of the local sights: the charming old-Montana farmhouse that faces the road here is said locally to have been Guru Ma's house.

NORTHERN NUTTINESS

Back at the Corwin Springs bridge, a right turn takes you to the King Arthur's Court chapel, conference center, and gift shop. In 2008, NBC News reported that you can buy, there, church merchandise ranging from a wallet-sized "Chart of Your Divine Self," for $1.25, to a framed portrait of Guru Ma for $239.95. The prices will probably have gone up. Here also is the largest of the bomb shelters, which does still exist, next to Mol Heron Creek (sometimes spelled Mulherin—it is named for an early settler, and "Mol Heron" is an odd local corruption). According to NBC News, the bomb shelter today houses what the group considers most important: twenty-two thousand hours of audio and video recordings of Guru Ma speaking.

The core of the church's faithful remains in the immediate area. Their animating pursuit is the translation of her message into the languages of the world. Since her every word was important, they will not be done until they have gone through that whole twenty-two thousand hours. So it may be that they will be there for a while.

It is fun to speculate about that future. During your trip through the park, you may have been puzzled to see, at one or another of the major stops, people who perhaps looked to you like the Amish. They were very probably Hutterites, from the Montana Hutterite "colonies," to use their term. These are small self-sufficient communities in which the Hutterites live a life removed from much, although not all, of the modern world. They make nearly everything they need by themselves and operate farms that, although traditional, produce quantities of pork, beef, dairy products, eggs, poultry, and grain. They live here in Montana and also in South Dakota and the western Canadian plains.

They look like the Amish, and the Mennonites, too, because they come from similar roots: they are sixteenth-century radical Protestants. They are Anabaptists, followers originally of Jakob Hutter, and hence the name. Despite the traditional life they

4

live, they have no objection to driving a modern vehicle through Yellowstone in the summer, and that is why you may have seen them at Old Faithful or Canyon. You will see them also at farmer's markets all over the region. Their participation in the farm economy is not trivial—but still, they always stand out.

If we could transport ourselves back to the 1500s, we would probably have found them extraordinary even then. The Radical Reformation from which they sprang often looked dangerously bizarre to contemporaries. It was resisted violently. The Hutterites would object, naturally, but we might think of them as a cult that is so old, we now find them charming. The rural west has always been a place where unusual religions went to settle outside the pale. Another place where that happened is Mormon Utah.

So perhaps . . .

Perhaps, in four or five hundred years, visitors to Yellowstone and New Montana will find themselves puzzled to meet men and women dressed in the clothing of the 1980s: Sperry Topsiders and pastel shirts on the men, gigantic hair on the women. These people will come to the farmer's market and play for you a tape of Guru Ma on a Sony VHS recorder. If you are interested, they will of course be glad to sell you a wallet-sized "Chart of Your Divine Self," for $1,295. The framed portrait of Guru Ma will cost something more.

5

GEYSERS ARE STRANGER THAN YOU THINK

Grotto Geyser at the Upper Geyser Basin is one of the strangest sights in a strange place. SCOTT HERRING

5

Much of what we value about Yellowstone is new—not to the park, but to humanity itself. As noted, for generations, everyone's favorite Yellowstone animal, very nearly the symbol of the park itself, was the bear. When the average person thought of Yellowstone, Yogi and Boo-Boo will have come to mind as soon as anything else, and the single most-loved activity—in, say, the year 1960—was throwing marshmallows at roadside beggar bears. Yet the generation that founded the park, in 1872, would have found this odd. Bears, back then, were vermin—varmints, literally.

In 1881, a year before the park's tenth birthday, a future cattle baron named William Pickett left Bozeman, Montana, in the late spring and traveled first east, then south. His route made an arc around the national park, ending close to the present East Entrance. As he went, he was scouting for a place to establish a ranch, and he was shooting grizzly bears. He was making them his own personal project, and his goal, at least within his ability to reach it, was to exterminate them. He shot every bear he saw, and in the end killed twenty-three. We know about this hunting trip because Pickett wrote an extended memory of it in a book published in 1913, *Hunting at High Altitudes*, a book edited by George Bird Grinnell, one of the really important early figures in wildlife conservation and a great friend to Yellowstone National Park. But Pickett is not apologizing in the book. He is bragging. He established his ranch on the east side of the park, in Wyoming, and spent the rest of his life there, shooting every single grizzly bear on sight. His was a normal attitude toward bears during that time.

Even more extreme is the contrast between our attitude toward the new stars of the park and the one common in those early years. That we now nearly worship wolves would have struck the first generation of Yellowstone aficionados as insane, literally—just stark raving *nuts*. We wear wolf T-shirts, put wolf screen savers on our computers, post loving wolf videos online, hang wolf photographs in our homes, put wolf magnets on our refrigerators, and spend thousands of dollars visiting the park with a major goal being a mere look, from a mile away, at the new darlings, the Yellowstone wolves. The founding generation, back there in 1872, would be left shaking their heads in incomprehension and dismay to see their heirs worshipping an animal they would have thought lower than a varmint—worshipping *demons*, almost literally.

People today are normally surprised to learn that hunting was legal in the park until 1883. Commercial hunters, during that first decade, killed animals like elk in the thousands. It was not the animals the founders were interested in protecting. It was the geysers.

And the hot springs, and the mud pots, and the travertine terraces at Mammoth, and the whole thermal show. But their experience of these things was radically different.

It is worth noticing that even a first-time visitor, approaching the single most iconic geyser—Old Faithful—finds the performance to be not terribly surprising precisely because Old Faithful is the single most iconic geyser in the park and in the world. That first-time visitor will have seen the geyser erupt on video, probably over and over. The park website has Old Faithful all over it, and the geyser has had its own webcam for years. Approaching it for the first time, we know what to expect. People who work in the park actually get tired of the geysers, and people who work in the village at Old Faithful often call the place "Old Filthy" (or more affectionately, "Old Stinky").

Those first explorers, however, had no idea what to expect. Only vague rumors had filtered out of the Rockies about this place. A big part of their delight came of sheer surprise.

They were surely delighted, though, and their rapturous response has had the effect that, from the very start, we are led to expect too much. Paul Schullery was a ranger for years and wrote a series of books about the park. In one, *Mountain Time*, he expresses a feeling that a great many people share: "The geysers, I am embarrassed to admit, have not captured me to the extent they captured the park's founders." He finds himself an appreciative audience to everything else in the park, "But geysers and hot springs, as fabulous and precious as I know they are, leave me looking for something else to do.

> Why is this? Are they just too awesome for my feeble perceptions? Could be, but I doubt it. I think it has to do with their rarity, the very novelty that makes them so extraordinary. . . . They are so rare, so alien, that we see but we do not absorb. We don't deny it happened—yes, it shot water 150 feet into the air—but we don't know what to do about it.
>
> Watch the crowd at an Old Faithful eruption. Amid the rattle of hundreds of shutters, some people feel a need to applaud, to do some act, like a gorilla beating on his chest in displacement of flight or aggression. Many people occupy themselves with photographs to show back home. There are "ooh's" and "ah's" and other scattered sounds. But even before the water has entirely subsided many people turn to leave.

You may have had that experience yourself. You need not feel bad about it. The solution, I have discovered, is to branch out and look for that hidden detail that is really strange. Not just the usual. Yes, the geyser basins are filled with volcanically superheated water doing extraordinary things found here and in only a handful of other places in the whole world—but what makes them *really* strange?

Well—did you know that the whole massive, world-changing revolution in the field of genetics, and the industries that have spalled off it, worth hundreds of billions of dollars, came in part from a single, unspectacular, miscellaneous Yellowstone spring that no one visits? That no one can even find because it is nowhere near a boardwalk and never will be? That is so obscure it goes by three different names, and no one has ever tried to sort it out? That's strange.

"And You've Just Had Some Kind of Mushroom"

The spring in question is Mushroom Spring or Mushroom Pool or, according to Montana State University, "MS_15," which makes it sound like an international criminal gang. It could hardly be more different from that.

It lies well off the asphalt at the section of the Lower Geyser Basin that is usually referred to by the small sidetrack that serves it, Firehole Lake Drive. Mushroom Spring is part of the White Creek Group of features. That name alone will throw you off the track because Mushroom Spring is much closer to Tangled Creek. All attention is focused away from it because it is on the other side of the road from the most famous feature in the area, Great Fountain Geyser, and another favorite, White Dome Geyser. Everyone is normally looking in the exact opposite direction.

In 1965, a young biologist from Indiana University named Thomas D. Brock applied for his first research permit in the park, from which much else would flow. You could not have guessed it at the time. Ours is an era when science is lavishly funded and scientists may grow absurdly wealthy, but it was not always so. Brock wrote a charming memoir in 2017, *A Scientist in Yellowstone National Park*, illustrated with his and his wife Louise's photographs, and one of the charming aspects is just how folksy even highly consequential science was back then. Brock was educated in botany but had developed an interest in the microbial communities in natural springs. When they could, he and Louise traveled the country to take samples from various springs that were in one way or another attractively bizarre to him. When they did, they traveled in a Volkswagen microbus and slept in it. Most couples living the #vanlife today (look up that hashtag on Twitter) live as if in a mansion compared to them.

Yellowstone inevitably caught their attention, and Brock began working there in 1965. They lived, first, at Old Faithful in a rock-bottom "Camper's Cabin" (they no longer exist) that served as their laboratory as well. There was only one electrical outlet—in the light socket in the ceiling—so they could only run one experiment at a time. The conditions of their collecting permit forbade them from working in view of the public, for the very good reason that the public would wander out there to see what they were doing and kill themselves in a hot spring, so they dodged around like fugitives, eventually reaching the less heavily visited Lower Geyser Basin. Their guide to the thermal areas was a book known to Yellowstone people but no one else, a 1935 volume called *Hot Springs of the Yellowstone National Park*. They used it throughout their time in the park, having checked out the book from the library and copied it on a first-generation Xerox machine. Brock includes a photograph of their copy. The acid in the paper has turned it a horrifying shade of yellow, the color of mustard gas.

Brock contacted a scientific colleague who was working in the park and struck it rich: this colleague "had a field laboratory just inside the Park boundary near West Yellowstone, and there would be space for us. His field lab was in a building owned not by the Park Service but by the Yellowstone Park Company at an area called 'The Barns.'" The correct name of their new home was the Driver's Bunkhouse (it, too, no longer exists). Here was scientific treasure: "The facility not only provided plenty of electrical outlets, but tables, and kitchen facilities. We could even sleep there (on the floor, using our sleeping bags and foam pads)."

Brock eventually landed a National Science Foundation grant with enough money to hire help, although he had been determined to get back to Yellowstone, even if he had to use his own money. The couple now had the cash for a cabin in West Yellowstone, where they used the kitchen and bedroom as a laboratory. They were using radioactive bicarbonate in some of the experiments—Brock had a license from the Atomic Energy Commission—and did the radioactive work in the bedroom. In photographs, the cabin appears to be no more than five hundred square feet. They made their meals in the same kitchen but washed the radioactive glassware in the bathtub. It was here, and at the Lower Geyser Basin, that the most important work was done.

Mushroom Spring (Brock called it that, not "Pool," and certainly not "MS_15") was unusually perfect for the kind of work the Brocks were doing: they were trying to evaluate the whole ecology of the hot springs. Among their most important discoveries was learning about the nature of the organisms themselves. There was a general sense, among people who thought about it at all, that anything living in the almost unbelievably hostile environment of the springs—remember, the water dissolves human bodies until there is nothing left— must be just hanging on. The Brocks found that that was not true. The life-forms they found there were living in that water because it is their preferred place. In a sense, they *like* it there.

In later years, Brock wrote a pamphlet, *Life at High Temperatures*, explaining what they had found for the general public (the park bookstores sold thousands of copies, and it is now available for free online, from the University of Wisconsin, the school at which Brock finished his career). He uses the term, "procaryote," that scientists use for the large group of microorganisms to which bacteria belong: "Even if the source pool looks white and sterile, microscopic study usually reveals large numbers of procaryotes. . . . It is amazing that in addition to living in boiling water, these procaryotes are growing surprisingly rapidly; a population can double in as few as two hours." Where might all this lead?

5

The presence of procaryotes in boiling water (100 degrees C or 212 degrees F) makes us wonder if there is an upper temperature for life. Temperatures even hotter than 100 degrees C occur in the thermal vents found at the bottoms of the oceans. Because of the high pressure in the ocean depths, temperatures of over 300 degrees C (572 degrees F) are found. Careful study has shown that at such high temperatures, no living organisms are present, but evidence exists of procaryotes living at temperatures as high as 115 degrees C (239 degrees F). In fact, cultures have been obtained that can be easily grown at this temperature in the laboratory.

It is an interesting fact that 115 degrees C (239 degrees F) is near the temperature at which hospital sterilizers are operated, yet here are procaryotes that actually *prefer* such temperatures!

Procaryotes can grow over the complete range of temperatures in which life is possible, but no one organism can grow over this whole range. The bacteria that cause disease, for which the hospital sterilizer is intended, are completely unable to grow at the high temperatures of hot springs. Likewise, the bacteria living in hot springs are unable to grow at the temperature of the human body.

All this has since led people to wonder about other planets and their moons. Some are thermally active or were in the past. We have been led astray by science fiction. We can hardly help expecting life on other planets to be humanoid or just plain human, like the English-speaking aliens of the original *Star Trek*. It may be that life on other planets in our solar system will be found in a Yellowstone-like spring far, far away.

Those creatures they were finding in obscure, unspectacular Mushroom Spring, and elsewhere, raised the most fundamental questions:

GEYSERS ARE STRANGER THAN YOU THINK

How is it possible for living organisms to survive at such extremes of temperature? Actually, we are only surprised that life thrives in boiling water because of our anthropocentric orientation. It is true that humans and other animals are very heat-sensitive, but the biological world is much more diverse than we realize from our experience. Life, and especially procaryotic life, is able to adapt to environmental conditions that are deadly to humans.

In fact, many scientists believe that life as we know it might first have arisen three billion or so years ago in high-temperature environments, and that the first organisms on earth might therefore have been thermophiles. Such thermophiles would then have continued to exist on earth in the intervening period, finding refuges in the hot springs that continue to dot the earth. In addition, these thermophiles would have been the forerunners of all other life forms including, eventually, humans.

Brock, Louise, and their helpers studied Mushroom Spring for two years, even during the winter, and when the cold months arrived, they returned to primitive living. Brock's memories of that time have a surreal quality, now that the major problems at Old Faithful during the winter are crowding, noise, and pollution. Winter in Yellowstone in the mid-1960s was still much the same as it had been a hundred years earlier:

> Those were the days before there were any winter facilities at Old Faithful. The roads in the park were not plowed but kept open by the snowcats that came up occasionally from West Yellowstone or Park Headquarters at Mammoth. There was a single Park Ranger at Old Faithful in the winter, who got around by snowcat.
>
> My research site, Mushroom Spring, was about 10 miles away from Old Faithful. The Park Ranger gave me a "lift" to the entrance to the Firehole Lake Loop Road, but

5

I had to "walk" the last two miles on snowshoes. Among other things, I had to detour around a large bison who was browsing in some of the grass made snowless by thermal activity.

He lived at Old Faithful, where there was plenty of space, of a sort: "The bunkhouse was an empty NPS building in the Service Area of Old Faithful. Shower and sleeping facilities were in another building. Because there was no heat in the shower area, the water had to be kept running constantly to prevent freezing. It was quite exciting stepping out of the hot shower into the cold building!"

It was in 1966 that he and an undergraduate assistant found a new species at the exact spot where water flowed out of the spring. Temperatures there were close to their hottest. The assistant was the one to locate the new species, from samples of the bacterial mat that the kid had brought back to Indiana. For generations to come, people will be chuckling at his name: Hudson Freeze. They have already been chuckling for decades.

Brock and Freeze—Brock called him Hud—named the new species *Thermus aquaticus*, announcing the find in the *Journal of Bacteriology* in 1969 (and Brock was generous in giving credit to Freeze, who was only an undergraduate but is Brock's coauthor in the journal—professors are not always good about that). Scientists had long thought that life could not survive above 131°F, but here was a creature they could not even get to grow in the lab until they incubated it at temperatures between 158°F and 167°F. They called it an "extreme thermophile," an organism that loved heat.

The Brocks and the students had kicked off a scientific revolution that has since only gathered steam, as it were. It all comes ultimately from those little-visited Yellowstone pools they were able to sample because the tourists could not see them.

GEYSERS ARE STRANGER THAN YOU THINK

Much more was to follow. They had no way of foreseeing, back there in the 1960s, what was to come out of Mushroom Pool.

In the 1980s, researchers were looking for a way of amplifying a DNA sample to such an extent that it would be possible to analyze the DNA in ways that had not been achievable before. A basic problem was that, in any sample of living tissue, the amount of DNA present is vanishingly small. When researchers strip away all the sample—a vial of blood, a leaf, a tissue biopsy, and so on—the amount of pure DNA left to work with is in the range of a nanogram or two . . . and understand that one nanogram is a billionth of a gram, and it takes twenty-eight grams to make a mere ounce. If a scientist were analyzing the genetics of, say, a kind of grass, that person would have to collect multiple football fields of grass to come up with enough DNA to work with.

What was needed was a way to take a small sample and make it much bigger. The key was thermal cycling. DNA, you may remember, is shaped like a ladder twisted into a helix. Heat the DNA until the ladder divides in two down the middle of the rungs, and the DNA can be copied, and enough duplicates made to be the equivalent of those football fields. The problem was the heat. When DNA copies itself in nature, it uses an enzyme called a polymerase. However, heat in thermal cycling runs almost to the boiling point, through thousands of repetitions, and almost all the polymerases in the world cannot stand the heat. It destroys them.

Back there in the mid-1980s, researchers were trying to make regular polymerases work. It was, however, like adding oil to an old car on the verge of death. It was an endless process. What if there were a polymerase that could be run all the way up to the boiling point, thousands of times, and keep on ticking?

And there it was. The Brocks, without knowing it, had turned up the solution in Mushroom Spring.

5

Thermus aquaticus has inside it an enzyme known as *Taq*-polymerase, which had been isolated in 1976. It is now so important that it is part of everyday conversation in laboratories and on university campuses everywhere, and so has acquired nickname: *Taq*-pol, or simply *Taq*, normally pronounced "tack." The "*Taq*" is itself short for *Thermus aquaticus*. The optimum temperature for *Taq*-pol is 161°F, and it does not come apart, even at 203°F, about as hot as Celestine Pool was when it burned David Allen Kirwan, the man who jumped in after the dog. Recall that it burned him so badly that he started to literally fall apart almost immediately and died the next day. That kind of heat is pleasant weather, for *Thermus aquaticus*.

The field of genetics was then off to the races, and in 1993, PCR—short for polymerase chain reaction—earned for its inventor, biochemist Kary Mullis, the Nobel Prize for Chemistry.

PCR turns up everywhere. It sped up the Human Genome Project and indeed made it possible to begin with. It has unlocked the history of pathogens like HIV and can be used to detect them. Doctors use it to screen for and diagnose genetic disorders. It powers biotechnology companies like 23andMe. In 1994, when Nicole Brown Simpson and Ronald Goldman were murdered, it was there to take the blood drops found at the crime scene and link them to OJ Simpson. If you are old enough, you may recall the images on the TV news coverage of the trial (images that the TV people never really explained) of a test result that looked like marks on a Scantron form. Those were pictures of the gel electrophoresis that was the end stage of the PCR that had amplified those tiny bits of evidence into a usable result.

There are other kinds of polymerase now that are a rival to *Taq*. A famous one is known as "Vent Polymerase" because it comes from a microorganism that lives around hydrothermal

158

vents on the ocean floor. But *Thermus aquaticus* has without a doubt changed the world.

There is a debate among scientists and other interested parties about what we owe to the places from which such discoveries come. The idea is that since taxpayers and visitors pay to protect Yellowstone and all the other parks, they should get something back from the use of resources like *Thermus aquaticus*. The *New York Times* reported on this issue from Yellowstone in 2006. It told the story of PCR, noting that "despite how spectacularly useful it has turned out to be, no royalties have gone to Yellowstone or the National Park Service." The paper spoke to Tom Olliff, chief at the time of the NPS Center for Resources in Yellowstone. "In bio-prospecting circles, it's called the great *Taq* rip-off," Olliff said. "The director of the National Park Service told us not to let that happen again."

The problem lies in the definition of "use" of the park's resources. "While the commercial use of specimens from the parks is prohibited," the *Times* continued, "commercializing the results of research on those specimens is not prohibited or regulated. Companies cannot patent the organism, but they can patent the results of their research. For example, the Park Service does not allow the sale of ginseng collected in the park but creating and selling synthetic ginseng based on research using the park's ginseng, collected with a permit, is not banned."

The Park Service is today guided by a *Benefits-Sharing Handbook*, last updated in 2018. It seeks to regulate the situation. Scientists would, in general, rather not be limited in what they can do with the "resources" they collect. One feature of Thomas Brock's tenure in the park is the relative freedom under which he operated. The government did not want him visible while he worked, but what he and Louise and his students did out of sight, back there at Mushroom Spring, was—very largely—nobody's business but their own.

5

5

There may be another *Taq* out there, or at least a find of equivalent importance . . . but when Brock and Hud collected that odd little bug from Mushroom Spring, they had no idea that they held such intellectual dynamite in their hands. No one did or could possibly have known. It would have been hard to share benefits when, for decades, there were none.

So we can say this: if history repeats itself, it will surely be a total surprise.

And They Called It Wonderland
People have gotten out of the habit of referring to Yellowstone National Park this way, but visitors used to call it Wonderland. They came to Yellowstone expecting—and getting—extraordinary things. The name, however, also makes you wonder. You wonder why they behaved the way they did.

Complaining about tourists is a staple of conversation among people who work in the park. It has also been a staple of authors commenting on tourism in general, and American tourists specifically. The surprising truth, however, is that tourists are generally better behaved today. Tourists back when they called the place Wonderland could be barbarians.

Just look at the strange things they did to the geysers and hot springs.

In the old days, Old Faithful herself was subjected to degrading treatment. An early guidebook (Henry Winser's 1883 *The Yellowstone National Park: A Manual for Tourists*) reports Old Faithful "being made a laundry. Garments placed in the crater during quiescence are ejected thoroughly washed when the eruption takes place. Gen. Sheridan's men, in 1882, found that linen and cotton fabrics were uninjured by the action of the water, but woolen clothes were torn to shreds." Soldiers who were stationed there later joked, in letters home, that the dirty uniforms they stuffed down Old Faithful came up pressed, folded, and bearing a laundry mark. And people used the naturally hot water to do laundry elsewhere around Old Faithful's home, the Upper Geyser Basin.

Thing is—the water in the geyser basins is not just "hot water." As we have just seen, it is teeming with life. *Thermus aquaticus* is harmless. It cannot grow inside humans because we are too cold; you would have to run a temperature of 158°F for it to even show an interest. When the water is a little cooler, though, it gets all sorts of algae, parasites, and other kinds of bacteria in it. It can play host, for instance, to *E. coli*, the stuff in fecal matter and sewage, and also, incidentally, the producer of the enzyme they tried using in PCR before they found *Taq*-pol and that did not work because it could not stand the heat. It is perfectly fine, though, with *warm* water. Exposure to a certain amount of *E. coli* will not hurt you, but it is not the kind of thing you would seek out.

Now that the Boiling River is done for a while, at least until the river reroutes itself (they always do eventually), the only opportunities for getting into a natural hot spring are illegal. A spot where people have done this, illegally, for generations is Huckleberry Hot Springs and Polecat Creek, just south of Yellowstone National Park in the John D. Rockefeller Jr. Memorial Parkway. In the 1980s, scientists collected *Naegleria fowleri* there. They found it again in 2002, and as recently as 2019, they found its DNA in the water. What this bug will give you is amoebic meningitis, more properly primary amoebic meningoencephalitis. Less properly, the news media calls it the brain-eating amoeba. It lives in hot springs, and as you might guess, people do not generally survive it.

Now, amoebic meningitis is rare, and it is only recently that we have figured out it lives in places like Huckleberry Hot Springs. Still, why would you want to sit in that? And finding *E. coli* there is pretty common. Returning from an—illegal—trip to the hot springs, the first thing employees do is throw the clothing they were wearing in the washing machine because it

5

is always left utterly vile by its soak in the spring. So what is the appeal of using hot springs as laundromats?

Early park visitors certainly did, to such an extent that a popular feature at Black Sand Basin was Handkerchief Pool. You might guess how it got that name: yes, for decades, visitors dropped handkerchiefs in the pool, watched them disappear, and watched them reappear, boiled certainly, and apparently clean. It was so popular that a circular concrete perimeter was poured around the boundary of the spring, like the masonry ("coping," they call it) around a backyard hot tub. Lee Whittlesey, the retired park historian, summarizes what happened over the years. What developed at Handkerchief Pool was repeated elsewhere in the geyser basins:

> Over the years, hundreds of Yellowstone visitors watched their handkerchiefs go down into the pool and then come up again. The pool became so famous that scientists came to the park to study it. By 1906, tour guides were telling visitors that this was where the devil took in washing, and by 1913 some were calling it the "Devil's Laundry."
>
> Sometime in late 1926 or early 1927, Handkerchief Pool became dormant.

Nevertheless, visitors continued to throw handkerchiefs and other objects into the pool.

> On June 21, 1929, Ranger Carlos Davis removed 1.5 bushels of foreign objects from Handkerchief Pool, including "one broken bottle, portion of a spark plug, over one hundred hair pins, nails, stove bolts and nuts, a small horseshoe, badges, about one dozen handkerchiefs and bits of material not belonging to the surrounding formation" and U.S. coins totaling $1.98. This cleaning somewhat restored the circulation of the pool, but it still remained dormant even with additional work in 1933.

GEYSERS ARE STRANGER THAN YOU THINK

> In 1950, Park Geologist George Marler pried a log out
> of its vent, and water jetted once more into the bowl of
> Handkerchief Pool.

The circular concrete perimeter that lined the spring was demolished long ago, and the boardwalk at Black Sand Basin no longer goes anywhere near Handkerchief Pool, although it is still on maps. The strategy, it seems, is to give it a long break, and one cannot help but sympathize with its plight.

All the most famous features, and plenty of the less famous, were treated this way. In 1877, Old Faithful was visited by Frank Carpenter, a visit we know about only because Carpenter wrote about it in a book, *The Wonders of Geyser Land*. Naturally, Carpenter and his companions crammed their laundry into a pillowcase and crammed the pillowcase into Old Faithful Geyser. The pillowcase became a 19th century version of a cluster bomb: the laundry was blown a hundred feet into the air, and when they gathered it up, they found it to be, seemingly, clean. Next, they went to work cramming into Old Faithful a significant portion of the local environment. Carpenter describes the event in a breathless present tense: "We collect an immense quantity of rubbish and drop it into the crater. We have filled it to the top with at least a thousand pounds of stones, trees, stumps, etc. . . . the earth begins to tremble . . . and away go rocks, trees and rubbish to a height of seventy-five or eighty feet in the air." It provided what Carpenter called "entertainment of unusual magnitude and duration."

This is something he was writing about. In a book. He was not trying to keep it a secret.

A lengthy report on vandalism in the thermal areas ran in the January 2009 issue of *Yellowstone Science*. It identified the summer of 1946 as an especially awful time for this kind of thing. The authors, Alethea Steingisser and W. Andrew Marcus, quote the park geologist, George Marler, venting on the subject: "To name all the thermal features where vandalism is in evidence would be a cataloguing of most of the pools, springs and geysers in the Upper, Midway and Lower Basins. Just as a slowly advancing delta destroys the lake, just as certainly continually man-added debris will destroy the pools, springs and geysers of Yellowstone." Marler recognized that the people doing the damage were a small percentage of the park's visitors. It did not matter. Even "granting he comprises but one percent or less of the traveling public, still this army of thousands is spreading a pestilence which if unchecked will produce a vastly different Yellowstone a few generations hence."

The destruction surged in 1946 because of the end of the war. Gasoline and tires had been brutally rationed. The sudden lifting of the ration regime sent the nation out onto the roads in an orgy of automotive tourism. Steingisser and Marcus think that Marler was angry because the garbage was a literal burden:

> Marler's strong sentiments are due in part to his responsibility for cleaning debris out of thermal features in 1946, when he twice removed rocks weighing more than 40 pounds from the vent of Turban Geyser. In 1947, he reported hauling 55 wheelbarrows full of rocks and debris from springs and geysers in addition to a large tree from Emerald Pool, stating that "the culprits had resorted to considerable labor to drag this tree to the pool and shove it in."

We might have a contest to crown the single most abused thermal feature in the park. Steingisser and Marcus think the title belongs to Minute Geyser, in the Norris Geyser Basin:

> During the late nineteenth century, it erupted once per minute, sometimes up to 40 feet high. A stagecoach stop located there sometime later encouraged passengers to throw coins and other items into the vent. . . . When

Geysers Are Stranger Than You Think

new roads were constructed, Minute Geyser remained relatively close to the main access road and was continually vandalized. In 1935, a park naturalist noted, "I found about 10 boulders ranging up to the size of a man's head, almost completely filling the smaller of the two openings."

By the late 1960s, the rubble that had been stuffed into the geyser had been fused together by the minerals in the water. Eruptions shifted to a side vent and became sputtering and irregular. The eruptions reach maybe a foot high. It is a wretched shadow of its former self.

Another candidate for the most abused feature of all would surely be Morning Glory Pool. It can be found at the end of the paved trail—actually the former road—that extends northwest from the Old Faithful Inn. Early visitors describe the name as unusually appropriate, the water exhibiting a beautiful deep blue. We have to take their word for it because the color is no longer particularly dramatic. The problem is circulation, which is useful not just for laundering handkerchiefs. Without circulation, the temperature and chemistry of the water changes, and as Thomas Brock could tell you, hot water has its own special ecology.

Morning Glory Pool came under attack early on. According to Lee Whittlesey, "The spring originally had a scalloped border, described by geologist Arnold Hague as a sinter fringe 6 to 10 inches wide and 2 to 5 inches high, broken in only two places for runoff water. It seems incredible that souvenir hunters could have dismantled this entire thick rim, but it happened." You can confirm that for yourself. There is no scalloped ridge around Morning Glory Pool, not even a trace. But it is the water itself that came under the most concentrated attack. For this issue, the go-to source is T. Scott Bryan's classic *The Geysers of Yellowstone*. Morning Glory Pool is known to occasionally

165

behave like a geyser—many hot springs do—which helped when it came time to try to save it:

> Morning Glory Pool is one of Yellowstone's most famous hot springs. Before the highway and large parking lot were removed from the area in 1971, Morning Glory was visited by more people than any spring or geyser other than Old Faithful. . . .
>
> Its popularity may have spelled the demise of Morning Glory Pool. In the past it was hot enough to prevent any growth of cyanobacteria within the crater. The color of the pool was a delicate pale blue, unlike that of any other. But so much debris has been thrown into the crater that the vent has been partially plugged. Hot water has smaller egress into the crater, and the temperature has dropped. Cyanobacteria can grow down into the crater, and the color is less beautiful than it used to be.
>
> Because of its known geyser potential, Morning Glory was artificially induced to erupt in October 1950. The purpose was to empty the crater so it could be cleaned. The list of material disgorged included $86.27 in pennies, $8.10 in other coins, tax tokens from nine states, logs, bottles, tin cans, seventy-six handkerchiefs, towels, socks, shirts, and "delicate items of underclothing." Since 1950 several additional attempts to induce eruptions have been made, all without success. Coins and rocks can be seen lining small benches on the crater walls and cleaning them out is a continuing job—2,785 coins were removed during 2004 alone.

So people today continue to vandalize—but a penny's worth at a time. They do not stuff a thousand pounds of rubbish down Old Faithful.

You may wonder how they clean springs like that. First, they are careful. For light cleaning, the rangers have a mechanical arm. Heavier jobs, like Morning Glory Pool, require a more forceful intervention.

Lowering the water level may work. One of the strange features at the Upper Geyser Basin lies at the end of a trail that branches off the boardwalk at Geyser Hill. It leads through a section of forest that went through the 1988 fires mostly untouched, and the trees, on a warm day, are something of a relief, after a long tour of the geyser basin in the sun. Up the hill, ahead, is Solitary Geyser. It was formerly a spring, until the construction of a pool and bathhouse down below, on a flat on the other side of the Firehole River—and yes, that is correct. For decades, an increasingly elaborate pool-and-bathhouse combination served the geyser-going public. In 1915, as it was being completed, water was diverted from Solitary Spring; a pipe carried it down the hill to fill the pool. What had been Solitary Spring quickly became Solitary Geyser: the pool suddenly erupted. By lowering the water level, the pressure on the water deeper down was also lowered. That pressure was keeping the water from boiling. When the pressure was removed, the water deep down flashed into steam, driving the water above to the surface in an abrupt surge that, to us, becomes a visible eruption. The diversion ended in the late 1940s; still, Solitary continues to erupt for reasons no one entirely understands. The thermal features are always strange.

So removing water will cause a hot spring to turn into a geyser. However, in a situation like that at Morning Glory Pool, such interventions can only accomplish so much. The rangers are in the position of a doctor trying to treat a patient with multiple gunshot wounds but using only a pair of forceps, or maybe just tweezers. They need to be able to go much deeper than they can.

Another trick is available. Soap tossed into a spring, or into an irregular geyser, will cause an eruption. This abuse was another that the early visitors indulged in. They threw so much soap into the springs and geysers that the stores had a hard time keeping soap in stock.

It is said that this trick was discovered by accident. A man was operating a laundry concession at the Upper Geyser Basin. He was using one of the springs as a vat. He added soap, and his laundry detonated in his face. You guessed it: the dirty clothes were blasted all over the landscape.

That seems to have happened an awful lot back then.

There Are So Many Ways to Die Here

It is hard to keep track of them all.

For instance: the news media would have you worry about the Yellowstone "supervolcano," which is presently living a quiet life underground, as the massive magma plume that is the ultimate energy source for the geyser basins. It erupts about every six hundred thousand years, and since the last maximal eruption happened something close to six hundred thousand years ago, the news media trots it out occasionally as a new end-of-the-world scenario with which to frighten the audience—Ebola, killer bees, and the Mayan apocalypse for a new generation.

The people who deal with questions along these lines, probably more than anyone else, are the earth scientists at the US Geological Survey. Most people probably do not really know what the USGS is, which is a shame because they do wonderful work. It is the federal agency charged with studying the landscape of the United States, especially its natural resources and natural hazards. It is a bureau of the Department of the Interior, like the National Park Service, but it issues no regulations; its purview is exclusively research. We do not think of them often, but let another volcano in the Cascades begin to simmer, or let another fault line shift under Southern California, and the USGS will be in your living room because they are the ones who know about that kind of thing. It is among the oldest of the federal alphabet-agencies—much older, for instance, than the CIA or the FBI.

The USGS funds the Yellowstone Volcano Observatory, which it runs along with eight other member agencies, including the universities of Utah and Wyoming, Montana State, and the National Park Service. About the Yellowstone volcano, geologists cannot do much, nor can anyone else. They run increasingly sophisticated monitoring. If the volcano were going to explode, it would presumably give us a fair amount of warning; Mount St. Helens sent out earthquakes and blew off steam for two months before it erupted. When the Yellowstone volcano does erupt, even running away will not help. As a happy side effect, the USGS is learning more and more about the geology of the park. Hence, they will tell you that you should not worry about the volcano. If you have to worry about something geologic in Yellowstone, worry about hydrothermal steam explosions.

What are they? If the news media people were on the top of their game, you would know. Because they are fearsome things. Consider Indian Pond. It is easy to visit. It is right next to the East Entrance Road, close by the spot where wolf 812M, the rogue Mollie, was filmed harassing the stick-wielding, shouting man. The Storm Point Trail, a short, gentle loop well-loved by families, runs alongside Indian Pond near its trailhead, ending at Mary Bay on Yellowstone Lake. Even without knowing its history, a visitor to Indian Pond will find it looking . . . oddly ominous. Given that this is Yellowstone, that too-round shape is evocative. What it evokes is an explosion, like the crater left by the blast of a large bomb—a mighty large bomb.

The impression is correct. Indian Pond is the remnant of an epic explosion that took place here 2,900 years ago. It is not the biggest. Due east, uphill and away from the road, is Turbid Lake, almost four times the size of Indian Pond. And under the waters of Mary Bay, scientists have recently found the largest hydrothermal explosion crater in the world. The fireworks went off here 13,800 years ago, just as the glacial ice was departing. The blast left a crater a mile and a half across.

Such an explosion can throw debris a mile or more into the air, and the debris can land as much as two and a half miles away. They do not give warning. The earth just suddenly blows apart in a cataclysm of steam and rock.

"Fireworks" is actually the wrong word. What happens is a large-scale version of the same kind of physics that caused Solitary Spring to turn into Solitary Geyser. According to the USGS scientists at the Yellowstone Volcano Observatory, "Hydrothermal explosions occur where shallow interconnected reservoirs of fluids with temperatures at or near the boiling point underlie thermal fields. These fluids can rapidly transition to steam if the pressure suddenly drops." The massive crater under Mary Bay, for instance, is thought to have been created when the glacial ice melted enough to reduce the pressure that held down hot water there, and the sudden release caused a kind of super-eruption: "Since vapor molecules take up much more space than liquid molecules, the transition to steam results in significant expansion and blows apart surrounding rocks and ejects debris. Hydrothermal explosions are a potentially significant local hazard and can damage or even destroy thermal features."

The distribution is not random. Scientists have identified at least twenty-five craters in the park. They occur in association with the Yellowstone caldera. They also pop up where hot water runs between Norris and Mammoth. These two thermal areas share their source of hot water; the water runs along a fault between the two, and blasts have happened there, too. The big ones go off about once every seven hundred years. The USGS thinks they may represent the end-stage of a geyser basin. Eventually, such a basin will have its water sealed over by clay minerals that form caprocks and lock the water within its system. Any drop in pressure can then cause the water to flash into steam and blow apart the earth above it with violence that, at the outer extremes, really resembles the detonation of a tactical nuclear weapon.

Seven hundred years sounds like a timescale so large that humans need not worry too much, but smaller blasts happen every year or two. At Norris Geyser Basin, for instance, is a vivid display of the kind of violence that can result from a steam explosion even at a smaller scale.

In the Back Basin section of Norris is a feature that at one time was a small spring that erupted irregularly and unspectacularly. Its name was Porkchop Geyser. The names the early explorers gave to thermal features are often now nonsensical because the feature has changed (and maybe the name was never a good match anyway), but "Porkchop" fit because it looked almost perfectly like that cut of meat.

Geysers have personalities. Some are stable, and some are erratic. Some are prone to fits. Some go through regular crises, and some—like the famous faithful one—can be counted on to stay the course no matter what happens. They do change. They are born; they live; they grow old; they die. Some die quietly, just fading away like General MacArthur's "old soldiers." Some die a violent death.

Porkchop had a crisis. It had been an unassuming creature, a pool about ten feet across that erupted now and then and would go quiet for years. When it did go off, the eruption was not more than ten feet high. The vent at the bottom, from which the water issued, acted as a throttle on the size of the eruption. It was only an inch or two wide.

Now, the Norris Geyser Basin is a strange place, a place of extremes. The water is unusually acidic in places, and it is the hottest of the geyser basins; hotter temperatures have been recorded here than anywhere else in the park (on land—as we will see, Yellowstone Lake hides places even hotter). Remember, the water in a random spring literally dissolved that guy who fell in while trying to hot-pot and did it in a single night. The tallest geyser in the world—Steamboat Geyser, which erupts irregularly, but to three hundred feet—is just up the hill from Porkchop.

The basin has been studied for a long time. The temperature in Porkchop stayed the same from the 1920s through the 1950s, but after the 1959 Hebgen Lake earthquake, about which we will hear more later, it dropped, and Porkchop stopped erupting. Then it changed again. Something happened in the ground, and the temperature began to rise. Porkchop began erupting again. The temperature kept going up through the 1970s, and the eruptions started happening more frequently. Still, Porkchop kept getting hotter.

Suddenly, in March 1985, it freaked out. The spring drained, and the eruptions became continuous: it became what the geologists call a perpetual spouter. The eruptions were now twenty or thirty feet high. At times, also, it got loud. It roared so loudly that it could be heard a mile away. It became one of the sights and sounds of the park, especially during winter. The constant eruption produced a mist that built an ice cone twenty feet high.

Porkchop needed an intervention of some kind, but geysers never get those. Instead, four years after it began, the crisis peaked. Geologists have studied these events closely, and the USGS tells the story of what happened:

> On September 5, 1989, at 2:40 PM local time, eight visitors to Yellowstone National Park watched as the eruptions of Porkchop Geyser suddenly increased to heights of 20–30 m (65–100 ft). Immediately thereafter, the silica sinter surrounding the geyser was thrown into the air as the geyser exploded. It was over in seconds, but during that period rocks over 1 m (3 ft) in size were uprooted, and some smaller material was thrown a distance of over 60 m

(200 ft) from the vent. The explosion left a crater over 10 m (30 ft) across that was surrounded by a rim of jumbled blocks ejected during the explosion. And the porkchop shape was no more.

You can see the result: the wreckage is still visible all around Porkchop, which is a pool again, a much larger pool. It looks a little like a scale-model version of Stonehenge. What had happened was that the throttle on the geyser failed, and when the height suddenly increased, the volume of water ejected did, too. Remember that these explosions happen when there is a sudden decrease in pressure. The removal of the water provided that decrease. The rest of the water under Porkchop's vent flashed into steam and blew Porkchop apart.

These things happen often enough that one provided what could be the most improbable event in the whole history of the park. On May 17, 2009, a group of geologists was visiting Biscuit Basin, near Old Faithful. They were here for a meeting of Earthscope, a professional society, and were on a two-day field trip that was finishing here at Biscuit Basin. The boardwalk was absolutely full of geologists. One of them, Hank Heasler of the Park Service, was addressing the group. He was even talking about hydrothermal explosions and how rare they are. Out of nowhere—that is how these things happen—Black Diamond Pool exploded. Black water erupted upward, accompanied by waves of heat and rocky debris. It was photographed multiple times before it settled, even though the geologists were about as ready to run as anything. One of them remembered, "I heard this roar. I really thought it was a truck coming down the boardwalk."

Even the "small" explosions are not so small. You can see the remains of a series of such explosions at Midway Geyser Basin; they were the largest hydrothermal explosions to take place since the park was established. The crater that resulted is merely a large spring today, but still—even just sitting there, steaming and boiling—it is one of the most dramatic sights in the park.

Excelsior Geyser Crater has a violent history. It has, in the past, been the largest geyser in the world by far, sending up masses of water three hundred feet high and three hundred feet across. Look at the present Excelsior Geyser Crater and imagine it erupting from one end to the other, with that ocean of water lifting three times higher than Old Faithful. These eruptions are often described with just that word, "eruption," but the USGS classifies the events of its major eruption cycle, in the late nineteenth century, as explosions.

When we look at an eyewitness report, we can see why. Superintendents of Yellowstone were required to prepare an annual report for the Secretary of the Interior. From 1877 to 1882, the superintendent was Philetus Norris (as in Norris Geyser Basin and Mount Norris). In his report for 1881, he writes much of Excelsior. He was aware that what he was seeing was extraordinary: "During much of the summer this eruption was simply incredible, elevating to heights of from 100 to 300 feet sufficient water to render the rapid Fire Hole River, nearly 100 yards wide, a foaming torrent of steaming hot water, and hurling rocks of from 1 to 100 pounds weight, like those from an exploded mine, over surrounding acres." That is no ordinary eruption. Nor was this one, which he recalled from earlier in his time as superintendent, in 1878:

> I then distinctly heard its spoutings when near Old Faithful, 6 miles distant, but arrived too late to witness them, though not its effects upon the Fire Hole River, which was so swollen as to float out some of our bridges over rivulet branches below it.
>
> Crossing the river above the geyser and hitching my horse, with bewildering astonishment I beheld the outlet

at least tripled in size, and a furious torrent of hot water escaping from the pool, which was shrouded in steam, greatly hiding its spasmodic foamings. The pool was considerably enlarged, its immediate borders swept entirely clear of all movable fragments of rock, enough of which had been hurled or forced back to form a ridge from knee to breast high at a distance of from 20 to 50 feet from the ragged edge of the yawning chasm.

He then complained that his accounts of the geyser were received by outsiders "with annoying evidence of distrust."

He was telling the truth, we know. We can also see, from descriptions like this, that the geyser was not merely erupting. It was blowing itself apart, and it stopped in 1890. When you visit Excelsior, try to imagine what happened here—and know, also, that in 1985, the geyser produced a series of smaller eruptions and went through a period of violent agitation between 2004 and 2006. Is it getting ready to blow again?

The chances are . . . unknown. We never know when the next explosion will happen, but Yellowstone is an outlandish place. If we can have an explosion right in front of a gang of geologists, then Excelsior can blow, too.

The USGS has drawn the logical conclusion:

Fortunately, no one was injured by the blast from Porkchop Geyser, but the event illustrates one of the most significant yet least appreciated hazards in Yellowstone: hydrothermal explosions. Even small explosions can be harmful to anyone standing nearby. These sorts of events usually happen in the backcountry and are not witnessed by people, but occasionally they occur in developed areas— like the 2018 explosion of Ear Spring, near Old Faithful, which, in addition to rocks, ejected several decades worth of garbage that had fallen or was thrown into the pool.

So worry more about being blown up by a steam explosion, and less about the volcano, even if that documentary you may remember (*Yellowstone Mega-Blast!* on the generic cable channel) never said a word about steam.

The weirdest geyser basin is the one we cannot see.

Before we leave the thermal features, we should give them one last opportunity to show how bizarre they are.

Take Grotto Geyser, to start. It is down the valley from Old Faithful and is easy to find: the boardwalk that runs past Grand Geyser takes you right there, as does the paved trail leading to Morning Glory Pool. It is hard to miss because of its unique "cone," which is not the right word. As local writer Janet Jones puts it, "It looks like Dr. Seuss was allowed to design a geyser." Another comparison would be to the English sculptor Henry Moore; it looks like the famous 1938 *Recumbent Figure*. How did this happen? The generally agreed-upon explanation is that the geyser was born amid a grove of trees. It killed the trees when they drew up the silica-rich water, and it turned them to stone, pretty much literally. When the new spring erupted, it also coated the trees with silica, and before they could topple, the added weight pulled them over and turned them into the loops, like the handle on a coffee cup, that make Grotto so distinctive. One of those trees remained upright, and that is today the single vertical column that protrudes from the center of the formation. Strange to think, but inside that white geyserite lies a little forest, utterly entombed.

You can see the same kind of process happening all up and down the Firehole River valley, wherever the thermal water is cooking. When hydrothermal activity starts under a new piece of ground, it kills the trees above. Entire groves die this way, and they have a local name. When you see a group of blackened and dead trees with white geyserite a foot or two up the trunks, that is a "bobby socks forest." It gets that name from the cute little socks they have up to the ankles . . . of their otherwise blackened and corpse-like legs.

Consider, also, Poison Spring. It is away from the boardwalks among the upper terraces at Mammoth Hot Springs. I visited it once with a scientist who specializes in hydrothermal activity in the park. It is in a shallow dip in the landscape, where the travertine of the hill is fractured to make a little cave. In front of the cave is a milky spring that bubbles like a witch's caldron. All around is a riot of bright green vegetation. "I found all these dead birds, all around here," my scientist friend said, pointing at the grasses and other plants around the spring. The vegetation is nature's own Machiavellian ruse: it attracts birds, which breathe fast and poison themselves on nature's bounty. "I thought I'd found something fantastically new. Which is absurd, given how close this is to everything. Of course, they've known about it for decades."

The problem, from a bird's point of view, is that the cave and water produce tremendous amounts of carbon dioxide. And maybe it is a problem for creatures larger than birds: "I wouldn't hang around down there," he said, gesturing toward the area around Poison Spring. "The water actually isn't all that hot. The bubbling you see isn't boiling. It's CO_2 being released." Oxygen is only a portion of the atmosphere, of course. In the atmosphere, carbon dioxide—CO_2, that is—today is in the high 300 parts per million range. Before the industrial revolution, it was half that, or lower. "Around here," my friend said, "I've measured 200,000 ppm during the day, and 350,000 ppm at night."

"What happens," he continued, "is that, as the carbon dioxide displaces oxygen, it begins to bind to your hemoglobin. Eventually, your body shuts down. You pass out and don't get up again if there isn't someone there to help you."

As we left Poison Spring, I asked after a similar place, one that kills animals a good deal bigger than birds. Yes, he said—it

actually exists and is not just a fable. It is a ravine that meets
with Cache Creek, which itself flows into the Lamar River
in the northeast part of the park. It is really in the middle
of nowhere, which may be all for the best. It is called Death
Gulch.

It was discovered (or rediscovered—the Crow and Shoshone
will have known about it) in 1888 by a geologist named Walter
Weed, who reported it in an 1889 issue of *Science*. Weed rode
his horse up Cache Creek until he found the opening to the
ravine, where he got a surprise. He uses an old spelling for
"grizzly," but the bear remains the same:

> The gulch ends, or rather begins, in a "scoop" or basin
> about two hundred and fifty feet above Cache Creek; and
> just below this we found the fresh body of a large bear,
> a silver-tip grisly, with the remains of a companion in an
> advanced state of decomposition above him. Nearby were
> the skeletons of four more bears, with the bones of an elk
> a yard or two above; while in the bottom of the pocket
> were the fresh remains of several squirrels, rock-hares, and
> other small animals, besides numerous dead butterflies and
> insects. The body of the grisly was carefully examined for
> bullet-holes or other marks of injury, but showed no traces
> of violence, the only indication being a few drops of blood
> under the nose. It was evident that he had met his death
> but a short time before, as the carcass was still perfectly
> fresh, though offensive enough at the time of a later visit.
> The remains of a cinnamon bear just above and alongside
> of this were in an advanced state of decomposition, while
> the other skeletons were almost denuded of flesh, though
> the claws and much of the hair remained. It was apparent
> that these animals, as well as the squirrels and insects, had
> not met their death by violence, but had been asphyxiated
> by the irrespirable gas given off in the gulch.

GEYSERS ARE STRANGER THAN YOU THINK

Other parts of the park have these similarly bizarre concentrations of gas. A construction worker was killed by such a concentration in a pit dug in 1939 as part of the construction of a bridge over the Yellowstone River. My scientist friend found another such concentration in an otherwise nameless gulch near Mud Volcano; he was just walking through with his instruments when the numbers suddenly went off the charts. Here, he found, is an invisible river of carbon flowing, unknown to almost all, a few hundred feet from the road. The ground here is oddly sterile, the lodgepole pines sickly, and an expert on trees I talked to about it thinks that the carbon concentration is so intense that the flow permeates the ground like water and chokes the trees off at the roots, another bizarre example of Yellowstone life dying of nature's largesse.

But you can never tell what might turn up in a geyser basin. You would probably not guess that oil flows at the surface, and yes, it is that kind of oil: petroleum, like the stuff welling up at the surface of the La Brea Tar Pits, if in smaller quantities and without the sabretooth cats and mastodons. What we know about the phenomenon goes back to a 1970 report by geologists JD Love and John Good. There are three such places in the park, although none are easy to get at. One is deep in the backcountry. One is deep underground: it was exposed when the Tower Bridge was constructed over the Yellowstone River just northeast of Tower Junction, the same place where the construction worker was earlier killed by gas. One, however, is near Tower Fall at Calcite Springs, which is off-limits itself—and difficult to get at anyway—but is easy to see from above, on either side of the Yellowstone River canyon. There is even an official viewpoint next to the Grand Loop Road.

The ground is so hot here that sulfur turns into a liquid and seeps with some regularity to the surface. You may hear it suggested that it is impossible to see the oil from the Calcite Springs Overlook, on the road, but in fact an oil geologist could

5

spot it easily, if you happen to have one along. Photographs that the geologists Love and Good took when they investigated the oil seepage closely look a little like the opening of *The Beverly Hillbillies* (when Jed is shootin' at some food / And up through the ground came a bubblin' crude).

Love and Good were well-named for this task because they had a great time. They were allowed to get down next to the oil flow, where they were in geological heaven. From their report: "The orifices from which the oil emerges are along fractures in soil and rock. Temperatures of vapors 1 foot inside the orifices range from warm to hot. Several of the hottest . . . that were measured were 93°C, but the average was 80°–85°C." That would be very "warm" indeed, between 176° and 185°F. "The oil is highly fluid, has a strong but pleasant petroleum odor, and is light brown. It is accompanied by sulfurous gas and steam in the hottest vents and by small amounts of water in the cooler ones. The conduits and fractures are invariably lined with layers of beautiful euhedral yellow sulfur crystals, some as much as 2 inches long. Many crystals contain globules of oil and are generally oil stained." A euhedral crystal is a well-formed one, with flat faces and sharp angles. It would look like a diamond on which a jeweler has finished the first cuts. For Love and Good, it appears, the oil stains may have been a plus.

But as the title of this section says, the weirdest geyser basin is the one you cannot see. It is only very recently that we have learned anything about it at all. The violence there is glorious.

I am referring to the bottom of Yellowstone Lake. Until the last three decades, we knew less about it than we do the bottom of the deepest trenches in the world's oceans, which had at least been visited. The technological challenges in this kind of exploration are—if not as expensive—comparable to spaceflight, and it makes sense that humans began flying in space at about the same point in history that they began visiting the bottom of the sea.

GEYSERS ARE STRANGER THAN YOU THINK

Getting a look at the bottom of Yellowstone Lake has been a knock-on effect from similar efforts in the ocean. The same technologies are involved, and some of the same people.

Tentative probing began in 1871, when one of the early explorations of the park, the Hayden Survey, brought the artist and naturalist Henry Elliott to the shore of Yellowstone Lake. Elliott did not stop at the shore, sailing all over the lake and taking soundings that allowed him to make its first "bathymetric" map, meaning simply a map that gives depths—not easy in Elliott's era, when depths were taken with a piece of cord with a weight at the bottom. He used the *Annie*, an improvised vessel eleven feet long, with a sail made from a woolen blanket, a mast made from a lodgepole pine trunk that someone turned up in the forest, and oars made by hand on the spot. Yellowstone geologists have a soft spot for Elliott, who should probably have been killed in that boat and instead produced a map that later proved highly accurate.

It was difficult, however, to do much more than probe those depths. At its deepest, the lake is 394 feet, and it is almost unbelievably cold, spending a good portion of its year frozen over. One thing you will not see in its waters is people swimming, or even wading. There are beaches at, say, the Lake Hotel where employees hang out and sunbathe during the summer, and beaches where the hotel guests hang out (the employees have segregated the beaches quietly but more or less on purpose because they deal with those same guests all day). Nobody ever goes in that water, which has been hostile enough to keep even devoted scientists at arm's length. For well over a hundred years, the bottom of the lake remained a thing we could mostly just theorize about. Consider those giant lake trout, the ones that might have wiped out the native cutthroat, that were in the lake for years before anyone noticed.

5

It turns out the lake conceals an amazing irony. On its surface, on a calm day, it is a picture of deep blue serenity. On the bottom, it is a weird, sometimes violent moonscape.

Between 1950 and 1991, multiple agencies produced maps of the lake, but the technology available could only do so much. In 1997, though, matters took a turn toward the weird. Researchers were again scanning the floor of the lake, this time at Bridge Bay, when they got returns they could not explain. They put a new kind of technology to use: a robotic submersible. They were looking at the video images being sent to the surface when a bizarre sight appeared. It was . . . well, it was hard to describe at first, but it looked like some kind of spire. How? Why? They are, as the researchers suspected, thermal features. What we see as a spire is an accumulation of silica from the hydrothermal water, combined with the remains of microscopic creatures that lived there. The Park Service later sent divers down to recover a small spire (the largest are twenty-five feet tall). It proved, among other things, to contain an amazing range of toxic elements: arsenic, barium, manganese, molybdenum, antimony, thallium, and tungsten all turned up in the sample.

In 1999, efforts to get literally at the bottom of the thing kicked into higher gear; beginning in that year, the USGS produced the first high-resolution bathymetric map of the lake. This new generation of explorers had access to GPS and other luxuries, like computers you could pick up and carry around without hurting yourself, which used to be impossible. They also had multibeam sonar. The word "sonar" is short for SOund NAvigation and Ranging—that is, bouncing sound waves off objects in the water to determine how far away they are, a technique that of course played a big role in the Second World War, but this is not your grandfather's sonar. Multibeam sonar, when mounted on a boat, sends out multiple sound waves that spread away from the vessel in a fan, allowing the operators to map a wide swath of the bottom at once, and with greater clarity than before. They also used seismic waves to map what they would not be able to see, even if the water were not there: these waves told them what rocks lay under the silt and mud and glop generally that the glaciers left behind.

This effort ended in 2002, the researchers having taken 240 million soundings—rather more than anyone could take with a piece of cord and a lead plumb-bob. Since then, the exploration has continued, and intensified. Every kind of technology that might help has been deployed. The Woods Hole Oceanographic Institute brought in a sophisticated research vessel, the RV *Annie*, rather more seaworthy than the original 1871 *Annie*. It carried with it a deep submersible, the *Yogi* (and there he is again, the cartoon bear who has come to be an icon of Yellowstone). The advent of submersibles has defeated the defenses the lake always threw at researchers: the robots can dive deep, and the cold does not kill them.

What they have found is a dynamic landscape of fire and ice. If the water were removed, we would see here one of the larger geyser basins in the world. There are lava flows. There are places shaped by glaciers. There are hydrothermal vents in huge numbers. At the deepest part of the lake—the scientists have named it the Deep Hole—the temperature of these vents is off the charts. As the USGS reported, "The hottest vent measured was a whopping 345°F (174°C). This is much hotter than any surface hot spring at Yellowstone because the weight from the overlying lake water acts like a pressure cooker lid and allows temperatures higher than boiling to be reached. Indeed, these are the hottest hydrothermal vents measured in a lake anywhere in the world!"

There are submerged ancient shorelines. There are those weird spires. And there are hydrothermal explosion craters in such numbers that in places, the maps of the lake floor look like the surface of the moon. The research has focused recently on, among other things, the nature of these craters, and the events that caused them. The crater at Mary Bay, mentioned above, was created, they think, by a singularly dramatic series of events. There was a massive earthquake, then the equivalent of a tsunami in the lake which eroded the outlet area, where water flows out of the lake. The sudden drop in the water level reduced the pressure enough that the thermal water flashed into steam, and a nuclear-sized explosion followed.

Geologists are in the unusual position of discovering, in large numbers, new features that need a name (like the Deep Hole). That has not happened since the 1870s. One of the larger explosion craters—over two thousand feet across—is thus now named Elliott's Crater, after Henry Elliott, the lake's first mapmaker. He had the odd habit—odd among nineteenth-century explorers—of *not* naming features after himself. The geologists felt he had not done himself justice.

Elliott's Crater remains hydrothermally active. There are hot vents both in and around the crater, and smaller craters on its floor. Research has revealed that Elliott's Crater has been active for eight thousand years. If we could see it, it would be one of the important thermal areas of the park, and indeed of the world.

Will it blow again? The chances are that it will. It is not clear what the effect would be, but you might want to visit Yosemite that week instead.

6

LANDSCAPE BIZARRE

Gibbon Falls, where the Gibbon River tumbles over the edge of the caldera rim.
SCOTT HERRING

6

Yellowstone is, of course, unique and a land of extremes. It is worth pausing to recognize just how unique and extreme it is.

It was the first national park in the world. For a long time, it was the largest in the nation and the world. Were it not for the gigantic parks in Alaska and the relatively recent expansion of Death Valley National Park, it would still be the largest park in the United States.

It is home to the largest concentration of mammals—sixty-seven species of them—anywhere in the country, again outside of Alaska. (But we ought to leave Alaska out of this list, to be brief, and to be fair—it is a land of even more extreme extremes.)

Yellowstone National Park contains the largest concentration of geysers in the world. About half the geysers in existence are here. It has the largest hot spring in the country (Grand Prismatic) and the tallest geyser (Steamboat) in the world.

Yellowstone Lake is, as noted, the largest high-elevation lake in North America. In spite of the damage done by the lake trout, it has the largest population of wild cutthroat trout in North America.

Bizarrely, those trout are a Pacific Slope species trapped in a lake that drains to the Atlantic—but that, as we will see, is a strange story of its own.

The headwaters of seven major rivers can be found in the park, which sends water to the Mississippi River and the Columbia River both.

The Yellowstone River itself is the last major undammed river in the United States, and it's the longest undammed river. It has diversion dams, but nowhere is it stoppered. You could take a boat the whole way from just below its headwaters in Wyoming to the point where it joins the Missouri River in North Dakota . . . if you did not mind being killed going over the falls in the canyon.

Greater Yellowstone is thought by many to be the largest intact temperate ecosystem on the planet. Now that the wolves are back, it has all its original animals.

It has the largest herd of wild, free-roaming bison in the country. It is the one place where they have lived continuously since prehistory.

Grizzly bears, the largest carnivore in the country, survived here when they were hunted to extinction everywhere else except Glacier National Park, and now number, in Greater Yellowstone, something over a thousand.

We could go on. It was precisely because it is a land of extremes that it was ever preserved in the first place. It had to be mind-blowing for that first generation to even consider the designation "national park" because they were also inventing that concept. There had been parks before Yellowstone—Robin Hood, after all, is supposed to have been declared an outlaw for poaching in the equivalent of a royal park. Every medieval king and nobleman either inherited one or created one if he could possibly find a way. The idea of preserving a piece of the landscape was not new, but this "Yellowstone National Park" thing was. Preserves had been preserved, before, for some specific reason, like saving deer for the king to chase, or—more recently—saving wood to make ships for the nation's navy. The new national park was being saved for its scenery alone, and it was being saved for everyone.

There is an old story about Yellowstone that says the national park idea was born around the campfire that was warming members of the 1870 Washburn exploring party as they camped at the confluence of the Firehole and Gibbon rivers. Having seen the wonders of the place, they formulated a plan to see it set aside as a park, so that this ground would never be defiled by private development. We get the story from Nathaniel Langford, a member of the expedition. He published an edited version of the diary he kept during the trip many years later, and it is from the—edited—diary that the story comes.

Historians have come to doubt this tale, mainly because Langford is the only one who seems to have noticed that this world-changing conversation ever took place. Still, people took his word for it for a long time, so much so that the summit above the confluence of the Firehole and Gibbon is called National Park Mountain. Maybe, then, it is appropriate that National Park Mountain is not really a mountain. It is a high point rising from the plateau behind it. It looks like a mountain because it is a corner of the plateau, and standing beneath, the corner is pointing right at you. Like Langford's diary, the plateau is faking you out.

It seems natural, though, that such a story would have been widely accepted and believed for generations. Making this huge chunk of land into a "national park" was such an odd thing to do that an origin myth was needed to explain it. In fact, as we have seen, it was the thermal areas that led to the creation of the national park. Most of the unique features of the place listed above became important to the public later. Preserving animals and fish and mountains and lakes, and so much of the rest, have been a happy accident. Much of present-day Yellowstone is all about these happy accidents. They draw in the crowds today, but they are not what motivated the founders.

That first generation, after all, had no idea what had actually happened here. They were totally unaware of the greatest, most dramatic Yellowstone extreme of them all:

It is also home of the most powerful volcano in the history of the planet.

The Volcano Might Not Kill You, But It Sure Is Strange

Properly speaking, what we see in Yellowstone now is not a volcano, but a caldera.

What happens is this: when a volcano explodes massively and ejects vast quantities of rock and ash, it actually is not done yet.

In the case of the Yellowstone volcano, which has had eruptions larger than anything in the history of the earth, the material in the magma chamber under what is now the park was blasted outward. So much was blown clear that the magma chamber, having emptied, collapsed downward. There followed a long period in which different kinds of lava flowed at different times around and out of the caldera to make much of the landscape we see today. The caldera itself is hard to spot because these lava flows have largely filled it in, but there are some places where you can look right at it. Gibbon Falls, for instance, on the Grand Loop just north of Madison, jumps off a remnant of the caldera rim. The lava flows are visible all over the place. One of them created the plateau west of the Firehole River, the corner of which—perhaps appropriately—is National Park Mountain.

As noted, we really should not worry about the Yellowstone volcano. Yes, it erupts every 600,000 years or so, and the last super-eruption was 631,000 years ago—but when geologists talk about these events, they will qualify their estimate by saying "plus or minus 100,000 years." Unless you plan on living that long, you do not have anything to fret over. In Yellowstone, the traffic on the roads is far more dangerous than the geology.

Nevertheless, the hot spot under the park is one huge element that makes the place what it is. It is not the only thing, but it is a big thing making the place as bizarre as it is.

For instance: did you know that the park is heaving? Like a person's chest, breathing in and out?

Weird, but true. After the caldera collapsed 631,000 years ago, the magma chamber began to refill. It did so at two points that had been the centers of the trouble. One was named for a creek in Hayden Valley, the big open area north of Yellowstone Lake. The creek is Sour Creek, a good name for the purpose. What resulted was a resurgent dome, a lump in the landscape that swelled upward like a contusion. It rose hundreds of yards, until it peeked above the level of the caldera rim. Another rose at Mallard Lake, in the hills above Old Faithful, those hills themselves partly a result of the resurgence. Both the Sour Creek resurgent dome and the one at Mallard Lake are surrounded by line upon line of faults, where the rock has been fractured by the rising dome. On a map, there are so many fault lines that the oval resurgent domes look like fingerprints.

This sort of behavior was no great surprise to the geologists. The magma system underneath the park did not stop working just because the lid blew off—it has done that over and over, leaving a trail of violence stretching almost all the way to California. Again, the hotspot under Yellowstone sits still. Every part of the planet's surface is in motion, and as the North American plate moves over the hotspot, it creates a trail of volcanic fury that makes it look like it is the magma source that is moving. In fact, it is the other way around. Although they have increasingly sophisticated ideas about them, geologists cannot yet explain hotspots. They have two competing theories: one possibility is that the name is correct, and the source of the volcanism in Yellowstone and elsewhere is a spot deep in the earth that is unusually hot. Alternatively, the roof above may be unusually thin, letting the magma through. If you can decide which is correct, you can have a professorship and the honor of having resolved one of the major fights in earth science.

This is what excites TV producers: if the magma chamber is filling, then the end is near, right? This is just like those weeks before Mount St. Helens went, when the volcano got more and more anguished and everybody ran away, right? It's going to go off like a pile of hydrogen bombs, and we can somehow still film it, right? *Right?*

The scientists cannot say they are wrong. Still, again, it may be due, yes, plus or minus a thousand centuries, literally.

The ground does not just go up. It goes up and down—again, it heaves. It does so every year because the ground absorbs water when the snow melts, but it does so more dramatically over longer periods of time. The inevitable analogy is that Yellowstone is breathing in and out. Measurements were taken in the 1920s, and when they were taken again in the 1970s, the caldera had risen twenty-eight inches. Ominous . . . but then it went down again. Between 1985 and 1995, it subsided at about the same rate it had risen. More recently, scientists have moved the record back way, *way* past the 1920s. On the northern shore of the lake are a series of lines on the land, looking a bit like tree rings. They show up loud and clear on a satellite image, radiating back from the shore of the lake, matching the shape of the beach as they stack one atop the other from south to north. The more obvious are even visible on Google Maps, and on the ground itself, in the big open area north of the Indian Pond explosion crater. They were put there after the glaciers left because otherwise the glaciers would have obliterated them like an eraser removing chalk from a board. What are they?

They are old shorelines, and there are some underwater, too. When the caldera "breathes in," the ground rises, and the lake tips like water in a bowl. When it subsides, the opposite happens. Looking closely at those shorelines, the geologists have been able to arrive at pretty good dates because the shores are full of things that can be dated, like ash from ancient volcanic eruptions, and archeological sites with distinctive kinds of artifacts in them. What they have found is not what one would expect: since the glaciers retreated—even after all that weight was removed—the ground has actually gone down.

Where the cause of this heaving is concerned, the USGS has bad news for the producers of shows with names like *Yellowstone Mega-Blast!* In 2020, they tied it together with the stars of the geological show:

> But what could cause such variation? Magma intrusion is certainly a possibility, but that does a poor job of explaining why the caldera also subsides in these cycles and

is overall down relative to thousands of years ago. A more likely possibility is the hydrothermal activity that drives Yellowstone's geysers and hot springs. We know from multiple types of data sets that the hydrothermal fluids in Yellowstone migrate laterally. Hot water migrating from one area to another in the subsurface could cause the surface to move both up and down.

There is just too much going on underneath Yellowstone to boil down into a simple explanation because the forces that cause the boiling here are just too weird. In 2020, a team of scientists (Greg Vaughan of the USGS, along with Jefferson Hungerford and William Keller of the NPS) announced they had found a whole new thermal area. It is deep in the backcountry, right on the edge of the Sour Creek resurgent dome. It, too, is visible on Google Maps, easily: it is just to the west of Tern Lake. Looking at the satellite image, it is clear how very new it is because the area is a riot of formerly healthy trees, now killed by the heat and left lying around like Tinkertoys on the living room floor.

What did it mean? Was this an omen, a suggestion of some new danger brewing underneath? Vaughan, Hungerford, and Keller considered the possibility but found no compelling connection, and even a whole new thermal area is no big surprise in the park. "Yellowstone is behaving just as we would expect," they concluded. "Thermal areas in Yellowstone are known to be dynamic, as evidenced by this study. . . . They heat up; they cool down; and they sometimes migrate as new fluid pathways to the surface become available. The newly emerging thermal area described here does not signify an impending eruption nor any significant changes to the deeper magmatic system."

Statements like this from Yellowstone scientists are becoming more common. They are necessary when the general public has been trained to expect that mega-blast.

The Ground Does Not Just Heave, Though
It also shakes.

Between 700 and 3,000 earthquakes occur in the area every year. Almost none of them is strong enough to feel. They of course have to do with the volcano, but not every single thing in Greater Yellowstone is about that volcano, and much that lies underground is, as the scientists put it, "not well understood." As the people of Los Angeles have discovered, over and over, a common way to learn that a specific earthquake fault exists is by having an earthquake.

The earthquakes in the immediate area of the park routinely occur as "swarms," quakes that cluster together in time and location. The news media also loves earthquake swarms, which happen regularly but are spaced widely enough in time that the newest one can be trotted out as the latest sign of the apocalypse, and the readers will have forgotten the last one. The greatest swarm of all occurred in 1985, and it is instructive what happened with that one. Geologists have learned much from the 1985 swarm, which was unusual in a number of ways. It was intense indeed, with three thousand earthquakes in a three-month period. On two separate days during that period, there were over two hundred in a single day. Now, remember how the caldera, as noted above, rose until 1985. The earthquake swarm actually marked the beginning of the caldera falling. The theory is that something, in effect, snapped underground, and hydrothermal water flowed away from the caldera and into other parts of the Yellowstone netherworld. It was water, not lava, that was making the ground shake.

Oddly enough, the news media is now so hung up on the supervolcano that they no longer think much about super-earthquakes, even though the earthquakes can be—have been—like something out of science fiction.

The famous one (or it used to be and should be still) was the 1959 Hebgen Lake event. It happened on August 17 at the very height of the tourism season but happily in the middle of the night. The official Richter magnitude is 7.3, but those numbers never do justice to an earthquake as powerful as this one. It was comparable in power to the earthquake that destroyed San Francisco in 1906 and remains one of the biggest quakes in the history of North America. The roads were empty, which was a good thing because the roads were buried. If it had not occurred in maximally rural Montana, Wyoming, and Idaho, hundreds—maybe thousands—would have been killed.

The lake that gave the earthquake its name, Hebgen Lake, is a reservoir on the Madison River. The engineers who built it in 1914 thought the fault line that runs along the north shore of the lake was inactive. It was not. At 11:37 that night, August 17, 1959, the fault slipped massively.

The terrain here is pulling apart, and when the fault slipped, the ground dropped twenty feet. In the lake, the water was agitated violently, the whole lake basin—the whole gigantic lake basin—having been suddenly tipped northward. Try that with a basin of dishwater and see what happens. What geologists call a seiche developed in the lake. That is their term for a thing (not unlike a tsunami) that happens when an enclosed body of water like this one is shaken with that kind of violence. Massive waves washed back and forth, bearing down on the dam and blasting over it in a way that left witnesses thinking, in panic, that the dam had failed. Downstream, the whole town of Ennis evacuated, the fear being that even if the dam had not collapsed yet, it would. It survived, but it cracked to such a degree that engineers quickly drained the lake entirely. One of the memories people have of the event is the smell of dead fish.

Everywhere, the landscape itself fell apart. US Highway 287 was, for miles, no longer in existence. It runs along the north shore of Hebgen Lake and long segments ended up *beneath* Hebgen Lake, slumping, disintegrating, and falling to add to the general discord in the lake water. The people who lived around the lake had never had any experience of this kind of universal violence, and for them it was as if the world was ending. Many—perhaps most—thought the Soviet Union was attacking with nuclear weapons; it is hard to imagine what the Soviets would have been attacking in that lonesome part of the world, but no one asks rational questions at such a moment. Emmett J. Culligan, the tycoon founder of the water softener company, owned a ranch where he had spent money in the hundreds of thousands building the ultimate nuclear fallout shelter. He built it almost on top of what was now the epicenter. The fault line, running right under the 150-foot-long shelter, twisted it like bread dough. The shelter, now shelters, split apart down its entire length.

Immediately after the earthquake, a writer named Edmund Christopherson collected as many eyewitness reports as he could find and assembled them into a book called *The Night the Mountain Fell*. Some of the memories are funny, like that of the owner of a tourist camp that sat nearly on top of the epicenter: "In the confusion that followed when the first shock hit, Jerry Yetter, who operates the Duck Creek Cabins near West Yellowstone, jumped out of bed and knocked on all the cabin doors to warn the occupants of the quake. Only after he'd finished the job did he realize he was wearing no clothes at all. His wife, Iris, ran onto the front porch. The porch dropped into the basement. She climbed out, got into the car, and didn't stop until she reached Bozeman, 90 miles to the north." Apparently, she left Jerry behind.

All the way down in Idaho Falls, much of the town was awakened, including a woman who realized something was wrong when her sleeping parrot was knocked to the floor and began screeching obscenities. On the West Entrance Road, in the park, a pair of guys driving a truck full of Pres-to-Logs thought their engine had broken off its mounts, but still kept going—not their problem, one can guess—and were finally stopped when the Madison River canyon collapsed all around them. As the boulders toppled across the road and around the truck, they hid out behind some trees, which were themselves shaking worse than the truck. At the Canyon Lodge, frightened guests were oddly reassured by the voice of a tourist at the front desk who never stopped loudly complaining about his reservations—an unintended reassurance that normal life would continue.

Then there was the unique experience of another man who was asleep in a trailer right atop the epicenter:

> The only man who was enthusiastic about the earthquake from the start was geologist Irving J. Witkind of the U.S. Geological Survey, who was living in a trailer on a rise to the north of Hebgen Lake, above the Culligans . . . while he surveyed and mapped the area.
>
> When the first shock hit, he figured his trailer had somehow broken loose and was rolling down the hill. He charged out, intent on stopping it. From the way the trees were swaying in the absence of any wind, he knew it was a genuine earthquake. He hopped in his jeep and headed down toward the lake. He saw the scarp that the Whitmans soared off just in time to stop.
>
> "It's mine! It's mine!" he shouted as he got out of the jeep and realized the full measure of his fortune. His words will echo wherever geologists gather in years to come. Professionally, his once-in-a-thousand-lifetimes fortune in being on the scene of a major quake meant as much as discovering an unfound Pharaoh's tomb would to an Egyptologist.

Some memories are less funny. The reference to the Whitmans has to do with the experience of Rolland Whitman, who lived near the Duck Creek Cabins, almost on top of the epicenter. He was alarmed when, as the initial shaking slowed, he could not reach his wife's family in West Yellowstone on the phone. No one at that point—no one at all, not even the geologist Irving Witkind—understood what exactly had happened. Might the epicenter have been right under West Yellowstone? Whitman, his wife, and their six children got into the car and started toward the town—and instantly drove off a cliff. It had opened in their driveway, one of the places where the fault line had dropped. They came through the crash about as well as could be expected, especially since no one wore seat belts back then.

These were old-time rural Montanans, though. They were tough. One of the celebrities to come out of the quake was Grace Miller:

> On the night of the quake Mrs. Grace Miller, a widow who, in her seventies, is still sprightly enough to run, single-handed, the Hillgard Fishing Lodge cabin and boat rentals on the north shore of Hebgen Lake, found herself suddenly wakened about midnight. She didn't know what was happening, but she felt she had to get out of the house. She threw a blanket around herself. The door was jammed, and she had to kick to get it open.
>
> Outside the door she saw a big, 5-foot crevice. As she leaped across it, the house dropped from under her into the lake. More crevices kept opening in the moonlit ground as she walked away from the lake. "Rabbits were skedaddling in every which direction," she said, but her Malamute dog, Sandy, was so frightened he wouldn't even notice them.
>
> After quite a spell of hiking in the nightmare-like night, she found refuge along with about forty other people at Kirkwood Ranch, which itself was considerably damaged, but a safe distance from the lake. She was safe there, while next day skin-divers, alerted by worried friends, searched her floating house for her body.

6

Later next day she boated past her 9-room home—which contained everything she owned, floating on the lake.

"I hope it stays upright," she said. "My teeth are still on the kitchen counter, right next to the sink."

To this day, photographs of her house, bobbing around in Hebgen Lake, appear as illustrations when the subject of the earthquake comes up.

People were trapped everywhere. The worst damage caused by the earthquake happened downstream of Hebgen Lake on the Madison River, where an event of awesome power unfolded: the side of a mountain slid down to bury both the Madison and a campground full of sleeping families. We will return to this incident in the next chapter. It was an extreme version of what happened all over the region: everywhere, highways were buried. If a road ran alongside a cliff or even just a steep hill, the road was now entirely under the cliff or the hill. This problem was maybe at its worst inside the park, where most of the phone lines were down, and most of the roads were blocked, or in places cracked open.

At the Old Faithful Inn, the structure creaked and popped loudly. The superintendent, Lon Garrison, later expressed relief. "We had to evacuate the building," he said. "Hot water from a broken pipe in the attic was running down the floor of the east wing. Half an hour later the fireplace and chimney crashed through the dining room floor, activating the sprinkler system. The water damage was horrible. A few hours earlier, with the dining room full, the casualty list would have been gruesome. As it was, our only casualty was a woman who sprained her ankle leaping out of bed after the first tremor.

"Later in the week a ranger, exhausted from quake duty, skidded on a rain-slick pavement and went off the road," he continued. The man, District Ranger Davis, was okay. The car was destroyed. "We feel," Superintendent Garrison concluded, "that God had his arm around us all the way."

It was in many ways a primitive era in a primitive place. With phone lines down—and all phones were then landline phones—the outside world learned what had happened by ham radio. There were injured people downstream of Hebgen Lake, and upstream of the big landslide. Anyone along that section of the Madison River and what remained of Highway 287 was trapped. To signal the outside world, someone wrote "SOS" on the dam spillway with pancake flour. It got the attention of Dr. Raymond Bayles, a Bozeman medical doctor who had recently bought the Stagecoach Inn in West Yellowstone (you can still see it, one of the landmarks of the town). With the phones out, Bayles had chartered a plane to go check on the place and had the pilot tour Hebgen Lake. When he saw the SOS, he had the pilot land at West Yellowstone, gathered medical supplies and a nurse, and returned. The pilot managed to land in a field at one of the area ranches. Later, US Forest Service smoke jumpers—the crazy guys who parachute into forest fires—jumped into the area where people were still trapped, with first aid supplies and food. Many of the injured ended up in a hangar at the West Yellowstone airport. Even for a totally improvised hospital, the hangar was not well equipped. The bedridden patients were placed in beds atop hay bales.

One of the most striking effects of the earthquake, though, was what it did to the hot springs and geysers. It is not too much to say that they went berserk.

George Marler, the park geologist who we met earlier, angry at the garbage he had to fish from the thermal features, was the greatest expert on geysers of his generation, in the park and perhaps in the world. He observed the thermal areas personally after the earthquake, and in 1975 wrote, with USGS geologist Donald White, a summary of what had happened:

During the first few days after the earthquake, a reconnaissance was made of most of the thermal features in the Firehole geyser basins. Early results of the survey revealed that at least 289 springs had erupted as geysers. Of these, 160 were springs with no previous record of eruption. Some previously obscure springs had erupted very powerfully, and large pieces of sinter were strewn about their craters.

The beautifully colored and limpid water of hundreds of springs had become light gray to muddy. An early count revealed that 590 springs had become turbid. During the first few days after the earthquake, most springs began to clear, but several years passed before clearing was generally complete.

During the night of the earthquake, all major geysers erupted that had been recently active, and some that had been dormant for many years were rejuvenated.

There were many other changes. New hot ground appeared, much of it easily spotted by the suddenly dying and dead trees. Bobby socks began to grow. New craters formed, sometimes explosively. The water temperature in the geyser basins went up, then, over a period of years, went back down again. Some geysers shut down and intervals changed. Many erupted more frequently—sometimes much, *much* more frequently—but some had their interval lengthen. Most famously, the eruptions of Old Faithful grew further apart. The interval increased again after a less powerful earthquake in 1983, when, less powerful or no, the interval rose quite a bit. Starting at an average of 69 to 70 minutes, it rose for four months after the 1983 quake, until it finally stabilized at 77 to 78 minutes. Here is the source of the common belief that Old Faithful is "broken" now, that it used to erupt every hour on the hour until the government . . . *broke* it somehow. It never erupted on the hour—it knows nothing of clocks—and it remains magnificently predictable.

Not just hot spring water was affected. The quake revealed an astounding level of connectedness in the water systems of the world. Geologists specifically looked at the levels of water in wells after the event, and those levels were affected as far away as Hawaii and Puerto Rico. In nearby Idaho, they fluctuated by a full ten feet.

Among the park geysers, the most amazing change was what happened—temporarily—to Sapphire Pool. This hot spring, at Biscuit Basin just up the road from Old Faithful, is one of the prettier in the whole park, giving a sense of what Morning Glory Pool might have once looked like (before it really *was* broken, by the general public tossing rubbish into it). It had small eruptions, domes of water six feet high, a common kind of eruption around the geyser basins, nothing special.

After the earthquake, Sapphire was one of those features that went mad, in a delightful way. As T. Scott Bryan explains in *The Geysers of Yellowstone*, "No spring in Yellowstone was more greatly affected by the 1959 earthquake than Sapphire. On the day after the shocks, the crater was filled with muddy water, constantly boiling with vigor. Four weeks later, Sapphire began having tremendous eruptions. Fully 125 feet high and almost equally wide, these eruptions were among the most powerful ever known in Yellowstone." It was a little like Excelsior in the 1880s and had a similar effect: the geyser blew itself apart.

The name "Biscuit Basin" came from Sapphire Pool especially and refers to the biscuit-shaped nodules that once lined its crater, and still do, a little. The giant eruptions only lasted a while. Bryan continues:

> The force of the play decreased, too, and by 1964 no eruptions were more than 20 feet high. Still, it wasn't until 1971 that Sapphire finally cleared all muddiness from its water, at just about the same time that all eruptive activity stopped. Only time will tell whether or not Sapphire will

ever again undergo major eruptions. There is plenty of evidence that the geyser damaged its plumbing system. Prior to 1959 the crater was circular and 15 feet in diameter; today it is oval and measures 18 by 30 feet. The explosive activity that enlarged the crater and destroyed the geyserite "biscuits" that gave the area its name also eroded substantial amounts of material from deep within the plumbing system.

It was all a great delight to the geyser fans. So there was a happy side to the whole affair. But . . .

But there was a much larger unhappy side. The Hebgen Lake earthquake did $11 million in damage, $2.6 million of it in the park. The larger sum, $11 million, would be $115 million today. Businesses were destroyed; an antique dealer in West Yellowstone looked at his shop, where everything was destroyed, and left—just disappeared. Twenty-eight people died. The number would have been much, much higher if— here at the height of the tourism season—the quake had struck in the middle of the day, with everyone on those roads, the ones that were buried under all that displaced earth.

Perhaps, then, we should worry more about earthquakes. No one has yet been killed by the Yellowstone supervolcano.

The Real Estate Is Hot in More Than One Way
And you are not going to like it.

We should not pass on from this look at the ground and water in Greater Yellowstone without noting some of the other really strange things. For instance, did you know there are places in the park where a compass does not work?

We are not talking about a digital compass, or the compass built into your phone. Electronic stuff is often not what you want for serious travel in the backcountry, and "serious travel" in rough country like this is travel anywhere out of sight of the roads. In the late afternoon, in deep valleys in the park, a GPS will start to get flaky because at that time the satellites are too close to the horizon for the kind of extreme terrain that appears with great regularity in the park. And here is a trick wilderness educators teaching a backcountry travel class have recourse to. The instructor holds up a paper map with a bullet hole in it. How much of the map, he asks the students, is still usable? They debate and settle on something like 98 percent. "Now," the instructor says, "how much of this one is still usable?" And he holds up an old GPS with a bullet hole in it.

Cell phones are worse because there are wide swaths of the park where they do not work at all.

So serious travelers of the backcountry carry, at least as a backup, an old-fashioned magnetic compass and a paper map (generally without a bullet hole). Serious travelers also know that this most ancient and reliable aid to navigation in mysterious territory may, in Yellowstone, go just as crazy as the thermal areas did after the earthquake.

A case in point. A scientist friend who worked with me on this book was searching, with a map and compass, for an obscure thermal area in the backcountry with another person experienced in the vagaries of off-trail travel in this place. They were narrowing their search but were having more trouble than they should have. A thermal feature will let you know where it is: there is, first, the steam. Then, as you approach the area, the ground ahead turns white, the trees thin and show stress, and there is of course that smell, that hydrogen sulfide smell that everyone thinks of as the smell of rotten eggs, and which in truth is simply the smell of Yellowstone (it grows on you).

"Where is it?" one of them asked.

"It should be over here," the other replied.

"That doesn't make any sense." They debated, and it became clear that they were not referring to the same Yellowstone. There was a fundamental disagreement about just where they were.

My friend looked, then, at his map and compass and got a surprise. In the English language, we use the compass as a metaphor for reliable guidance. We speak of "true north," of a good person having a "moral compass," of being "blown off course" in life, or, alternatively, being on "the right course."

As my friend watched, all that went out the window. He moved just a little, and the compass needle spun like a baseball bat in the hands of a batter chasing a fastball. He moved a lot, and the compass might as well have been drunk: "It was as though a strong magnet were nearby and the compass was pointing at it instead of the North Pole," he told me later, in an email. "If I moved quickly, then the compass would over-correct and spin all the way around. There were also apparently several of the 'strong magnets' because as I walked around within a 20 square yard area, the compass jumped and pointed at them in turn."

He was actually unsurprised. They were near the South Entrance, and just below the Pitchstone Plateau, a place where even such accomplished navigators as migratory birds get confused. Kurt Repanshek of *National Parks Traveler*, writing about Shoshone Lake, just north of the Pitchstone Plateau, noted how delightfully odd the bird life there can be; rare sightings are a fairly regular occurrence, perhaps because the birds have a hard time getting away. "What some birds struggle with once they arrive in the area is the underlying geology," Repanshek explained. He spoke to Terry McEneaney, at the time the park's staff ornithologist, about the matter:

"It screws up birds that are migrating," McEneaney said. "What happens is there is a lot of electromagnetic rock in that area. If you go south down onto the Pitchstone Plateau a compass will go crazy. Migrating birds, birds like pigeons, that are very sensitive to electromagnetic changes, we've had a number of birds that have been a little confused down there.

"Particularly homing pigeons. One time I can remember a homing pigeon that couldn't fly out of there. It just kept flying in circles."

The Pitchstone Plateau has another bizarre secret. It is radioactive.

This is a subject that almost attains urban legend status, or maybe exurban legend. When Yellowstone people get together, and this subject comes up, a member of the group may mention—almost in hushed tones—a study that some scientist guys did that found plants and animals so radioactive that. . . .

It gets vague, but the story pops up in respectable places. It turns up, for instance, in *Rising from the Plains,* the third volume in John McPhee's Pulitzer Prize–winning series *Annals of the Former World. Rising from the Plains* is about the geology of the Rocky Mountains. The star of the book is Wyoming geologist David Love, and at the time McPhee was writing—1986—there were still plans afoot to tap the geothermal resources of Greater Yellowstone for power plants. Love was concerned not just about the geysers, but about the outflow, and McPhee describes him pestering public officials at public meetings:

> Love, who has made a subspecialty of the medical effects of geology, had . . . asked what consideration was being given to radioactive water from geothermal wells, which would be released into the Snake River through Henrys Fork and carried a thousand miles downstream. After all, radioactive water was known from Crawfish Creek, Polecat Creek, and Huckleberry Hot Springs, not to mention the Pitchstone Plateau. On the Pitchstone Plateau were colonies of radioactive plants, and radioactive animals that had eaten the plants: gophers, mice, and squirrels with so much radium in them that their bodies could be placed on photographic paper and they would take their own pictures. A senator answered the question, saying, "No one has brought that up."

No, they would not have brought that up. Too bizarre. You may recall that Polecat Creek and Huckleberry Hot Springs are the places where people hot-pot illegally and where the brain-eating amoeba turned up, so there is another strike against them . . . or is it? When Yellowstone people get together and those radioactive plants and animals come up, no one ever seems to know whether the story is true or not. Here is where we seem to enter the realm of folklore.

But it *is* true. Scientists really did find plants and animals that fogged photographic paper. It was in fact one of the weirdest pieces of weird science ever to come from Greater Yellowstone.

The study was performed by two zoologists from the University of Wyoming, Kenneth Diem and Garth Kennington, in the early 1960s and reported at a conference of scientists working in the national parks in 1976. They had collected their specimens from various locations on the Pitchstone Plateau and just on the other side of the south boundary of Yellowstone National Park. The rumors were correct: they had collected small animals, specifically pocket gophers, a common species in the region. They also collected samples of the kinds of plants the gophers were eating. The collecting was not friendly: "Northern pocket gophers were trapped with 14 cm Macabee gopher burrow traps. Traps were checked hourly and captured specimens were immediately preserved in a dry ice freezing chest until placed in laboratory freezer facilities."

They then took "autoradiographs," the term for a self-administered X-ray. They took parts of the gophers—femurs and teeth—and laid them atop Kodak X-ray film for six weeks. They did the same with the plants the gophers were eating— mountain dandelions and yarrow—for eight months.

The results? They all glowed like the moon.

So, yes, the gophers were radioactive—not to a Chernobyl-style extreme, but they were picking up some kind of radioactive material from the plants, and the plants were drawing it up from the ground. Diem and Kennington were limited by the technology of the era, but they tried to find out what the material was and thought it might be uranium. They then let the matter lie for a few years, until they learned of an artesian well in Idaho that issued water originating in rock that was much the same as that on the Pitchstone Plateau. The water comes from a young rhyolite lava flow, and the rhyolite on the Pitchstone Plateau is among the youngest in the park. Diem and Kennington got their hands on some of the water and after testing it found in it radium, uranium, and thorium. If water could do so, this water might glow like their gophers.

Plants do not take up uranium, but they will absorb its decay products, including radium. They thought this fact might explain their earlier results, in which they thought they were seeing uranium in their little friends. Radium does accumulate in bones. They reached some of the same conclusions David Love had ("Lastly, beyond the Park's boundaries, geothermal power developers may need to be concerned about natural radiation problems where thermal waters are closely associated with rhyolite substrates"). They otherwise recommended future research that would really dig into the gophers ("Comparative histological studies of tissues from the respiratory tract, digestive tract, circulatory system, and skeleton of gophers on rhyolite flows and adjacent nonvolcanic substrates would be valuable"). No one ever took them up on it, and their study remains something of an orphan.

It still comes up in those conversations among park people, but the details are always imprecise. The little creatures that were discovered to fog film are sometimes mice, sometimes squirrels, sometimes chipmunks, and are rarely identified as precisely as the study's "northern pocket gopher (*Thomomys taipoides*)." Some years ago, the subject turned up in a conversation on the message board of GOSA, the Geyser Observation and Study Association. One of the geyser gazers, David Schwarz, had this to say: "Is there anything useful to conclude from this? Well, if it's true, don't eat the chipmunks. If you must eat the chipmunks, try to eat young ones that haven't had very long to concentrate radioisotopes. Regardless, like farmed fish (often contaminated with small amounts of heavy metals), don't eat them too often, and your prognosis will be indistinguishable from someone who has never tasted radioactive rodent."

It remains excellent advice.

The thermal water does have radium in it, in places. It will not hurt you, or the kids either (the heat is much, much more dangerous), but it is there. One of the early pieces of research that the US Geological Survey did in the park resulted in a 1909 report that was clear about what it found: "Radioactivity of the Thermal Waters of Yellowstone National Park." A pair of scientists, Herman Schlundt and Richard Moore, spent part of their summer sticking quaint-looking instruments into springs all over the park. They found radium, thorium, and uranium in many places, although later researchers figured out that the instruments were so quaint that a good deal of what Moore and Schlundt thought was radium was actually radon gas, the stuff you may have in your basement. It was revolutionary work in its way, though, because the thorium they found, originally and most abundantly at Norris, was the first to turn up in a hot spring in the United States ever.

Schlundt returned in the mid-1930s with a new collaborator, Gerald Breckenridge, and went over the park again, this time with "modern standard instruments." They found much the same sort of radioactive elements that they had before. In their report, while they concede that "the amount of radioactivity in the spring waters of the Park is low," they note that it is strikingly high over time. They measured radium flowing from the Boiling River (they knew it by an older name, Hot River), and found that, given the heavy discharge there, over the course of a year, the Boiling River discharges 90 milligrams, and if they counted radon and radium together, they got 33.9 grams of "radium equivalent," a fair amount of the element that is thought to have killed Marie Curie. Another blow against the park hot-potting tradition.

A fun fact about Herman Schlundt: he was a professor at the University of Missouri in Columbia and worked in a laboratory in Pickard Hall, an elegant old red brick building that is one of the landmarks on campus. His old laboratory, however, is so radioactive that the whole building was closed to the public in 2013, and in 2019, condemned, historic or no. As of 2022, what the school newspaper calls the "radioactive building" remained standing. The university is today trying to formulate a plan with the US Nuclear Regulatory Commission for safe demolition, a process that is expected to take many years.

Other researchers have since found radium, radon, and uranium in the park hot springs. The quantities are never large. Some years ago, the USGS announced that they had used the mineral zircon to date the magma chamber under the park, which worked because the zircon has uranium in it (the rate of radioactive decay gives them the age). The geologists may have been sorry they mentioned that. The British tabloid newspaper the *Daily Express* ran the story with the headline "Yellowstone volcano SHOCK: Scorching magma chamber is RADIOACTIVE, USGS scientists reveal." The first line of the story: "YELLOWSTONE volcano's terrifying magma chamber, deep beneath the supervolcano caldera, is full of radioactive molten rock, scientists have shockingly revealed." Whenever that supervolcano comes up in the news, you need to keep your grains of salt close at hand. Lots of them.

Radium and uranium are not the only scary chemical elements to turn up in the park. As one might guess, there are some amazing things in the Firehole River. That river has to be unique in the world. It flows around the Mallard Lake resurgent dome like a moat around a castle. All the water flowing out of

Excelsior Geyser crater (4,000 gallons a minute, and so well over 5 million gallons a day) falls right into the Firehole, and that is only one spring. The river, almost the whole thing, flows down the middle of the premier collection of thermal water in the world. All that cooking summons up, from the strange ground beneath, some strange elements. In the past, there was enough mercury to make the fish unsafe to eat in places (mercury, though, is more likely to turn up in the lake trout, since it bioaccumulates—fish that eat other fish, lots of them, are eating lots of small doses of mercury, and it adds up). There is ammonia and boron in the Firehole—quite a bit of boron, in fact. There is at least some chromium and selenium.

The one that freaks people out the most, however, and that does show up in the water regularly, is arsenic. It is certainly in the Firehole. The drinking water for Old Faithful comes from the Firehole River directly, although it is filtered and treated before it comes out of the tap. The government drinking water report for Old Faithful for 2021 found arsenic, the only contaminant it had to report, with this footnote: "While your drinking water meets EPA standards for arsenic, it does contain low levels of arsenic. EPA's standard balances the current understanding of arsenic's possible health effects against the costs of removing arsenic from drinking water. EPA continues to research the health effects of low levels of arsenic, which is a mineral known to cause cancer in humans at high concentrations and is linked to other health effects such as skin damage and circulatory problems." Still, does it matter when everyone in the park is drinking bottled water? The park otherwise has some of the cleanest water in North America, tens of millions of acre-feet of it, and the park concession companies haul in truck after truck full of . . . water.

Where arsenic is concerned, though, the Firehole is only a first runner-up. A big study published in 2022 in the *Journal of Volcanology and Geothermal Research* found arsenic . . . oh, all over the place. The arsenic is released when thermal water flows over the rhyolite lava found everywhere around the caldera, but the chemistry of the water makes a big difference: some springs have virtually none, but others are full of the stuff. Old Faithful Geyser, by the way, is one of the features that tends toward the "full" side, and the Upper, Midway, and Lower geyser basins are among the areas with the most arsenic. When water boils, as it often does in the thermal areas, the arsenic in the water does not leave it, which has a good and bad side for humans: the steam in thermal areas has no arsenic in it . . . but the boiling tends to concentrate the arsenic and pass it on down the drainage. Many of the rivers, in consequence, are well above the Environmental Protection Agency standard, some of them *far* above.

The USGS wrote a summary of the research in its column for the general public (*Caldera Chronicles*). The metric measurements are a nuisance, but these are scientists, after all. The Greek letter is a "*mu*," and the measure "µg/L" is micrograms per liter. Here, we should note that the EPA standard for arsenic in drinking water states that the stuff is dangerous at over 10 µg/L:

> What is the fate of arsenic in thermal waters? Most of the water discharged from Yellowstone's thermal features ultimately ends up in a nearby river. As a result, the arsenic concentrations in the main rivers draining Yellowstone are also elevated because very little arsenic is lost over long distances. By employing the same methods that are used to monitor Yellowstone's rivers for thermal input, the arsenic concentration and flux can also be quantified. Downstream from thermal areas, the summertime river arsenic concentrations are elevated in the Firehole River (~380 µg/L), Gibbon River (~140 µg/L), Madison River (~250 µg/L), Yellowstone River (20-30 µg/L), and Gardner River (~110 µg/L). The total arsenic flux from Yellowstone is also large (~180,000 kilograms/year), and arsenic is

transported several hundred kilometers downstream from Yellowstone. As a result, arsenic impacts downstream water resources, requiring additional treatment at some drinking water treatment plants. There are popular swim areas in Yellowstone, including the Firehole and Boiling River Swim Areas. To minimize the risk of illness from swimming and soaking in Yellowstone rivers, the National Park Service recommends that you avoid swallowing river water and any activities that cause water to enter your nose. If you submerge your head, wear nose plugs or hold your nose shut.

By way of contrast, that figure, 180,000 kilograms per year, would be about 200 US tons. Of arsenic. Since the Firehole Swimming Area is usually closed, and the Boiling River is out of commission permanently, the arsenic in the park is not going to hurt you . . . but goodness, there is a lot of it.

As we have noted, though, Yellowstone seems to have a limitless supply of weird ways to hurt you. Here is a mighty strange one: fluoride—the stuff in your toothpaste, that is. It is good for your teeth in small quantities. Too much of it destroys them.

This problem affects humans a good deal less than it does the park's wildlife. It was an ecologist at Montana State in Bozeman, Robert Garrott, who began to figure this out back in the early 2000s. He was working on another project, in the Firehole and Madison River valleys, when he noticed he was not seeing as many older elk as he saw elsewhere; here, the elk died by the time they were fifteen, while elsewhere in the park, they lived to their mid-twenties. He and the other researchers he was working with eventually zeroed in on fluoride and another, even more common thing in the area, silica. In the geyser basins, there is silica everywhere. The plants take up and accumulate fluoride and silica, and there is silica dust all over, too. Especially during hard winters, the elk cluster on the warm ground of thermal areas. They take up fluoride, and the result is what a doctor would call, if it were to happen in a human, "fluoride toxicosis"—fluoride poisoning, that is, which attacks their teeth and jawbones. The silica further abrades their teeth like sand. The result is a one-two punch that kills the elk early. The MSU newspaper reported the research in 2004:

> "In ungulates, tooth wear dictates longevity," Garrott said.
>
> The elk's teeth slowly wear away in irregular patterns over many years, Garrott said. The elk may seem fine for a while, but the fluoride eventually catches up with them.
>
> "It is only as they get older, say eight-plus years, that the wear progresses to the point that they are inefficient in eating," Garrott said. "They crop and chew food fine, but their teeth don't break plant tissues down well because of wear. This fluoride toxicosis results in early old age, or, in other words, a reduced life span."

So really, *really*, you should not drink the geyser water.

There are plenty of other surprises in the ground, some of them unpleasant, some of them intriguing, some of them just strange. There is antimony occurring with the arsenic; it is a metal that is at least as toxic as arsenic, and maybe more. There are gases, argon, neon, and a vanishingly rare kind of helium, helium-3, that is as old as the earth itself. Given that Soda Butte Creek, in the northeast part of Yellowstone National Park, flows past Cooke City before it enters the park, there will be at least some of what brought men to Cooke City in the first place: gold and silver. It is still present in the mountains above town in vast quantities. The bulk of it is in Henderson Mountain, just north of Cooke City, where an active mine was proposed in the 1990s and led to such an environmental controversy that the proposal was eventually defeated. The contents of the mountain are staying there, and that mountain, according to the USGS, "hosts identified resources of at least 2.3 million ounces of gold, 8.9 million ounces of silver, and 130 million pounds of copper." Some of the gold will have tumbled into Soda Butte Creek. That is why gold prospectors panned creeks: the gold is heavy, and therefore wants to come down.

All this makes it unsurprising that the real estate is hot—in the physicist's sense of "hot." Hot, like Professor Schlundt's laboratory is hot. Hot like Chernobyl is hot.

In a town like Gardiner, astride the north entrance, every house has a basement. Away from the tourist eyesores that line the highway, Gardiner is in many ways a rural Montana village, and an old one. In this part of the world, a basement is a given. It is also a given that the basement is radioactive. The air down there is full of radon. The locals often do not even bother to test it; they simply assume that it is there because the magma plume deep underground . . . just *does* things like that. Your cute little Gardiner VRBO, if it has a basement, is hot. Perhaps *any* Yellowstone VRBO, if it has a basement, is hot.

Living atop the world's largest volcano, people get in the habit of expecting natural phenomena that are dangerous, even right there in the home.

Standing Astride the Divide—Over and Over Again

One odd cause of congestion in the road traffic is a phenomenon that actually is not quite "natural." It is the signs the National Park Service has erected at key places, especially the large signs that mark otherwise invisible lines on the map. People stop and photograph themselves in front of the signs, and in places people have to wait in line just to get the sign to themselves. The really popular ones are at the entrances, of course, but there are others, including, in no less than three places, the Continental Divide.

Many visitors have never been anywhere near the Continental Divide and are not even sure what it is. It is an abstraction and a reality at the same time. On one side of the divide, water runs to the Pacific Ocean; on the other, it runs to the Atlantic (specifically the Gulf of Mexico). People speak of the divide as if it were a line, or a road, or the spine running down an animal's back because we need a comparison to understand this thing-that-is-not-quite-a-thing. When standing atop it, the division may be dramatic since it is often a high mountain ridge. It may, on the other hand, be barely noticeable. Nevertheless, it is the parting of the ways.

It runs all the way up and down the New World, through North, Central, and South America. In the south, it starts at the farthest tip of Tierra del Fuego, then runs north up the spine of the Andes—and notice that we are talking about "spines" and "running." On the ground, there is no spine, and nothing is running. It is strange that way. The divide runs through Panama, including the canal; that is why the canal needs those locks, to pick ships up and over the summit. At the level of the water, in the canal, the divide is 85 feet above sea level, and to the north, in Nicaragua, it reaches its lowest natural point, at 154 feet. From there, however, it begins to climb, and in the United States, it runs along the backbone of the Rocky Mountains (although not necessarily along its highest points). It continues to run along the Rockies in Canada and touches the ocean again, at last, at its northern terminus, at a point just south of the Arctic Circle. Somewhere—no one knows exactly—on a beach facing Siberia across the Bering Strait, it finishes its long run from a point not too far north of Antarctica.

Yellowstone is one of the places where the Continental Divide does not look like anything special, with one big exception. The South Entrance Road crosses the divide once, and the road from West Thumb to Old Faithful crosses it twice. This happens because the park sits astride the high point in the Rockies . . . but at the same time, it is mostly a high plateau. Only in places does it look like what we would expect from a divide—like Glacier National Park, for instance, which is all Alp-like peaks and ridgelines (the Continental Divide goes through Glacier National Park, too, and Glacier even sends water to Hudson Bay). Driving from the South Entrance to Old Faithful, that first crossing of the divide is just a spot in the trees with the big sign for people to photograph. The division between the two watersheds is here a kind of bump. Past West Thumb, there is a long climb, but the second crossing of the Continental Divide is again nothing dramatic.

The exception is that third crossing of the divide, although it is more dramatic coming the other way, from Old Faithful to West Thumb. The road climbs out of the Firehole River valley and, over eight miles, winds up and up until it reaches a high crossing called Craig Pass. Here is one of the strange places in the park. The divide is not a notch in the rocks; it is, in fact, that lake you are driving over. The road crosses it on a bridge. The lake, Isa Lake, which seems to always be covered by lily pads, has two outlets. It is almost the only lake in the world to send water to two different oceans, both the Atlantic and Pacific— but not the way it should. The east outlet drains to the Pacific (to the Lewis River, then the Snake, then the Columbia). The west outlet drains to the Atlantic (to the Firehole, the Madison, the Missouri, and the Mississippi). Looking at it, just standing there and looking at it, is a little headache-inducing. All sense of direction gets scrambled.

Isa Lake looks, at first, like the solution to an old mystery, but it is not. If you look at a map of the park and zoom in on the forest south of West Thumb, you may note a small body of water called Riddle Lake. If you look even more closely, you will see that it is drained by Solution Creek, but the solution was wrong. It got that name during the 1872 Hayden survey of the park. One of the surveyors, Rudolph Hering (no relation) bestowed the names. Another of the surveyors, Frank Bradley, explained why: "'Lake Riddle' is a fugitive name, which has been located at several places, but nowhere permanently. It is supposed to have been used originally to designate the mythical lake, among the mountains, whence, according to the hunters, water flowed to both oceans." By "hunters," he means what we would call mountain men. Bradley continued: "I have agreed to Mr. Hering's proposal to attach the name to the lake, which is directly upon the divide at a point where the waters of the two oceans start so nearly together, and thus to solve the insolvable 'riddle' of the 'two-ocean water.'"

Problem: Riddle Lake is not on the Continental Divide. As these things go, it is not especially close, either.

The story of the lake in the mountains that drains both ways goes back at least as far as Lewis and Clark and was handed down through generations of wandering trappers until it began to take on the patina of myth. Isa Lake is not the answer to the riddle, either, because it appears not to have even been discovered by European Americans until 1891. But there is a spot, to the south, a very strange spot indeed, that may solve more than just one riddle.

Well to the southwest of Riddle Lake, and due south of Yellowstone Lake, is Two Ocean Plateau. In the Bridger-Teton National Forest, just beyond the southern boundary of Yellowstone National Park, is Two Ocean Pass, from which the plateau takes its name. The pass was visited by the famous mountain man Jim Bridger during his early wanderings through the area, and the retired park historian Lee Whittlesey thinks the name "Two Ocean" may have originated with Bridger.

Here was the solution to the riddle because here an extraordinary thing happens. Here, a watercourse called North Two Ocean Creek flows down a hill and enters a low spot known locally as Parting of the Waters. The creek divides into Pacific Creek and Atlantic Creek, and the names explain themselves. The water mingles and splits, some going to one end of the continent, some going to the other. As *Caldera Chronicles* puts it, "It is 3,488 miles to the Atlantic Ocean and 1,353 miles to the Pacific Ocean, quite the 'choose your own adventure' for a water droplet."

The area became a mecca for early scientists and fish biologists, who traveled to the pass and studied it starting way back in the 1870s. The leading guide in the early decades of the park, Billy Hofer, took his high-profile clients to Two Ocean Pass. He took Theodore Roosevelt there, for instance. He also took Warren Delano, a name which may sound familiar: he was Franklin Delano Roosevelt's uncle. Hofer also made the trip with scientists of that era, and it may be that one of them began to entertain the possibility that here was an explanation of one of the park's great mysteries.

When the first explorers arrived, there was only one kind of trout in Yellowstone Lake, the cutthroat—but that kind of trout belongs in water that flows to the Pacific. How did they get into a lake that flows to the Atlantic? And how did any fish get into the lake at all, given the spectacular barriers in the Grand Canyon of the Yellowstone—that is, the two big waterfalls? This is the issue referred to at the start of this chapter. Modern geologists have looked into this question, too, and reached some conclusions. As *Caldera Chronicles* explains,

> [T]he high alpine meadow at Two Ocean Pass doesn't look like a pass at all. The profile of the pass is so low that when the meadow is flooded in the spring during a wet year, a fish can swim from the Pacific watershed into the Atlantic watershed! This is how the Yellowstone cutthroat trout . . . is believed to have originally colonized Yellowstone Lake following the end of the Pinedale glaciation about 14,000 years ago. As the glacial ice receded, fish were not able to swim upstream in the Yellowstone River all the way to Yellowstone Lake due to the natural barrier of the Lower Falls. Thus, cutthroat trout likely colonized the lake by

swimming across Two Ocean Pass and then were the only trout species living in the lake for thousands of years.

It was quite a jackpot for those first fish to make the trip over the Continental Divide and down the creeks leading to Yellowstone Lake. Here was one of the the really big bodies of water on the continent, and it was completely empty of fish. There was nothing here but food. Fish can still make the trip, and one concern is that nonnative fish can use the route to enter Yellowstone Lake, which does not need any more such trouble.

A parallel situation exists elsewhere in the park, far to the north. It involves another fish that lives here, one we have not mentioned yet. It is both impossibly beautiful and impossibly rare.

That fish is the westslope cutthroat trout. It is not "endangered," at least not yet, but it is headed that way. The fish was once abundant. Among other places, it could be found all along the west side of Yellowstone National Park, but it has been reduced to a fraction of its former range. In the upper Missouri River drainage, which includes the park and the Yellowstone River, that fraction is 5 percent. In Yellowstone, the westslope cutthroat has either been eliminated or has interbred with other fish to the point it no longer is what it was. The villains in the story are not the usual ones (overfishing and habitat destruction)—the fish are doing poorly, after all, in the world's first national park. The problem is that so many of Yellowstone's fish are nonnatives that have outcompeted the native fish nearly everywhere in the park. Do not blame the National Park Service; the serious fish stocking commenced decades before the Park Service even existed.

Native Yellowstone cutthroat have also been moved into waters where they do not belong. Along with other, even more thoroughly nonnative trout, they have interbred with the westslope cutthroat. The problem, then, is more subtle than fish floating belly-up. The westslope cutthroat is in danger of having its genes erased, while fish that look similar to the real thing are alive and healthy.

So the species appeared to be sunk. Then, back in the mid-2000s, a genetically pure population turned up in the distant northern corner of the park, in what used to be an unnamed tributary of Grayling Creek, now called Last Chance Creek. But it was not the last chance: in that same year, another genetically pure population was discovered in two small watercourses named Oxbow Creek and Geode Creek. Both had been empty of game fish when the park first became a park, and both were located far from the westslope cutthroat's usual home. How did they get here?

What had happened here was almost magical—no, scratch that. It was *entirely* magical. The fish got into this odd place when Geode Creek was stocked in 1922 with what the hatchery people recorded only as "cutthroat trout." The hatchery guy drove the truck to the place he had been told to drive it, dumped the fish, and never gave it a second thought. It was just another load of fish. The westslopes were forgotten.

They are not easy to get at. There is only one spot where Geode Creek is accessible from the main road, and it is a scramble even there. Finding that stretch requires both an old-fashioned map and a good GPS. Even then, when you park where the satellites tell you to, you will see no trace of a stream, only dense forest—but eventually, over the noise from the road, you might hear the rush of water, once the car engine is off and you step away from the pavement. This is how the fish had remained hidden: average park visitors, even serious anglers, would never find the stream unless they happened to have a flat tire right *here.*

The local name for Geode and Oxbow Creek together is the "Oxbow/Geode Complex." It is called that because the waters mingle in a swampy area upstream. Here, the fish were able to expand their range by swimming from Geode to Oxbow Creek. They thus made the switch in the same way that fish are thought to have gotten into Yellowstone Lake by swimming over Two Ocean Pass. In both places, it would have been easier during a wet year, but they had time.

Still more magic was involved. Given a chance and the water to do it in, fish expand into every environment they can. Geode Creek empties into the Yellowstone, which is full of nonnative fish. The nonnatives would have interbred with the westslope cutthroats, and for that matter, the creek would never have been fishless back in 1922 anyway, when the hatchery truck came by—but for that magic. Downstream from the road is a cascade that makes it impossible for fish to migrate up out of the Yellowstone River.

There was one last bit of magic: the lower part of Oxbow Creek is blocked, too. The two creeks together made a secret Shangri-La where the westslope cutthroats were able to hide out for most of the twentieth century, safe from the genetic ravages all around them.

Can fish swim through a marsh? And why would they want to? But fish do that. Every angler has had the experience of watching a really big fish get excited and chase a lure right up to the angler's feet, thrashing through water a fraction of its height, then maybe changing its mind and thrashing just as fast back into more comfortable water. Seeing it happen, for the angler, is . . . *exciting*. Watch, also, films of salmon when they get up into the headwaters of their spawning stream, where they may have to power their way over gravel bars with hardly any water to do it in.

A spectacle that is fun to watch is the Yellowstone cutthroat trout that inhabit Pebble Creek, which flows through an isolated and dazzling valley in the backcountry off the Northeast Entrance Road. A trail follows the creek, crossing and recrossing it repeatedly, and when a hiker's feet disturb the cutthroat, they explode up and downstream. If their alarm is great enough, they will blast through water that may be less than an inch deep, creating their own whitewater as they go.

To adapt the famous line from *Jurassic Park*, life finds a way. Yellowstone fish have found a way, even when they had no idea which way they were going . . . until suddenly, they found themselves in an aquatic paradise.

7

THE DEPARTED

The grave of Joseph Trischman in the Fort Yellowstone Army Cemetery. The splotches are lichen, common on the older graves here. SCOTT HERRING

7

You may not think about it or even imagine it as a possibility, but there are graves scattered all over Yellowstone National Park. They pop up, sometimes by surprise, and it is always a disturbing experience when it happens. You could even call it "haunting."

Why would graves be a surprise? Probably because Yellowstone is a vacation destination. We do not expect graves on the beach at Daytona, or in the casino at Vegas, or in the rides at Disneyland. People, however, live in Yellowstone. Everything humans do, they do there, except that babies tend to be delivered at the hospital in Bozeman or Jackson Hole. Plenty of people have died in the park, and in the past, back when moving human remains around was more of a trial than it is now, they were buried there. There are, in fact, whole cemeteries.

(And besides, people scatter the ashes of cremated loved ones at Disneyland all the time, to the extent that it is something of a problem for the people who work there. This is a fairly open secret in Southern California. "Current and former custodians at Disney parks say identifying and vacuuming up human ashes is a signature and secret part of working at the Happiest Place on Earth," the *Wall Street Journal* reported in 2018. "Human ashes have been spread in flower beds, on bushes and on Magic Kingdom lawns; outside the park gates and during fireworks displays; on Pirates of the Caribbean and in the moat underneath the flying elephants of the Dumbo ride. Most frequently of all, according to custodians and park workers, they've been dispersed throughout the Haunted Mansion, the 49-year-old attraction featuring an eerie old estate full of imaginary ghosts. 'The Haunted Mansion probably has so much human ashes in it that it's not even funny,' said one Disneyland custodian." People scatter ashes at Las Vegas casinos, too. A favorite spot appears to be the fountains at the Bellagio.)

There are at least three cemeteries inside the park. One, perhaps the creepiest, is the one you are most likely to stumble upon completely by surprise. Atop a windswept hill in the sagebrush above Mammoth is a cluster of fourteen graves known informally as Kite Hill, and officially as the Mammoth Civilian Cemetery. The first funeral here took place in 1883, when the first big hotel was under construction in the village below. Only one monument is left there, and while many of the graves are easy to spot from the rocks that surround them, many have faded away. Five of the graves have known occupants. We have the names of five more, but not which graves they occupy. Four are just a mystery. With its forlorn and abandoned quality, amid the sagebrush desert, the cemetery is a fit place for morbid thoughts.

Back down the hill and a brief drive south, on the road to Norris, is the turnout for the corrals run by the hotel concessioner. The corrals are closed now, but not the big parking area on the road, where people still stop. A traditional thing to have happen there is this: a traveler gets impatient with the line at the vault toilet, dodges off toward the trees, and gets a shock. Here is the Fort Yellowstone Army Cemetery, where soldiers from the fort, civilian employees of the army, and their families were buried. It was in use between 1888 and 1957, although the army moved a number of the bodies to the cemetery at the Little Bighorn Battlefield in 1917, a year after the army handed over management of the park to the new National Park Service. Like the civilian cemetery up the hill from the hotel, it has an abandoned feel; there is more water here, so it is also a bit overgrown. Few people are aware it is here, and it, too, is a fit place for morbid thoughts. You will have them by yourself. No one visits.

The third cemetery is Tinker's Hill, just outside Gardiner. If you want to see a real-life frontier cemetery, this is the place, a little fenced reserve in which the native sagebrush and cactus does well. As is the case with many other burial grounds around the park, it exists in a kind of limbo. The land all around is part of that section of the park that we visited earlier, where homesteaders lived until the government bought the area and added it to Yellowstone National Park. The cemetery was managed by the Eagles' Club in Gardiner until the club disbanded (although their hall still exists, in Gardiner on Main Street, where you can still see the rather handsome eagle sculptures out front). A great many graves were identified by wooden monuments that have long since weathered into nonexistence, so there are at least fifty unmarked graves and maybe as many as seventy-seven. More substantial stone monuments, some dating back into the 1880s, are still there.

(My source for much of this is, of course, Lee Whittlesey's book *Death in Yellowstone: Accidents and Foolhardiness in the First National Park*, which leaves no stone unturned.)

We will revisit all these cemeteries in the rest of this chapter, and the graves of others who died here. These graves often exist in lonely isolation, forgotten and marked only by the stones that were commonly piled on frontier interments to keep the wolves away. The spirits will not reject our company.

The Secret at Fishing Bridge

Above, I wrote "at least three cemeteries" because a good deal depends on how one defines "cemetery." Very few people are even aware that there is a secret burial place at Fishing Bridge. How it got there is a long and tangled story, with what may be described as a happy—or at least satisfactory—ending.

It started when workers at Fishing Bridge dug up, by chance, something no one had ever seen in the park, and that has rarely been seen since. As is normal in such situations, they had no idea what they had found.

Many years later, in 1948, the park's chief naturalist during that era, David Condon, recorded what had happened for *Yellowstone Nature Notes*, the in-house newsletter for the park naturalists. *Nature Notes* was, during that time, charmingly primitive, with hand-drawn line art and news articles that were set on a typewriter, the whole then mimeographed for distribution among the park staff. "AMERICAN INDIAN BURIAL GIVING EVIDENCE OF ANTIQUITY DISCOVERED IN YELLOWSTONE NATIONAL PARK," it announced, although the discovery had occurred a long time earlier. Condon's description of what happened reveals how little anyone knew about the subject, and what a surprise it all was (and he was the Chief Park Naturalist):

> That the Indians of the west utilized Yellowstone National Park probably hundreds of years ago was brought to light when the grave of an American Indian was opened on August 27, 1941, by Mr. Alex Palmquist, a laborer who found the burial site directly in the path of a sewer trench which he was digging. Unfortunately, the major portion of the skeletal remains were removed from the trench before the incident was reported to authorities who might have secured more accurate information had they been able to remove them from their resting place.
>
> This find is considered to have definite significance for Yellowstone. It is in all probability the first Indian burial found in the Yellowstone National Park; and from the artifacts, the stratigraphy of the grave, and other evidence the burial is not of recent date.

No, indeed: it was not, although he was correct that it was the first native burial ever found in the park. Yellowstone is, in general, not kind to bones. The high Montana plains to the northeast are famous for their dinosaur fossils, and people sometimes wonder why there are none in the park. First, older fossils, like those of dinosaurs, would have been atomized in the caldera eruptions, and even younger bones do not last. The volcanic soil dissolves them.

Yet here he was, lying in his grave at Fishing Bridge: a man of the prehistoric past. The grave had turned up among the cabins, in what is today the big open area behind the store and gas station, the cabins having since been removed. Condon described what he had found, reconstructing the grave to the best of his ability (complete with that hand-drawn graphic art). He could tell the grave was old because he found a continuous layer of charcoal a half-inch deep all around the area and extending over the grave itself, the remains of a 1988-style fire that would have wiped out the surrounding forest. The trees here were old, with no sign of fire anywhere, and another four inches of soil had accumulated atop the charcoal, so the man had been lying there a long time. Over the grave, stones had been placed, of a sort that had to have been carried from elsewhere. Condon found what anthropologists call grave goods, finished tools left inside a burial, 105 of them in all, including arrowheads, a spearpoint, a knife, and a drill. He also found the remains of two dogs.

Condon did what he could, but no one would mistake this seven-page report for a professional analysis. Why he waited so long to tell the story is not clear, although we need not see anything sinister in it. Surely, it had to do with the nature of the Park Service during that era. There had, in the 1940s, never been any professional archaeological survey of the park; the first formal survey was done by a graduate student nearly two decades after the sewer workers found that grave. He wrote it up as his master's thesis, and think about that: the first survey was done by a guy whose training, as an archeologist—was the survey itself. It was on-the-job training. There was no archaeologist on staff in 1941. What the rangers knew about the prehistoric native residents of the park they had picked up on their own.

A common claim today is that they suppressed the memory of the natives out of sheer meanness. They did not. It was just not their job to spend the summer digging on hands and knees with a trowel and brush, and they had not been trained in the techniques anyway (also—the fictional Indiana Jones was an archaeologist of this era, and would you necessarily want him investigating native life in the park, with his bullwhip and maybe dynamite?). Condon worked in Yellowstone a long time, and later he helped one of his rangers, Wayne Repogle, reconstruct the route the Bannock tribe followed on its annual bison hunt, which led the hunters across the park. We know today that Repogle got parts of the route wrong, but he was hardly incompetent: he knew very well how to recognize a spot where ancient native people had spent time, and Condon was the one who wanted him looking for them. They had not suppressed their memory.

But the Fishing Bridge area itself was not done with its surprises.

On July 24, 1956, it happened again. An operator working for the Studer Construction Company (it still exists, doing paving work in Billings, Montana) was running a backhoe, digging a trench for a water line, in the campground this time, when the bucket suddenly turned up bones. The machine scattered them so badly that no grave goods turned up at all. They did find a dog that had been buried with the human skeleton. No investigation was even possible, though, and the only record from that time is a mention in the superintendent's routine monthly report to the director of the Park Service for July 1956. That was all.

The bones went the way of the Lost Ark: that is, they went into government storage, and were mostly forgotten.

They were examined in 1982 by an archaeologist who was laboring under the considerable handicap that he had the two events and locations confused. We only learned more about these people when the Native American Graves Protection and Repatriation Act became federal law in 1990. It mandated the return, for reburial, of native human remains, no matter how old they are, stating that such remains "must at all times be treated with dignity and respect," which, heaven knows, the Fishing Bridge remains had not. One requirement of the law was that federal agencies with such remains in their possession make a thorough inventory of them. Now, at last, it was possible to learn something.

The grave goods went to a Park Service archaeologist. The bones were examined by a pair of anthropologists, Patrick Willey and Patrick Key, who took them to California State University, Chico, and there at last examined the bones using the full range of modern techniques—at least for the date they were working, 1992. Today's sophisticated DNA analysis was not available to them, which was an issue because one of the reasons for the examination was determining to which present-day tribe these ancient people belonged.

They did what they could, which was a great deal. The bones from 1941, which had come to be called the Condon burial, after the Chief Naturalist who saved them, had been rudely treated. The acidic soil and the cycle of the seasons had weathered them, and the shovels of the laborers who dug them up had covered them in divots. They would have decayed even further, but some unknown person had coated them heavily with preservative. Willey and Key thought it was polyvinyl acetate—that is, Elmer's glue. They did not remove it because they were convinced the bones would be completely destroyed if they tried.

The language is somewhat dense—"The supraorbital torus, nasal indentation, mastoid process, nuchal area, cranial contour, cranial discriminant function, sciatic notch, preauricular area, auricular shape, and femur head diameter and midshaft circumferences are masculine"—but can be penetrated, given patience. Condon had been correct: it was a man, between thirty-five and forty-five when he died—pretty close to Condon's original estimate. He was not imposing, by our standards. He had degenerative joint disease of the spine and neck and must have had stiffness and pain. He favored one side of his back, and was getting a little crooked, although he never habitually lifted heavy weights. He was small by our standards, at five feet four inches tall. Condon had thought he was almost six inches taller—but Condon was not a physical anthropologist with a university laboratory and x-ray machines.

Who was this man? On this point, too, Willey and Key were able to shed some light, and it is remarkable what forensic anthropologists can work out from wear and subtle injuries to the bone tissue. The man was right-handed. He squatted regularly, as is normal in a society without chairs. The older speculation about him, which Willey and Key were supposed to either confirm or disprove, does sound odd. He had a flat nose and an upper jaw that jutted out in a way that was "extreme." For this reason, older reports had called him "negroid," but Willey and Key were able to point out that prehistoric native people in Wyoming looked like that, too. Taking everything into account, they declared that "the specimen is an American Indian." They even found the kind of flattening of the skull that indicated he had been tied in a cradleboard as an infant, a practice among plenty of North American tribes before the Europeans arrived. In a separate analysis of the grave goods, archaeologists reached the conclusion that the man belonged to what they call the Late Prehistoric period, a phase of Native American history that lasted from 1,800 to 150 years ago—not too precise but better than nothing. One of the earlier investigations had concluded he had been in the ground about a thousand years.

Willey and Key then moved on to the 1956 skeleton from the campground, who had even more of a tale to tell.

It was a woman, between forty and sixty when she died. She was covered in Elmer's glue, same as the man, and would have fallen apart otherwise. The Elmer's was something of a handicap to the investigators, but still, she immediately surrendered a secret: in her grave, she was not alone.

Among her bones, Willey and Key found a single rib from an infant.

They could not do much with it, and the real problem was that the gravesite had been chopped to pieces by the backhoe bucket. They continued with the woman. She was five feet tall, exactly—not five-foot-something, just five feet. The skull had almost all the features found in Native Americans. When they moved on to her general health, she began to come back to life—a painful, difficult, revealing life.

Her dental health, Willey and Key found, was "poor," which was something of an understatement. She had no less than six active abscesses among her teeth when she died, and one of the molars had rotted all the way out. The depression in the bone above the teeth called the canine fossa was deeper on one side than the other, and they thought the cause was the abscesses: the bacteria in one of them had gotten into her left sinus and gone on a rampage there, too.

It got worse. The problems she suffered had begun at an early age. X-rays of the long bones of her arms and legs showed the effect of delayed growth in childhood, for some cause they could not work out. Her skull was covered with what doctors call lytic lesions, four of them, one of them a triangle-shaped depression over two inches across, quite large as such damage goes. Willey and Key found that none of their own explanations were entirely convincing, although all are equally horrifying: she might have had a widely metastatic cancer, or she might have been scalped in a war with an enemy tribe. Yes, they scalped women, and yes, the victims often survived—having your scalp cut off is not inherently deadly (people who have survived say the scalp makes a *pop!* when it comes off). She might also have had a severe birth defect, or a fungal infection, or terminal syphilis. None of these causes entirely fit what they were seeing. However, she also had eight lytic lesions on her pelvis. The largest had been there long enough to permit bony buildup around the damage. A metastatic cancer made sense, with the lesions resulting from metastases originating in yet another place, somewhere in the soft tissue that was gone now—although it seems as if it should have killed her more quickly, because if it was cancer, it was anything but benign.

But she was tough. Willey and Key could not entirely explain the lesions, but the rest was clear. She had had children. She had osteoarthritis of the spine and neck. It was a serious matter. One side of her jawbone was starting to break down. Both fibulae, the long bones in the calf, were bowed, really dramatically bowed, although some of this change may have happened while she was in the ground.

Based on the bones alone, Willey and Key could not say what tribe she belonged to, or the skeleton of the man whose remains Condon had rescued in 1941, but other factors point to the Shoshone, one of the groups that was in the park when the first white explorers arrived (the Sheepeaters, as we saw, were Shoshone). Especially before horses arrived on the continent, they buried their dead with dogs, which was not that common. The Crow, another Yellowstone tribe, did so too, but both the 1941 and 1956 skeletons were strikingly short, which does not fit the Crow quite as well. Genetic testing could have resolved the issue, but maybe it was not necessary. It looks like the two were the many-times-great grandparents of today's Shoshone.

This brings us to the secret burial place at Fishing Bridge.

Only a select few in the Park Service know where it is, along with a few members of the Shoshone tribe who participated in the final act for their two ancestors. In 2006, disposition of the remains was placed in the hands of the tribe, specifically members of the Eastern Shoshone from the Wind River Indian Reservation in Wyoming, and the Shoshone Bannock tribes, who live on the Fort Hall reservation in Idaho (summer traffic headed to Yellowstone from the south flows through both places like a steel river). The annual report for 2006 of the Yellowstone Center for Resources, the Park Service office that was placed in charge of this unusual affair, gave the only, very brief account of how it ended: "The tribes requested that the remains be re-interred near where they were exhumed. In October, ethnography and law enforcement staff facilitated the tribes' re-interment of their ancestors' remains. The tribes were grateful for the assistance from the staff and the respect shown by the National Park Service." Indeed, federal law or no, the NPS had bent over backward.

There they lie today, somewhere around Fishing Bridge: our first true Yellowstone people, returned to our oldest Yellowstone burial ground.

There is a lesson we can take from their story, and specifically that of the woman, although the lesson is not easy to see at first. The reports are bare and scientific. Willey and Key are interested only in the "osteological evidence"—the bones, that is. No one would have been happy if they had gotten creative. It is the same for everyone else who worked on the burials, going all the way back to Condon. What is revealing about her story is not in fact in any formal report. It can be seen, though, between the lines, in the analysis of her remains.

One fact that it reveals about her is, in truth, obvious: it reveals that she was a wreck. But it can transmit to us only what was written into those bones and was still there to be read centuries after she died and was buried in the caustic Yellowstone soil, there also to be subject to the other brutal Yellowstone elements, and finally to the tender mercies of the twentieth century: the construction guys, the backhoe bucket, the Elmer's glue, the decades of storage. If we had the rest of her, of course we would know more—but we can be sure it would be a tale of physical woe. The eight lesions on her pelvis, and the others on her skull, especially that big triangular patch strip-mined from the top of her cranium, tell us that something was drastically wrong.

We do not even know what killed her. Something else went wrong, fatally wrong, and left no sign of its passage in the skeleton. It was therefore likely not sudden and violent. Enough of her survived that violence would have left some sign. It was, instead, another health catastrophe.

Furthermore, whatever was wrong enough to have caused those lesions cannot have failed to be painfully wrong as well. That is the main theme of the various tales told by her remains. The abscesses in her teeth were painful. The infection that may have wandered up into her sinus was painful. The osteoarthritis in her spine was painful. The similar degeneration in her neck was painful. And whatever caused all those lesions on her pelvis and skull must have been epically painful. Compared to all that, childbirth might not have seemed all that bad.

She was not, by our standards, old, but the decades she lived had been rugged ones. Her people did not have horses yet. One reason she and the man from the Condon burial were interred with dogs was not to insult the people, but to honor the dogs, on whom the Shoshone depended for everything horses would eventually do. Anthropologists Peter Nabokov and Lawrence Loendorf call the Fishing Bridge burials "archaeological evidence that the bond between Yellowstone National Park's Indians and their dogs was intended to continue even into the afterlife." Her people walked everywhere, and while the dogs carried much of what they needed, the humans carried the rest.

They lived a purely wild life, eating what they could find. Anyone who has tried doing that in the backcountry in Yellowstone can report on how difficult it is; a major challenge every single day was to find food with more calories in it than you expended finding the food. Obesity was not a big problem. Shelter and tools were what you could create out of the natural environment, and while they were great craftsmen—the tools buried in the Condon grave are testimony to that skill—the environment was what it was. They did what they could with what they had. They softened animal hides, for instance, by chewing them. They had an advantage in some of the things they did not have, and that we do: heroin, methamphetamine, cocaine, alcohol. Because they did not eat refined sugar, their dental health was famously good—but that boon missed the woman in the grave, whose teeth were a travesty.

And so she suffered.

The tribes of this part of North America did not really have painkillers. They chewed willow bark for pain, which has a chemical in it that is today used to synthesize aspirin. There were, here and there around North America, the same kind of drugs (datura, peyote, mushrooms, and so on) that people get stoned on today, but they are mostly absent from the high, cold plateau of Yellowstone. Native healthcare was mainly spiritual. "Herbs, manipulative therapies, ceremonies, and prayer are used in various combinations to prevent and treat illness," an article in *The Journal for Nurse Practitioners* explains, outlining what one would in general have found among the tribes of North America at the time of Columbus. "For thousands of years, traditional indigenous medicine has been used to promote health and wellbeing for millions of Native people who once inhabited this continent. Native diets, ceremonies that greet the seasons and the harvests, and the use of native plants for healing purposes" were their ways of achieving the overall goal: "to promote health by living in harmony with the earth." Americans and Europeans love that kind of thing—but imagine using that to treat metastatic cancer that was lodged widely in the bones, or whatever it was that created those scars. It may have been something worse.

And so she suffered. Yet somehow, she made it to what, given her condition, we should really regard as an advanced age, perhaps as much as sixty years. It is, however, not such a mystery how she made it that far. We know how it happened. It happened because she belonged to a society that supported her.

She ate, even when she could not, by her own exertions, gather the calories she needed to keep going. She had shelter and a fire and clothing when her own exertions failed there, too. She would have died much, much younger if she had not had that support, especially given where they all lived: on a frigid plateau near the top of the continent. Aside from the problems with growth early in life, one thing Willey and Key did not find was evidence of malnutrition.

When her heart finally failed, they put her in the ground with one of their dogs and a child, on the peninsula between the great lake and the great river. They took care of her even then.

We know all that, and one more thing about her:

She was loved.

The Western Way of Death

We have romantic ideas about life in the Old West. Never do we pause to imagine what it was like to go to an Old West dentist.

It is unlikely this state of affairs will ever change. The Wild West has had a tremendous vogue in entertainment that has gone on decade after decade. It started with dime novels and Wild West shows that were wildly popular when the cowboys and Indians were still chasing each other around out west and continued through decade after decade of film and television. The vogue seemed to at last burn out in the later 1960s, but then one of the most popular films of the decade ended up being *Butch Cassidy and the Sundance Kid*. Nor was there any improvement in "realism" (did the real Sundance actually look as good as Robert Redford did in 1969? Did his hair look like that?). Nor would there be, through films and TV shows good and bad: *Heaven's Gate*, the third *Back to the Future*, *Wild Wild West*, *The Lone Ranger* (twice), *Westworld*, and for that matter, Kevin Costner's hit series *Yellowstone*, along with hundreds in between. We want our West romantic, not honest.

(Locals around Yellowstone get a kick out of *Yellowstone*, by the way. The people on the ranch use a helicopter to commute to Bozeman, for goodness' sake. Given where the fictional ranch is located, Bozeman is a really easy drive—by pickup truck or limousine both.)

The graves of Yellowstone are actually a good tutorial in what the Old West was really like. Their stories can be grim once you learn them. Probably without exception, people who really know Yellowstone would give anything to experience it in the deep past, to take a time machine back and ride, perhaps, with one of the early exploration expeditions. However, having made the ride, only a few of us would volunteer to stay permanently. Life was too rugged.

Just look at what killed these people.

Consider what happened to Fannie Fitzgerald, who is buried in the Tinker's Hill cemetery outside Gardiner. Fannie's gravestone is the oldest in the cemetery. She died at twenty-two, on July 11, 1888. When she died, she had just given birth to her son David, and what killed her was childbed fever. The more formal name, in her era, was puerperal fever (from the Latin for "childbirth"); doctors today call it a postpartum infection. It happened all the time, and the cause was simply dirty conditions. If, while giving birth, a woman was exposed to contaminated instruments, bedding, or for that matter a contaminated doctor, a raging infection could follow, and without antibiotics to fight it or even some idea of what might be causing it, women died after giving birth—ironically, more often in the Early Modern world than, say, the Middle Ages because women started giving birth in hospitals, which were, originally, filthy. Puerperal fever played a big role in medical science growing out of its early barbarism. Famously, the Hungarian physician Ignaz Semmelweis noticed that there seemed to be some connection between cadavers and infection. Incredibly, doctors at his hospital examined patients and delivered babies after cutting up dead bodies. When he made them wash their hands first, the death rate from puerperal fever, among other things, collapsed. He blamed "cadaverous particles" on those filthy hands, but the idea did not catch on right away anyway. Fannie Fitzgerald died more than forty years later, but the idea was nowhere near reaching rural Montana, and who knows how dirty the room was when she gave birth?

Nearby is the grave of the son she gave birth to, David, who died on July 26, 1888, just fifteen days later. We do not know what killed him exactly, but children died then. Babies died routinely. Medical science was what it was, and Gardiner was, in that era, truly the middle of nowhere. Heartbreakingly, David's gravestone includes, as its only decoration, a sculpted lamb with its legs resting under its body, a common way for grieving parents to memorialize their child.

Cemeteries like Gardiner's are filled with children, as is the Fort Yellowstone Army Cemetery. Of those who remain buried there, close to half are children. A visit to the place can be awful that way. In the cemetery, we find "Sarah Clark, infant child of E. W. Clark," "Floyd M. Wheate, infant child," "Don Wales, child of F. E. Wales," who died of "exhaustion," "Ralph David Korn, son of Adam Korn, Sergeant 1st Class," who died of scarlet fever, "Baby Ellis," "unknown baby," and so on.

Elsewhere in the area, we find the same tales of tragedy. Take the cemetery in Aldridge, for instance, the coal mining town we visited earlier in this book. Doris Whithorn, the old-time local historian who wrote about Aldridge, has whole chapters full of people dying horribly, in ways we can normally avoid today. "In the spring of 1900," she writes, "the coal camps were visited by the scourge of contagious disease, as frequently happened in that day." What is striking is the way the patients were treated, just as a matter of course. A "pesthouse," for instance, is a word that is gone from the language. It was a spare building where people with infectious diseases were locked up (*pest* and *pestilence* come from the same root):

> During the latter part of January Frank Robinson was taken with the smallpox at Horr. He was confined in an old tool

house on the mountain and later removed to a pesthouse that had been fitted up near the racetrack at Horr. . . . In April there was another case of smallpox at Horr which caused considerable alarm. This time the victim, Will Davis . . . was taken to Livingston to be confined in a county pesthouse for treatment. . . . He was transferred in a common boxcar and the county had to pay $30, or at the rate of 15 fares, for hauling him to Livingston. The county authorities were said to deserve special credit, as they thereby obviated considerable expense for the maintenance of more than one pesthouse.

In November 1902 Harry, the 10-year-old son of the Thomas Sidebothams, died of diphtheria. Several members of the family were afflicted and fear of contagion kept many sympathetic friends away.

Imagine being sick with a disease that has a terrifyingly high fatality rate and enduring its worst ravages while locked up in a toolshed on the side of a mountain in the Northern Rockies in January (Aldridge was at sixty-four hundred feet above sea level).

It was pretty common to be killed by horses, those gentle, sweet creatures who preteen girls get hung up on. They killed people all the time. What may be the loneliest grave in the park is on a bench above the Yellowstone River and the Old Yellowstone Trail, near the point at which the road crosses Reese Creek and thereby leaves the park (Guru Ma's house is just ahead). On the bench, amid the cactus and sagebrush and rattlesnakes—prairie rattlesnakes use a den nearby—is a pile of rocks. There are plenty of rocks out there, but these are . . . not natural. They have certainly been there a long time: they are splotched with lichen and have that relaxed look that shows they are settling into the earth. They stretch out a full six feet but are as wide apart as a man's shoulders. It is, of course, a grave.

It shows up on maps but was long a mystery. Even the professional archaeologists called in by the NPS to survey the area were perplexed. As often, Lee Whittlesey figured it out, with help from his mentor, the eminent park historian Aubrey Haines. The story, bare though it is, was handed down by word of mouth from one generation of park rangers to the next. It is the grave of a cowboy who was thrown from a bucking horse and buried by his friends here, near the house belonging to their employer, the Reese family. It happened in 1905.

The house is gone now, along with most other easily visible traces of the life lived here for decades. This is one of the parts of the park that were homesteaded. Reese Creek got its name from the Reese family. The traditional life of the old West played out here: the family had cattle, and furls of barbed wire, also covered in lichen, are stashed around the area. The traditional death of the old West happened here, too, or at least one kind of the many.

The cowboy's name was Corwin: that is almost all we know about him. He got up one morning, went to work on the ranch—and died. His work kept him on horseback, and this time his horse got the better of him. His friends planted him in the ground, another part of their workday too, and here he has lain ever since. The ranch did not, of course, have a time punch clock. Its employees had a different way of punching out.

The view from the grave is wonderful. One wonders if his friends planned it that way.

Horses were of course the main way of getting around the park for decades. The soldiers at Fort Yellowstone were cavalrymen. The trains delivered the tourists to stations where they climbed aboard horse-drawn stagecoaches. Those who could afford it hired a guide and toured the park at the head of a pack train. There were even some "Jingle Bells"–style horse-drawn sleighs in the winter. Given the size and power of the animals, it is unsurprising that, among those thousands and thousands of people who toured the park in the era of the horse, some would come to grief.

Whittlesey, in *Death in Yellowstone*, has a whole chapter devoted to the topic. He found records of nine deaths by horse, four by stagecoach, and a lucky thirteen by wagon. "Horses, of course, had to be dealt with carefully," he explains, continuing:

> Incidents, often called "runaways," were fairly common, as auto accidents are today. Stagecoach companies usually reported up to four stage wrecks per year, 1880-1916. Huntley Child, who grew up in Yellowstone to eventually manage the Yellowstone Park Transportation Company, remembered many years later that during his tenure the company experienced "about one accident per year." Indeed, statistics in 1909 indicated that there were thirty fatalities for every one hundred million horse-traveled miles in the United States, compared to about one-sixth that today for automobiles. The park stagecoach companies tended to be close-mouthed about stage wrecks because few or none of them carried liability insurance. Thus, they often attempted to "settle" quickly with an injured passenger. Causes of accidents tended to be inept drivers, sudden wild flights of teams, mechanical failures of equipment, or intoxication.

Read together, the accounts are a record of relentless mayhem. In the summer of 1891, a soldier at Fort Yellowstone was killed instantly when his horse kicked him in the stomach. In 1894, an officer left Gardiner and never made it to the fort. One of the army scouts found him on the road, unconscious; he had apparently been thrown, then dragged when his foot got stuck in a stirrup, although we have to speculate about that, because he died without regaining consciousness. In 1895, W. A. Babcock, president of the Babcock Company of Cleveland, was in a large party near Slough Creek; when the group entered a narrow pass with a steep drop on one side, the guides told everyone to dismount and walk. Babcock stayed in the saddle. The horse slipped and plummeted forty feet downward, and when it hit the earth again, Babcock was underneath, and was crushed.

And so it went. In 1893, a private from the fort, while drunk, nearly collided with a bicycle on a park road. The bicyclist leapt to one side, and when the soldier tried to jump over the bicycle, the horse's hooves got tangled in the spokes, throwing the soldier, fatally (Whittlesey notes that "the bicycle was totally wrecked"). In 1890, one of the miners at Cooke City, visiting Cinnabar near the north entrance, playfully tried to lasso a companion's horse. Both his horse and the target startled, and in the runaway that followed, the miner's head was slammed against the wall of a building, breaking his neck instantly. In 1910, a cowboy who tended stock for the park mail carrier left to find some lost horses. His own horse returned to the stable without its rider. The cowboy's body was found a week later, the front part of the skull crushed in, apparently when he was thrown.

There were others, but you get the picture. The bulk of the wagon deaths came of the victim being run over by the wagon and crushed, messily, to death. The stagecoach wrecks were more like the vehicle collisions we have to live with today, but with some variation on the theme. A representative wreck occurred when a stagecoach was coming down Targhee Pass, approaching the final run to the West Entrance to the park, on an August night in 1899. Joseph Lippman, an attorney from Salt Lake City, and his wife, a woman of about thirty who was said to be unusually beautiful, were in a rush (as summer visitors are today) and had persuaded the stage company to make the run after dark, even though they were told it was dangerous. "The stage went on its course through the dark canyons and over steep inclines, lurching from side to side on the miserable roads until the occupants were well-nigh prostrated with nervousness," the *Salt Lake Herald* later reported (as quoted in *Death in Yellowstone*). "They had just traversed a level plat . . . and entered upon a road cut through masses of tall pines, which only made the darkness more impenetrable." The *Herald* continued:

> Suddenly the wheel of the coach struck a large boulder that had rolled down from the mountain side, and the conveyance was heaved to a dangerous angle, when a piece of the harness broke, and the horses started to rear and plunge. The wheel at one side got off the road, and slewed down the mountainside a few inches, and Mrs. Lippman, terribly excited, struggled to escape. She put her head out of the window or upper part of the door, just as the horses gave another plunge forward. It was then the fatality occurred, though not until later was it known. The driver succeeded in stopping the horses before they had run over thirty-five feet, but for that distance Mrs. Lippman was dragged and the occupants thrown from side to side and out of the coach. Mr. Lippman was unconscious when his wife's body was picked up and tenderly laid across a seat in the coach by the other members of the party.

Mrs. Lippman's head had struck a tree trunk. Her neck was broken already when the coach landed on top of her, and the horses dragged it over her like a steamroller. Four others were injured. The driver, a man named Roger Sherman, decided he never wanted to drive again and asked the company to reassign him. It is a testimony to his experience as a driver that he was able to get the horses under control so quickly. He was, however, tormented by grief.

There were other quaintly horrible frontier deaths. There is a well-marked grave near the Nez Perce Creek picnic area. It is the resting place of Mattie Culver, the wife of one of the hotel winter-keepers, who died of tuberculosis in 1889. It was winter when she died, so her body was stored outside in two barrel-halves, frozen stiff, until the ground had thawed enough to dig the grave. A number of people were killed by Indians, their graves now unmarked. There were saloon brawls. The blame here can be laid, in great part, on frontier rotgut liquor. Doris Whithorn's history of Aldridge tells a number of these stories, including the death in 1903 of Frank Cheplak, who started a drunken fight and was killed when he was clobbered over the head with one or more chairs. Whithorn found a newspaper account of the affair, and the people involved had some of the most charming names this side of Dr. Seuss: "Anton Krumparichnick, John Stanfield and John Racoon were in John Yonskovitch's saloon in Happy Hollow the night of the fight. They were not drunk but had been drinking some ginger ale. While they were talking at the bar, in came Cheplak, very drunk and noisy. He wanted to fight somebody—didn't seem to mind much who. One witness said he talked rough and wanted to fight everybody. So, the boys pitched into him and warmed him soundly with chairs."

That death was maybe justifiable . . . but then there are the murder victims.

A fair number of people have been murdered in or near the park, often under sordid circumstances, or, in some cases, circumstances purely tragic. One of the latter is the death, in 1899, of little Joseph Trischman. It is one we can still connect with today because of the monument to him in one corner of the Fort Yellowstone Army Cemetery.

The graves in the cemetery are often plain, some of them starkly so, like the white marble tombstone, done in the style the army used, with only two words on it: "Unknown Infant." There are several like that, the others, for the most part, not quite so anonymous. Among these graves, only a few stand out. One is Joseph Trischman's. It is lined by a rectangular fence, ornate in its way, and somewhat worse for wear for its century-plus in the Yellowstone weather (the joints are rusting, although the bars themselves are holding up). Inside is a marble tombstone with the words "Joseph / Son of Geo and Margie Trieschman / Born July 29, 1893 / Died June 3, 1899." Beneath are two lines of verse: "'Tis' a little grace, but Oh Take care / For the hopes are buried there."

The monument is spotted with lichen now, bright orange against the white marble, and in the spring the grave is covered by the plants that grow wild in meadows at this elevation. For a while, the plants are bright green. Atop the marble is the one touch everyone remembers: a pair of child's shoes and socks, empty.

In *Death in Yellowstone*, Lee Whittlesey calls it "One of the most gruesome of all Yellowstone death incidents," one that is "little known but can truly be called riveting." The Trischmans are today remembered as one of the prominent families in park history, but the story does not begin auspiciously, to say the least. George Trischman was a wheelwright and carpenter at Fort Yellowstone. In the spring of 1899, he was living at Mammoth, but his children were a long trip away, even riding the railroad, in Billings. The whole family was widely separated because his wife, Margaret, was in Warm Springs, Montana. In the madhouse.

It is not clear what exactly happened to her, but earlier that year, she had broken down. She took a butcher knife, a big one, and hid behind the family's Billings house, where she slashed her own throat. She had been aiming for the jugular vein but missed, inflicting instead a hideous gash. She passed out. When she came to, she invented a story about being assaulted but was not believed. She was sent instead to Montana State Hospital in Warm Springs, near Anaconda.

Whittlesey picks up her story, which is worth quoting at length:

A few months later, asylum physicians announced that Mrs. Trischman had recovered. Elated at the prospect of having his family reunited, George Trischman traveled to Warm Springs on May 28, 1899, to pick up his wife. He had decided to move the family from Billings to Fort Yellowstone, so his children were placed on the train to Livingston. The family met in Livingston, and on Tuesday, May 30, they all rode the train to Cinnabar.

Mrs. Trischman's recovery was regrettably temporary. Four days later, on Saturday evening, June 3, at about 5:00 p.m., Mrs. Trischman seized 5-year-old Joseph, the youngest of her children, and cut his throat with a large hunting knife. In the presence of his brothers and sisters, his head was nearly severed from his body. Margaret G. Trischman then chased her other three children with the knife in an attempt to do the same to them. They ran in terror to the home of a neighbor, and the woman, giving up the chase, returned home. She was found a short time later, calm but insensible to her surroundings, and in a state of mind that prevented her from understanding the deed she had done. Heartbroken, George Trischman allowed her to be confined in the guardhouse at Fort Yellowstone.

The nightmare had not ended for the family. The US District Attorney investigated the matter, and Margaret Trischman was found to be insane. A touching aspect of this whole affair, though, is the way George Trischman refused to give up on her. He was along for the ride when the tragedy entered its final act:

Placed on the train bound for the government hospital at Washington, DC, she jumped from it on July 8 between Point of Rocks and Dailey's Ranch in Paradise Valley and landed in the Yellowstone River. Although the train stopped and backed up in order that Deputy James Morrison and Mr. Trischman could look for her, no trace of her was found, even though the search continued for many months. A year and a half later, George Trischman even traveled to Glendive, Montana, to examine a body that had been found in the river in hopes that it was that of his wife. It was not.

It happened nearly at the dawn of the new century, but as Whittlesey notes, it was very much a tale of the earlier frontier: "The Trischman story classically illustrates the historical reaction by some men and women to traveling and living in the 'hostile Western wilderness': men become savages and women go insane." Except that, tried to his limit, George never did become a savage.

One might think that the experience of being chased by their maddened, knife-wielding mother, after seeing what she had done to little Joseph, would have soured the other children on Yellowstone permanently. It absolutely did not. Elizabeth and Anna Trischman stayed until 1953, running an eccentric and ultimately sort-of famous soda fountain and curio store on the upper terraces at Mammoth Hot Springs, called, in a stroke of genuine wit, the Devil's Kitchenette. The other child of George and Margaret, Harry Trischman, became one of the army's civilian scouts, and when the National Park Service was created, he became a ranger. He stayed so long that he became part of the landscape: Trischman Knob, a mountain in the backcountry south of Old Faithful, was named in his honor. It was one of his favorite places in the park.

So the family left its stamp on Yellowstone. They literally put their name on the landscape. Sadly for them, the name was written in more than one place.

The Unmarked Grave—The Unquiet Dead
One story even a casual visitor to the park is likely to hear is the one about the ghost in the Old Faithful Inn.

The details never change much. The story begins in New York in 1915, where the fiery daughter of a wealthy shipping magnate was engaged to be married to the young son of another well-heeled family. She was in love, however, with a much older man who worked in their house as a servant. The father knew the servant was only after her money. He was heartbroken but allowed her to marry the servant (one of the more improbable details) on one condition: he would give them a dowry, but there would be no more money after that, and the couple would also have to leave New York forever.

The couple departed on their honeymoon trip, ultimately arriving at the Old Faithful Inn, where they stayed in room 127. The cad of a servant had, as the father predicted, spent the whole dowry on high living, and they soon had no money, even for the hotel bill. Violent quarrels now erupted between them; the employees of the Inn listened through the door as the couple screamed at each other night after night.

A staff writer at *Outside* heard the story and related the climax in the pages of the magazine:

> Then one night the argument was louder and more violent than usual. The husband stormed out of the hotel room, slamming the door. This was the last anyone would see of him. The hotel staff gave the new bride her privacy for a couple of days, but then they became worried and took a peek inside the room. It looked like a hurricane had thrown every bit of bedding and clothing about the room, but the bride was not in the bedroom. A hotel maid ventured into the bathroom and her screams brought many of the staff and guests to find the bride in the bathtub, bloody, and missing her head. Although they searched the hotel, her head was nowhere to be found.
>
> In a couple days, attention was directed to the highest point of the hotel. Up in the Crow's Nest is where the band played, but now the only thing that wafted to the lobby below was this horrible odor. You guessed it. . . . Further investigation revealed the bride's head.

And so, guests have ever since reported seeing a headless bride in a flowing white dress drifting about the hallways, and sometimes descending from the Crow's Nest carrying her head.

Problem: a beheading at the park's premier hotel would have left a paper trail, and there was no murder at the Inn in 1915. The source of the story is, in fact, known and mundane. An assistant manager at the Inn, George Bornemann, told Salt Lake City's *Deseret News* in 1991 that he had invented the story in the early 1980s. "People always come in here and are always expecting a ghost story," he said. "I made up that story, about the woman without a head. I've heard people tell it back to me, who I've never met, so it's made the rounds." It has been over thirty years since he confessed to inventing the headless bride tale, but the headless bride still wanders the halls. She is about as unkillably immortal as a ghost can get.

The older hotels tend to have legends similar to the headless bride attached to them. At the Lake Hotel, there is the elderly bellman who helps a travel-weary couple to their room. Before they can tip him for his wonderful service, he vanishes. Later, they see an old photograph at the front desk. They see the bellman in it. They ask who he is. An employee of the hotel, they are told . . . but he has been dead for years.

That one owes something to Jack Nicholson's fate at the end of the film *The Shining*. It is not the only haunting legend attached to the Lake Hotel. The place is in fact lousy with ghosts. President Calvin Coolidge stayed there during a visit in 1927, and he likes to reappear. A woman in flapper attire of the 1920s stalks the halls, as do the spirits of others who drowned in the lake. There is even a whole ghost orchestra that plays for the guests, in death as they did in life.

The Mammoth Hotel has poltergeists. The staff, it is claimed, is forever fighting guest room doors that will not unlock but mysteriously open themselves a short time later. Furniture moves around, and the story is told of a manager who retrieved a box of lightbulbs from a storage room, left after locking the door, then returned a moment later to find the door blocked. Forcing it open, he found a box of toilet paper had been pushed against the door from the far wall, in a room no one could have entered. There is also the sound of a girl laughing in otherwise empty hallways, and of little footsteps. A girl named Emily is supposed to be responsible. She lies now in the Fort Yellowstone cemetery just up the hill. Emily, daughter of Captain H. A. Sievert, died at the age of two in 1903; she was laid to rest right next to Joseph Trischman.

Probably every old building in the park has stories like these attached to them. Employees in the park tend to be dismissive about these stories, when they are not inventing them, although there are plenty of true believers. Furthermore, looking through the windows of the Old Faithful Inn after the staff has closed it and left for the season, on a late autumn day with the snow swirling and absolutely no one around, can be a jittery experience no matter what you think about the headless bride.

There are stories, also, about people who vanish in the park. There is, in fact, a whole class of stories—like a literary genre—about disappearances in national parks. A journalist named Jon Billman wrote a book on the subject, working partly with Bigfoot hunters to establish some basic data on park and wilderness disappearances. Doing so was necessary because the government was hiding things. The *New York Post* gave the book (*The Cold Vanish*) a boost, writing that both Billman and the Sasquatch hunters speculate "that the Park Service conceals the true data on how and where people disappear and how many have actually been found because it 'would shock the public so badly that visitor numbers would fall off a cliff,' Billman writes."

If visitor numbers fell off a cliff, anyone who has anything to do with the parks would, in fact, be delighted, but let us move on. The belief that vast numbers of people disappear in national parks has taken off in places like Reddit and TikTok, where especially weird theories have flourished, sometimes mutating and taking on new forms. A TikTok video by a user calling herself @jaybaebae96 went about as viral as one of those things can. In the video, she is answering the question, "What's a thought that freaks you out the more you think about it?"

"Feral people," she answers simply. She continues: "There are feral people living in our national parks. In 2021, there are feral people that are cannibals living in our national parks. Since I have learned this, I have not stopped thinking about it. I love to go outside. I love to go hiking. I will probably never go to a national park for the rest of my life because I am absolutely terrified of being eaten by a feral person. I've gone down so many rabbit holes on this and I can't." Her voice breaks. "I can't stop thinking about it. I can't stop thinking about it. *I can't stop thinking about it.*"

Many do believe it: that there are thousands of "feral people" living in the national parks, leading lives entirely cut off from civilization—until it comes time to eat, at which point they quit the backcountry, stealthily creep into the frontcountry, then seize and run off with a tourist to eat. People also believe that hundreds of thousands of people have disappeared in the national parks. Theories come and go about what has happened to this army of missing people: kidnapping by UFO beings is always going to be there as an explanation, and another popular one is portals to another dimension, through which people wander and disappear. The army of feral people, though, is one that has periodically stormed through social media.

It plainly has some staying power. Some people trace the idea back to the disappearance, in 1969, of six-year-old Dennis Martin, who vanished while on a family camping trip in Great Smoky Mountains National Park. He was last seen running behind a bush to hide with some other children, who were planning to ambush the adults; when he did not reappear, his father looked for him, but he had vanished. He disappeared so completely that all anyone found—during the largest search effort in the history of Great Smoky Mountains National Park—were some questionable footprints and a shoe and sock. No one knows what happened, but his father thought he had been seized and carried off. One witness reported hearing an "enormous, sickening scream" that afternoon and saw an unkempt man running from the scene.

The case remains unsolved and is unlikely ever to be cleared. It seems a long jump from Dennis Martin to thousands of feral humans eating tourists, also by the thousands, but that is where we are.

There are, of course, no feral humans in Yellowstone or any other park. Genuinely "feral" people have existed, usually children abandoned or orphaned in the wild, who in some way survived; when they reenter society, they often turn out to be impaired in some way (they cannot learn to speak, for instance). The phenomenon is vanishingly rare. A woods-hermit is a different thing. Someone who has chosen to live in the wilderness is never completely cut off. Take Ted Kaczynski, for instance, the Unabomber. He lived as primitive a life as it may be possible to live in contemporary North America, but he still bicycled into town to use the library and had other, more infamous uses for modern technologies. A genuinely feral human would, lacking clothes, be killed by the Yellowstone weather, and if the creature were capable of making a fire, the rangers would eventually come to visit.

Plenty of people have disappeared for real, in and near Yellowstone National Park. They have regularly left no trace, or so little trace that the searchers who were looking for them can only speculate about what happened. Their grave is the park itself.

We looked at such a case toward the beginning of this book, that of LeRoy Piper, who bought that cigar, stepped outside the Fountain Hotel, and was never seen again. Take, also, the disappearance of Daren Dixon, who vanished during the first week of July in 1993. He worked as a busser at the Roosevelt Lodge, which in the context is a highly respectable job; the bussers, like the waiters, are the public face of the establishment, and the busser is informally on trial for a waiter job, one of the best in the park. He was in his second season and was liked by everyone. He quit suddenly without providing a reason, which would normally be a red flag for law enforcement, but again, consider the context: during the summer, people quit all the time. He stayed in the immediate area, or what in Yellowstone counts as the immediate area. He was seen by friends in Cooke City on July 4, and when the rangers found his car, it was next to the Lamar River, between Cooke City and Roosevelt. His wallet was in the car.

Here is the key detail: his wallet was there, but his fishing gear was not. He loved to fish. The other key detail is that 1993 was an epically wet year. The snow and rain had only stopped that week. The rivers were cold and full. The search went on all summer, involving rangers and fire personnel both, but they never found a trace, and the case remains unsolved. It was, however, fairly obvious what had happened. He had fallen into water so cold that he had only minutes to escape before hypothermia set in. The water was so fast, however, that he was never going to escape at all.

That story is sad (rumors about Daren persisted for months, and then years). Some of the other mysteries are just strange, even when we have some sense of what might have happened.

Take the case of Dave Edwards, who was the winter keeper for the boat operations on Yellowstone Lake belonging to E. C. Waters, the early park entrepreneur. On November 12, 1906, Edwards was in a rowboat on the lake, rowing alone, when he suffered a fatal heart attack. The soldiers at the nearby Lake station found him, and he was buried along the lakeshore. There is a grave in the woods nearby—but the grave is empty. It claims to be Edwards's grave, and it is not.

Waters, Edwards's employer, intended to disinter the body and ship it to Edwards's home in Iowa. That never happened. History moved on, and Edwards stayed put, next to the lakeshore, near the Lake Hotel. History moved along far enough that the genteel world of 1906 vanished in the rearview mirror as automobiles invaded the park. When the time came to build a gas station next to the hotel and store, Edwards's grave was in the way. Workers were hired to move it.

The story goes that they got to drinking that night. They got to drinking and thinking. Digging a grave is never easy, and digging up an occupied one is worse; it is still a great deal of work but with something unpleasant at the bottom, and all the while you cannot guess how unpleasant it might be. The workers drank some more and made a decision. They moved the monument, but they left the body where it is, and the service station was built on top of it.

The service station is closed now, although it is still there; its last season was 1989. For decades, the cars and motor homes rolled through. Couples fought, kids ate junk food, lost people got unlost, the service station people solved one automotive catastrophe after another. And it all happened atop Edwards's grave. The service station should be another in the long list of buildings to which a haunting legend is attached, but it sits mostly empty now. Older buildings in the park tend to be converted for some new use, so when the living return to the building, maybe they will find that it is already occupied.

That one has its comical side, but there are many unsettling, even haunting mysteries. Above Gardiner, to the north, is a nearly random net of gravel roads, dirt roads, and jeep tracks that snake up into the Gallatin National Forest, which starts literally on the edge of town. One of the roads summits an unnamed pass beneath a knob that is one of the only named features on the landscape: Parker Point. Here, the road forks. One fork wanders off in the general direction of Jardine but peters out shortly. The other fork is longer, meandering around to the north, then the west, finally dead ending beneath Sheep Mountain, one of the taller summits in the area. Both roads are, one can guess, only here because this part of the forest was logged. The logging happened so long ago that the only clue the lumbermen were even here are the now silvered and decayed stumps, which are gradually rotting from within.

The forest, in many places, is deep, beautiful, and primitive. No one comes up here except hunters during elk season, and locals who know the place is here. The roads are buried in snow much of the year. Then, only cross-country skiers come here, and few enough of them.

That second road, the one that dead ends beneath Sheep Mountain, clings to the side of a steep ridge as it exits the nameless pass. On one side is a dense second-growth forest, and enormous trees that the loggers let be. On the other side is an open area, with some of those bright silvery stumps; the trees here have not come back, and the result is something that may be even better, an open meadow, splashed with flowers during the spring.

Among the stumps is a strange, disturbing sight: a single white cross.

It stands in the middle of that meadow, guarded by a circle of those stumps. It is a neat, well-made white cross secured in place by a lead pipe sunk into the ground at its back. The grave is outlined by rocks, although so much time has passed since the grave was made that the rocks are beginning to disappear into the soil. There is no name, no date, no indication at all of why it is here. Yet it was made with great care. Is it a lumberman killed by one of the trees that now, long dead, surround the grave with their stumps? Who knows?

There are similarly forgotten graves in that area along the north boundary that was homesteaded before the federal government added it to the park. We have already visited with

Corwin the cowboy, killed by that horse at the Reese homestead in 1905. In the early years, the homesteaders tended to bury their dead near their houses, a practice that may seem strange to us, but our practice of allowing mortuary professionals to eliminate our dead with the least amount of fuss might have seemed strange to them.

So there are graves out there that are about as lonesome as Corwin's. Recall how the Nez Perce warriors burned the Henderson homestead, before the cavalry ran them off. After that setback, the Hendersons moved into the outbuilding where their hired hands lived, quite a comedown in life. This area is visible today only as a collection of disturbances on the ground, far from the road or anything else identifiable. Among the disturbances is an oval on the ground that is clearly a grave. It is unmarked. Who lies here? Who knows?

We know a little more about another former homestead, closer to the road and closer to the place where the dusty Old Yellowstone Trail rejoins the paved twenty-first century. Here is an area that the very oldest people in Gardiner recall having been a dairy, long, long ago. Here also are traces of human life: broken masonry, outlines of foundations, and the purple glass that tells the observer that this trash dates from the homesteading era (clear glass once contained manganese, which glassmakers mostly stopped using in the early twentieth century; it is the manganese that turns purple). Life here cannot have failed to be a struggle; the ground is so utterly bereft of moisture.

Here, again, is a spot on the ground that looks like a grave—but here also is confirmation, a small, quite small rectangle of marble with a single word on it: "Alice." The marble has cracked and broken completely in two, the break bisecting the name right through the middle. Who was Alice? Her grave will be even more lonely now because at some point over the last few years her headstone disappeared.

For the most unsettling graves of all, though, we have to shift to another place we visited earlier. Near the epicenter of the 1959 Hebgen Lake earthquake is one of the strangest burial grounds in the country.

That night, when the ground slipped downward, the most amazing violence did not happen along Hebgen Lake or at the dam, as dramatic as that was. The really epic event happened down the Madison River, where nature decided that one lake was not enough. We learned a little about it earlier, but here is the full story.

Six miles downriver from the dam at Hebgen Lake, the canyon walls are steep. That night, August 17, 1959, they were forested densely from top to bottom. We look at a slope like that, and it appears entirely stable. How could it otherwise be covered with trees, top to bottom? As people who hike off-trail know, where trees grow, the slope is gentle enough to be climbed—painfully, perhaps, but there is no need for ropes. Earlier, on the afternoon on August 17, none of the peak-of-the-summer-season travelers and campers along the highway below would have looked up and seen a threat at all. It was just a mountain—a steep mountain—actually a ridgeline, one without a name.

It was, furthermore, convex along the upper reaches of its slope. It bulged. The rock underneath was, as the geologists might say, "weakly affixed." The ridge was made of different kinds of rock that stuck together for now. In the wake of the earthquake, the Geological Survey sent one of their people, Jarvis Hadley, to report on what happened here in the canyon. He looked at the rock and concluded that the local geology "had produced a dynamically unstable slope ready for a period of unusual rainfall, a violent flood, or an earthquake to set it in motion."

On the night of August 17, its wait came to an end.

When the ground began shaking that night, that weakly affixed rock came loose. It is thought that a barrier of stronger rock held weaker rock back, and when the shaking started, that buttress, made of a mineral called dolomite, failed. The convex surface became concave as a massive section of the mountain, two thousand yards wide, broke free and rushed downward, toward the river below. It was, Hadley wrote, "one of the largest landslides ever recorded in the United States."

This was not a California winter mudslide. The material was bedrock, together with what geologists call colluvium, various sizes of broken rock mixed together. Eighty million tons of rock blasted down off the ridge, burying a mile of the river up to two hundred feet deep. Hadley did some math and figured out that the front of the landslide accelerated to a hundred miles per hour. It pushed a wall of air in front of itself, air that was also moving at a hundred miles per hour, literal hurricane strength. When the landslide reached the other side of the canyon, it at first did not stop. It raced up the far side, piling up a mass of rock that reached, at the very top, four hundred thirty feet above the riverbed. The Madison River stopped. The rock formed a dam so immovable that even the Madison, a major river, merely piled up against it and began to rise.

The new lake was a problem to worry about during the coming days. Up and down the canyon, hugging the shore of the river, was US Highway 287, and not many other roads because the canyon was too narrow for much else. Below the ridgeline was a US Forest Service campground, Rock Creek. It was naturally full, as it would be on August 17 today if it still existed, which it very much does not. The people here were asleep, in trailers, in tents, and in the open on the ground. Additionally, at least thirty people were camping along the riverbank farther downstream.

The landslide drew a bead on them all.

7

In the same book-length USGS report in which Hadley analyzed the landslide, Irving Witkind was called on to give an account of the human side of the earthquake. Witkind was the geologist who was mapping the area when the quake struck and was delighted ("It's mine! It's mine!") by his good fortune to be in the middle of it. He was not insensible to the human tragedy unfolding around him, and that is what he described in the report.

He recalled, first, what an idyllic month it had been so far: "During the early and middle parts of August 1959 the weather was nearly perfect—cool sunny days and clear calm nights. On the night of August 17, the moon was full. Tourists crowded the area, so much so that late travelers through the Madison River canyon could find no available site at any of the campgrounds and reluctantly continued on."

As earthquakes do, the shock caught everyone by surprise, and they were also more or less completely unprepared—except that they were camping, and so they were ready to some extent for a period of roughing it. When the earth started shaking at 11:37 p.m., there came a few seconds of absolute confusion followed in some cases by panic. Nearly everyone—and perhaps absolutely everyone—had no idea what was happening at first. Even Witkind, the one person who might have caught on right away, thought the trailer he was sleeping in had come off its jacks and was rolling downhill. As we saw, many, many people had the thought that the Soviet Union was attacking or that the world was in some other way coming to an end—and for the people in the path of the landslide, in places like the Rock Creek campground, how might the actual end of the world have been different?

As Witkind notes, for many, the night was mainly just frightening and unpleasant. However . . .

> For some travelers the night of August 17 was more
> tragic. Mr. and Mrs. F.R. Bennett and their four children,

en route from their home in Coeur d'Alene, Idaho, to Yellowstone National Park, camped that night in the Madison River canyon near Rock Creek Campground, which was later partly buried by the Madison Slide. The parents were sleeping in their small house trailer, and the children were in bedrolls on the ground nearby when Mrs. Bennett was awakened by a loud noise. "Some time later" she heard a great roar and, alarmed, went with Mr. Bennett to check on the children. Just as they left the trailer a tremendous blast of air struck them. Mrs. Bennett saw her husband grasp a tree for support, then saw him lifted off his feet by the air blast and strung out "like a flag" before he let go. Before she lost consciousness, she saw one of her children blown past her and a car tumbling over and over. Her son Phillip, 16 years old, was buffeted about by the air blast and immersed in water, but somehow, with a broken left leg, he managed to crawl into a clump of trees, where he burrowed into the mud for warmth. He and his mother, sole survivors of the family, were rescued the next morning.

The blast was the wall of air, moving at a hundred miles per hour, that traveled ahead of the wall of broken rock. The effects were astounding in ways we will have a hard time understanding, and many of the most awful of them never got any publicity because there were too many weird things happening all at once.

For instance, the people camping at Rock Creek and along the river were in danger of being buried, but they were also in danger of being drowned. The seiche-waves in Hebgen Lake were washing over the dam, and at the same time the landslide was hitting the river and sending water in the other direction. This was not a "splash" of water. The whole Madison suddenly reversed course. As if the situation were not confusing enough already, the formerly placid river was attacking from both directions at once:

7

Rev. E. H. Ost and his family were among the survivors at Rock Creek Campground. Awakened by the first tremor, the family left their tent. As they stood in the bright moonlight, about 20 seconds after being aroused, they heard a tremendous grinding noise and, with it, the sound of water. No wave of water was moving downstream; instead, Rev. Ost saw water moving upstream. He shouted to his family to hang onto trees. His daughters, alerted by the call, scrambled upslope. Water swirled through the campground, rolling and tumbling their car about 50 feet upstream, but Rev. and Mrs. Ost held firm to the trees and soon were able to pick their way out of the debris. With other survivors, they climbed to higher ground. Dawn revealed the east edge of the Madison Slide about 100 yards from the Osts' former campsite. By 6:00 a.m. all the cars in the campground were submerged beneath Earthquake Lake.

One elderly couple climbed onto the roof of their trailer and rode it as the water carried it two hundred yards upstream. When the trailer sank, they climbed into a tree, and were forced ever higher as the water rose. Rescuers found them after they had been treed for five hours.

The full moon was now obscured by dust raised by the landslide, and the night grew as dark as it had been bright.

Some of the events of that night are the kind we would reject as improbable in a novel or movie. The Rev. Ost moved his family to high ground, then returned to the rising water, where his neighbors in the campground, the Fredericks family, were in a terrible way. Edmund Christopherson, in his book *The Night the Mountain Fell*, tells the story:

> He heard Mr. Fredericks call for help for his son, Paul. With a flashlight he borrowed, he was able to see the difficulty. The surge of water and trees had caught 15-year-old Paul

and pinioned him in a sitting position in the water, with one log across the small of his back and another across his lap. The ends of the log were jammed between a smashed trailer and the Ost car, so solidly they wouldn't budge.

Paul cried out with pain as the two men tried to pull him loose. The water kept rising as the men tried to pry the logs apart with sticks. A 2 × 12 plank, ten feet long, even though full of spikes, seemed a promising tool to pry with, but with it they were only able to gain an inch or so further separation of the logs that held Paul prisoner.

The men felt Paul's and their own helpless panic as the water swelled up to his chest, his neck, his chin. Raised in a soundly religious family, Paul bravely faced the realization that he was gasps from death. In desperation, Ost called on Mel Fredericks to pull as hard as he could, not to care if Paul cried, or if they pulled his arms or legs out of joint. In this last, desperate straining try they found that miraculously they could raise him six inches. The rising water had buoyed the trailer. In their next few feverish tries they were able to pull him loose and helped him to walk to high, dry ground.

These were the lucky ones. They spent a miserable night, but help was on the way. There were just under three hundred people trapped in the canyon. By late the next day, they were able to escape on an improvised road bulldozed by highway repair crews. Some, like the Fredericks and Ost families, were helicoptered over the slide and then taken by the Montana Highway Patrol to either the hospital or improvised dormitories. The badly injured were flown out, some to that aircraft-hangar emergency department we saw earlier, with the hay bales for gurneys.

Attention now turned to the new lake that was forming suddenly, quite suddenly, above the slide. On August 21, a Forest Service aircraft flew over the area, and someone on board leaned over and took a photograph. The earthquake had happened not even a week earlier, and the lake was already massive. In fact, it was already twenty feet deep at dawn on the morning after the quake, the level having been given a boost by the tsunami-like waves that had sloshed out of Hebgen Lake. The main reason for the quick rise, though, was the nature of the dam that was creating it. Human dams always let at least part of the river through. This one was stopping nearly every drop, and the Madison River downstream was bone dry, a bizarre, apocalyptic sight, and a smell, too—the fish were naturally all dead, and the valley smelled in places like a badly run cannery.

When three weeks had passed, the water was two hundred feet deep at its deepest and stretched almost the full six miles back to Hebgen Dam. What was going to happen to this incredible mass of water? The US Army Corps of Engineers was called in to do a strange thing: emergency spillway construction. They cut a new path for the Madison through the debris. The river refilled its downstream channel, to everyone's relief, and the Madison follows the Army's improvised passage to this day.

As people left the canyon, back on August 18, the miscellany of officials who were on the scene kept a census. They knew there were people still in the canyon, and there were calls coming in already from around the nation. The question was, who was still up there?

The situation that now developed was rather like the one that followed the terrorist attacks on September 11, 2001, when those with loved ones who had probably been in the World Trade Center hung "Missing" posters around New York City in the hope that at least a few might be lying injured in hospitals, unidentified. The sheriff of Gallatin County was a man named Don Skerritt, and he now took the lead in trying to figure out who might have been in the canyon. It involved a great deal of shoe-leather police work. "One of the leads was a spaniel discovered wandering in the slide area the day after the quake,"

Christopherson wrote. "The animal wore a Salt Lake dog license tag. . . . In response to Skerritt's teletype inquiry, Salt Lake police found that the dog supposed to be wearing the tag had been killed months before. Someone had hung the collar in a gas station. Subsequently this collar was put on another dog. Further probing developed that the dog in the quake area belonged to the Ray Painters of Ogden, Utah. Mrs. Painter, one of the casualties, died in the Bozeman hospital a couple of days after the quake."

Some of the methods were actually quite similar to the kind of techniques employed after 9/11. In 1959, they did move more slowly, and Christopherson, writing in 1960, notes that some of the mysteries remained unanswered:

> During the first weeks, Red Cross volunteers and personnel worked around the clock to answer the flood of inquiries. There were some 3,000 of them. They felt fortunate that no scout troops turned up missing.
>
> These queries, they painstakingly sifted, sorted, and winnowed down. With tireless persistence, they kept at it, writing to the source of each of the thousands of inquiries to find out if the missing had turned up. New inquiries kept coming in—and still do, asking about people that just plain haven't been heard from, and their relatives, or friends have thought of the slide as a possible explanation.
>
> Through tangible tie-ins, like postcards, letters, the use of credit cards in the area just before the quake, phone calls from the area, they finally got down to a list of those highly probable as slide victims whose bodies will never be uncovered.

They would never be uncovered because they were buried as completely as people can be. Photographs exist of searchers clambering over the landslide in the days after the earthquake. Against that wilderness of broken rock, they shrink to insignificance. By way of comparison, at the date of this writing, the US Navy has something between four and five million tons of ships in service. The slide was eighty million tons.

In the end, the searchers counted nineteen people who had either been in the Rock Creek campground or at the improvised campground along the river, and they were now unaccounted for. They were buried under the landslide. They are there yet.

You can still see it, pretty much all of it. The highway has been rerouted around the new obstacles that filled the canyon in the wake of the earthquake. The scar left behind on the canyon wall, where the landslide broke free, is still nearly as bare as it was in August 1959; just a few clusters of trees have colonized the raw wound. What was soon named Earthquake Lake—everyone calls it Quake Lake—is still there and is still filled with the trees that made up the forest that grew here before, some of the trees still standing, stark, silvery, dead. But it is not an evil place, where nature is concerned. Lakes form this way; large river systems often show signs of having been dammed by some kind of motion in the earth, including lava flows (there are a number of these in the Grand Canyon—the other one, the Grand Canyon of the Colorado). The river gradually chews its way through, and a few million years later it is back to the way it was. That is what will happen here.

Much of what transpired that night happened in the Gallatin National Forest, and in 1960, the federal government created the Madison River Canyon Earthquake Area. Later in the 1960s, the US Forest Service built, atop the landslide, the Earthquake Lake Visitor Center. Nearby is a memorial to all twenty-eight people who died in the earthquake as a whole. It is a plaque affixed to an indescribably massive piece of rock that may have been part of the buttress that failed that night, the barrier of stronger dolomite that held the weaker rock up. The rock is not the size of a house. It is the size of an office building. Somewhere underneath, far below, are the nineteen people who died in the slide and are as unrecoverable as victims carried down in a sunken ship in the deep sea.

Memories of the event are not as fresh as they once were, but this is a cemetery, same as the ones inside the national park. The families of the people who were hurt and killed that night are, some of them, still around. We should treat the place with respect.

At the same time, do not overdo it. Let the kids run around, and do also take in the scenery: the canyon, the valley downriver, the new lake, and the slide itself.

Strange as it all is, it is spectacular.

CONCLUSION

OUR STRANGE FUTURE

Excelsior Geyser Crater. If it were to blow again, the way it once did, the viewing platform would not be a comfortable place. SCOTT HERRING

CONCLUSION

What does the future hold for Yellowstone? More weirdness, surely.

There will be more outlandish urban/exurban legends and conspiracy theories. We have Bigfoot already. He, and she, has been resident in Greater Yellowstone for a long time, and if anything, Bigfoot congestion is worse now than it was before, to judge from a webcam video recorded in 2015 that appeared to capture a family of them. The video is all over the internet still, so you can look it up. A woman named Mary Greeley innocently uploaded a tape of some bison lumbering around, the way they do, amid a wintery landscape at the Upper Geyser Basin. In the background, Bigfoot hunters quickly noticed, are a group of bipedal but strangely inhuman figures, apparently stalking the bison—so at least, unlike the feral humans, the Bigfoots (Bigfeet?) are not cannibals. Sadly, in the video, when they first appear in the distance, their stride is precisely that of cross-country skiers, but, um, yeah.

If Wendigos make an appearance in the park, that will be something new. A Wendigo is a creature in the mythology of native people who speak Algonquian languages. It is usually associated with the Great Lakes and Canada, but the Cree are part of the Algonquian family, and big groups of Cree live in Montana, not far (by Montana standards) from the park.

A Wendigo is a thing uniquely horrible. It can be a spirit that possesses human beings, or it can be a monstrous creature that takes on human form. It makes its appearance on cold northern nights when, in the depths of winter, the food supply runs low and hunger threatens all. When that happens, the Wendigo possesses men and women and drives them to cannibalism. Alternatively, the Wendigo eats people without having to go to the trouble of demonic possession.

Basil Johnston, a Canadian writer and scholar of the Ojibway tribe, describes it in his book *The Manitous*, using an alternate spelling. In its appearance, it is a hideous thing, a giant "in the form of a man or a woman, who towered five to eight times above the height of a tall man. But the Weendigo was a giant in height only; in girth and strength, it was not. Because it was afflicted with never-ending hunger and could never get enough to eat, it was always on the verge of starvation. The Weendigo was gaunt to the point of emaciation, its desiccated skin pulled tautly over its bones. With its bones pushing out against its skin, its complexion the ash gray of death, and its eyes pushed back deep into their sockets, the Weendigo looked like a gaunt skeleton recently disinterred from the grave. What lips it had were tattered and bloody from its constant chewing with jagged teeth."

They have given their name to what psychiatrists call "Wendigo psychosis," which happens to people who belong to Algonquian tribes, typically in the depths of winter. Cooped up in a cabin with the food gone and hunger beginning to bite, on nights with the wolves howling and the full moon on the snow, a man would find himself possessed. He would turn on his companions and quite literally kill and eat them. It has happened, and it surely will happen again. We can be grateful that it is rare.

People who claim to know about such things say that we also need to worry about skin-walkers. A skin-walker is a witch, an evil presence luring people to destruction in the myths and rituals of native peoples of the desert Southwest. Such creatures take the good magic of the healer and turn it to evil ends. It is the eternal story: the skin-walker is a seeker of knowledge who is corrupted by power. In becoming a skin-walker, the witch takes on the form of an animal, but at the same time uses clever tricks to deceive the human victim, maybe calling out in the voice of a loved one who has died. The witch thereby lures the victim to his or her doom, reeling the person in like an angler reeling in a fish. The skin-walker may take the form of various animals, but often becomes a coyote, of which Yellowstone has plenty.

CONCLUSION

So, we have that to look forward to.

Or maybe we will just see old-fashioned kidnappings by UFO beings. There is a precedent, although it is a fictional one: think of what happens at the end of *Close Encounters of the Third Kind*. The hero, with plenty of hijinks along the way, drives his family station wagon through difficult traffic to Devil's Tower National Monument. Once there, he finds the government has built a landing place for the visitors, and in the end, he is whisked away by the aliens. There are plenty of places in the Yellowstone wilderness where the government could hide a spaceport and no one would notice. It is a wild place. Perhaps they have already done it.

There will continue to be regular problems with animals. Bison will continue to gore people and toss them through the air. Elk and moose will get in on the act. Bears will kill regularly. It may happen on the very day you are reading this book. About wolves, we will have to wait and see. The only certain prediction, where they are concerned, is that they will continue to be both loved and hated with an intensity that guarantees something strange will happen.

Strange, too, and wonderful, will be the surprises the geysers throw at us. Perhaps Excelsior Geyser Crater will do its thing again, blasting with a violence and a massiveness that will be like twenty Old Faithfuls erupting at once, and all in the same place. There would be only one unfortunate side effect of such a display: Midway Geyser Basin would be closed for the duration because Excelsior would be shellacking the boardwalk and pedestrian bridge with scalding water and boulders flung through the air like mortar bombs.

And up at Norris Geyser Basin, what about Steamboat, the largest geyser in the world? To say Steamboat has been irregular is something of an understatement. For much of the twentieth century before 1961, it shut down completely. It erupted through the 1960s and shut down again, and again completely, between 1969 and 1978. It got going again in the early 1980s, shut down in the second half of the decade, erupted five times between 1989 and 1991, took the 1990s off, and so on. For reasons no one can explain, but surely having to do with the strange and extreme conditions at Norris, it is fickle indeed.

Lately, however, it has been on a tear. It shut down from 2007 to 2013 and then again from 2014 to 2018—but in the latter year, something dramatic happened somewhere below, and Steamboat went into overdrive. It erupted thirty-two times in that year and then forty-eight times in both 2019 and 2020. It erupted right through the warm months in both years but also off and on all winter, which had the locals standing around Norris with five layers of clothing on, shivering and hoping to get lucky. It erupted a "mere" twenty times in 2021, then eleven in 2022, but you could go back through its history and find decades on end when it did not accumulate even eleven eruptions. It remains entirely unpredictable. It seems unlikely that it would ever become like Old Faithful, a creature whose performances can be forecast—but it would be wonderful if it did, and Norris is a centerpiece of Yellowstone strangeness. The whole area encourages the feeling that anything is possible.

And about Old Faithful itself—how long will it remain faithful? The US Geological Survey has an answer, one, oddly, that involves trees. Dead trees. Very dead trees.

The USGS staff unraveled this matter in *Caldera Chronicles* in 2020. "Natural geysers are rare because they need special conditions to form," they explain, "a supply of water, recent or active magmatism to supply heat, and the right geometry of fractures in subsurface rocks to permit episodic discharge." Because these factors are always changing, "geysers have periods of activity and dormancy"—as we saw above with Steamboat. "Transitions between activity to dormancy and changes in the interval between eruptions are often caused by earthquakes that modify the geometry of fractures in subsurface rocks and by changes in the amount of regional precipitation that flows as groundwater to geyser reservoirs."

For this reason, any geyser in the park, no matter how regular—or even constant, as some of them are—will shut itself on and off. Old Faithful is not immune, as the park naturalist George Marler learned over sixty years ago. Marler was the geyser expert who we met earlier, complaining, rightly, about vandalism of the thermal features. He discovered a piece of mineralized wood on the Old Faithful geyser mound, in this case not jammed there by tourists in a destructive mood. In a very early application of the radiocarbon dating method, he found the wood to be 730 years old. It had grown on the mound during what in Europe was the later Middle Ages. What that meant was the geyser must have, at that time, been out of commission. A tree could not have grown on the mound otherwise.

"Inspired by this observation," *Caldera Chronicles* went on, "a team of scientists collected and studied 13 mineralized wood specimens from the Old Faithful geyser mound." Three of the specimens were lodgepole pine, and the scientists thought the others probably were too, although this was not wood like the guys at Home Depot sell. "The specimens were then split into 41 samples and dated with the radiocarbon method. To the surprise of the researchers, all wood samples had similar ages and implied that lodgepole pine trees grew on the geyser mound in the 13th and 14th centuries." George Marler had been right, all those decades ago. He was in many ways an impressive guy.

So Old Faithful—was *not*, during that time. Why? "In the Yellowstone region, past climate reconstructions based on tree ring records reveal that a severe and sustained drought occurred in the mid-13th century, which coincides with the onset of tree growth on the Old Faithful Geyser mound." That same drought caused chaos among native groups all over North America (like the Anasazi, among others). "It would seem, then, that the pause in Old Faithful eruptions during the 13th and 14th centuries was related to diminished precipitation and groundwater supply to the geyser for several decades."

So, when there is another decades-long drought, it is a good bet Old Faithful will shut down. That will play havoc on the local tourist economy, although the locals may have other things to worry about. It calls to mind an old urban legend about Yellowstone and Yosemite. The legend states that a multinational corporation owns both parks, which is wildly incorrect. It was a matter of goofy misapprehension. In the year 1990, when the economy of Japan still had an aura of invincibility, the Matsushita corporation bought the US entertainment firm MCA, which owned, among other things, Yosemite Park and Curry Company, which you may recognize from various place names around Yosemite Valley. A minor, a very minor, scandal erupted when people objected to the *zaibatsu* of Japan buying American landmarks, and Matsushita agreed to put Curry into escrow while an American buyer for the small subsidiary was found. That forgotten affair translated into park visitors asking employees in Yellowstone, for years, whether the Japanese owners of Old Faithful were hard to work for, and did they plan on fixing Old Faithful so that it goes off every hour on the hour again? If the grand old geyser shuts down once more, people will find a way to blame the People's Republic of China.

And there is another thing we will get more of: zany behavior by park visitors. It is a permanent feature of life in the park and is usually not such an awful thing. One new feature in park life that will drive new varieties of strangeness in the future is the influx of people from all over the world. Foreign visitors used to just be Europeans and Canadians, but now only the very poorest parts of the globe fail to send a mass of tourists to Yellowstone in the summer. People come from such exotic locales now that the managers of the park's various bathrooms have discovered the need to post instructions on how to use the toilets. People for whom "the bathroom," back home, is a hole in the floor tend to want to stand with feet planted on either side of the toilet seat, squatting in midair for the duration, which is more than a little dangerous. Look for footprints on the seat during your next visit, if you doubt.

Changes in the park wildlife will lead to subtle, interesting, and, yes, strange developments. In much of the rest of the world, "changes in wildlife" would refer to some kind of decline, but in Yellowstone, the problems have to do with too *much* wildlife. The numbers of grizzly bears have surged steadily for years, and one noticeable feature of visitors nowadays is a greatly increased fear of the bears. It is a strange development, given that there has been no corresponding surge in the number of hikers, and no one is going to get mauled while in line at the ice cream bar.

Other animal populations have surged. For instance, there appear to be more eagles now, although this is admittedly an impression, if a strong impression. One place where they appear, bald eagles specifically, is just north of Gardiner. Few members of the general public are aware that Native tribes with a historical connection to Yellowstone—like the Nez Perce—are allowed to hunt bison under relaxed rules during the winter, when the animals wander down out of the national park. The bison have made this migration perhaps since the glaciers retreated; as shaggy and massive and weatherproof as they are, winter is the time to seek lower elevations. One place where the hunt happens is just outside the park across Reese Creek, an easy walk from the grave of Corwin the cowboy. Another is above Gardiner, in both cases on land inside the Custer Gallatin National Forest.

The hunters leave what they call gut piles, the parts of the animal that no one wants unless starving, and an amazing thing has happened in recent years with those piles. No human wants them, but the birds and coyotes and sometimes the bears do, and lately, they have drawn in improbable numbers of bald eagles. It is easy to spot the gut piles now because there on the rocks above them, the bald eagles sit, massive black-and-white sentinels, looking like the Maltese Falcon come to life, and often outnumbering the ravens and magpies. After the guts are gone, the eagles ride the thermals above the Yellowstone River valley, spinning ever higher until they at last lift out of sight, a dozen or more of them at a time.

It used to be somewhat difficult to spot a bald eagle in the park. Perhaps, in the future, it will not be. This sort of thing can have a comical side. Some years ago, in one of the Alaska parks, a tourist couple stopped beside the road. The wife let their Chihuahua out. The Chihuahua did what they do and went *Bark bark bark bark bark bark bark bark bark bark.* He should not, however, have been calling attention to himself.

Before the wife could react, an eagle swooped down out of the sky, grabbed the Chihuahua in his talons, and carried it away at the speed of, well, an eagle. Witnesses later recalled that the woman screamed in terror, while her husband "chopped the air with his fist and said 'Yeah! *Yeah!*'"

Maybe, as our Yellowstone eagles become more common, more such terror will stalk the land.

Most of all, though, we are certain to have more natural disasters. The volcano is not likely to erupt—again, yes, it is "due" to erupt, but the estimate is plus or minus a thousand lifetimes. What we will have is thermal steam explosions, for which no one is prepared in the slightest. There *is* no way to prepare, unless the USGS figures out a way to predict them, which is presently impossible. Imagine if the Indian Pond thermal explosion happened today, on a busy August afternoon. It would be like Yellowstone's own little nuclear war. The only thing to do would be to pick up the pieces afterward.

An even more likely danger is earthquake. It seems the region is living on borrowed time, where a big shake is concerned, although earthquakes are no more predictable than thermal explosions. As we saw, Yellowstone got more than a little lucky with the Hebgen Lake earthquake, which hit in the middle of the night and in the middle of nowhere. What might happen if the epicenter were closer to a big concentration of people, like that which occurs at Old Faithful every day in August? And what might happen if the hour were closer to noon?

It is at this point, in a piece of writing like this one, that the author is supposed to lament our terrible state of preparedness for the looming disaster. We are going to skip that. Whatever preparations have been made are bound to be inadequate because we are always like generals preparing for the last war, where this particular threat is concerned. The next earthquake will always be a surprise. That is the lesson of Southern California's experience with big temblors. After a long period of quiet, the ground under greater Los Angeles began shaking regularly in 1971, with the Sylmar earthquake. The most recent really powerful event was the Northridge earthquake in 1994. The city had had those intervening decades to prepare, and yet the Northridge event was still a nasty shock, in part because no one knew that particular fault was there. It was what the geologists call a blind thrust fault, hidden underneath the city. There is also only so much anyone can do. Shaking in an earthquake is always less violent in places that sit atop bedrock, and most violent in those atop loosely packed soil that has washed down from the mountains, "alluvium," in the language of the USGS. Northridge is in the San Fernando Valley, which is nothing *but* alluvium. The valley shook like Jell-O.

But you cannot move the city, and you cannot move Old Faithful, either. Further, an earthquake is the purest surprise nature has on offer. Every other kind of natural disaster gives you some warning that it is coming. A hurricane is visible when still far out to sea; a blizzard calls attention to itself when still gathering strength a thousand miles away; a tsunami does that weird thing in which the water disappears just before it comes roaring back; even a tornado is visible on Doppler radar. Earthquakes always come entirely out of the blue, jazzing your nerves top to bottom, so that even if no buildings collapse, there are always a few casualties from heart attacks. No, an earthquake will happen just as we have settled into the deepest complacency. The earth will have the last laugh.

And Yellowstone, strange to say, may be a good place for one. There are built-up areas, yes, but most people will be outside. That is one thing that makes Yellowstone what it is: unlike greater Los Angeles, it is almost all outside. Many visitors there carry with them the ultimate in redundant systems: an extra house, in the form of an RV or trailer or tent. The people who live in the park tend to be the kind—hunters and hikers both—who have a backpack and daypack in the closet filled with items like water purification tablets, first aid supplies, and the stuff needed to make a fire. In the communities outside the park, the people are sturdy rural types, the kind who survive disasters.

Also, oddly, there is a positive side to an earthquake in Yellowstone. The geyser basins, as we have seen, go wild after they are shaken. They do extraordinary things. We know from the experience of people like George Marler in 1959 that it is the event of a lifetime. The Upper Geyser Basin, after a major earthquake happening nearby, will be a weird sight, but an amazing one.

So, relax and enjoy the park. The only thing you have to fear is strangeness itself.

About the Author

Scott Herring is a distinguished writer, historian, and educator, currently serving as a continuing lecturer at the University of California, Davis. He specializes in teaching advanced writing to science students, helping them to articulate their research and findings in a clear and compelling manner.

Born and raised in Burbank, California, near the bustling center of metropolitan Los Angeles, Herring found his true calling in the serene and majestic landscapes of Yellowstone National Park. After completing his bachelor's degree, he embarked on a five-year sojourn in Yellowstone, living and working in various locations within the park, including the iconic Old Faithful. This immersive experience deepened his appreciation for the natural world and inspired his academic and literary pursuits.

Returning to civilization, Herring pursued his graduate studies at the University of California, Davis, where he earned both his master's and Ph.D. in English. His dissertation focused on literature about national parks, reflecting his personal and academic interest in these protected areas.

Herring has made significant contributions to the literature on Yellowstone National Park. He edited and authored several books, including *Rough Trip Through Yellowstone*, a detailed account of how the park's bison were saved from extinction, and *Yellowstone's Lost Legend: Uncle Billy Hofer, Renaissance Man of the Early Park*. The latter book is a biography of Thomas Elwood "Billy" Hofer, a wilderness guide, wildlife census taker, explorer, and expert skier, tracker, and naturalist

ABOUT THE AUTHOR

who became a fixture of Yellowstone National Park in the late 1800s.

In addition to his teaching and writing, Herring has been recognized for his excellence in teaching, winning the Academic Federation Award for Excellence in Teaching in 2013. Despite his extensive travels and experiences, he continues to reside in California, where he imparts his knowledge and passion for the natural world to the next generation of scientists and writers.